D1738165

Biographical Directory
of the Governors
of the United States
1978-1983

Also in this Series

*Biographical Directory of American Colonial
and Revolutionary Governors 1607-1789*
By John W. Raimo

Biographical Directory of American Territorial Governors
By Thomas A. McMullin and David A. Walker

*Biographical Directory of the Governors
of the United States 1789-1978*
Edited by Robert Sobel and John W. Raimo

Biographical Directory of the Governors of the United States 1978-1983

JK
2447
.B5733
1985
West

Edited by
John W. Raimo

ASU WEST LIBRARY

Meckler Publishing
11 Ferry Lane West, Westport, CT 06880
3 Henrietta Street, London WC2E 8LU, England

Library of Congress Cataloging in Publication Data
Main entry under title:

Biographical directory of the governors of the United States, 1978-1983.

  Includes bibliographies and index.
  1. Governors—United States—Biography—Dictionaries.
2. United States—Biography—Dictionaries. I. Raimo, John, 1946-
E176.B5733   1984   973.926′092′2   [B]   84-20717
ISBN 0-930466-62-4

Copyright © 1985 by Meckler Publishing

All rights reserved. No part of this publication may be reproduced in any form without written permission from the publisher, except by a reviewer who may quote brief passages in review. ·

Meckler Publishing, 11 Ferry Lane West, Westport, CT 06880
Meckler Publishing, 3 Henrietta Street, London WC2E 8LU, UK

Printed in the United States of America

CONTENTS

PREFATORY NOTE

In his introduction to the 1978 edition of the *Biographical Directory of the Governors of the United States, 1789-1978*, Professor James Shenton of Columbia University observed that "the opportunities to make a statewide mark have often made the governorship a stepping stone to the presidency." The election of former California Governor Ronald Reagan to the American presidency in 1980 serves to reinforce Shenton's contention that gubernatorial experience remains a crucial factor in developing political leadership on a national scale. Indeed, both the Reagan administration and the Carter presidency which preceded it offer strong evidence that policies first implemented on a state level frequently come to have major implications for the nation.

This sequel to Meckler Publishing's earlier four-volume set, which provided biographical data on America's chief executives up to 1978, covers the 87 individuals who served between January 1978 and January 1983. Although this has resulted in a certain amount of overlap with the earlier volumes, it permits a bit more detail and perspective on gubernatorial administrations which in 1978 were too recent to reveal significant trends and issues. Our wish to include meaningful facts on a governor's tenure has also led us to exclude all *new* chief executives who took office after early 1983. These governors, who are listed in the Appendix to this volume, will appear in Meckler Publishing's next five-year sequel, scheduled to appear in 1989.

Our cohort of 87 chief executives includes three women (Grasso of Connecticut, Ray of Washington, and Roy of New Hampshire). Of the three, only Vesta Roy, who served as acting governor of New Hampshire for eight days following Hugh Gallen's death, actually assumed office between January 1978 and January 1983. Still, while there is little reason to expect that women will easily achieve parity in gubernatorial politics, it is perhaps revealing that Martha Layne Collins won the Kentucky governorship in November 1983 at the expense of James Bunning, a former major league baseball pitcher. Had Bunning won that election, he would have repeated the success of no fewer than three governors elected in 1978 with a background that included professional sports (James of Alabama, Hughes of Maryland, and King of Massachusetts)! Readers of this work will no doubt discover other tantalizing facts, and it is our hope that this information will be of some value to observers of American political life.

The dedicated research efforts of the seven scholars mentioned below have made the present volume possible, and each essay concludes with the initials of the appropriate author. I would particularly like to thank John Healy and Marie Marmo Mullaney, who together contributed most of the sketches. The research that they and others have done here illustrates again the importance of Professor Shenton's argument that ''to understand the dynamics of American politics, one must understand its functioning on the state level.''

John W. Raimo
University of Vermont
November 1984

CONTRIBUTING AUTHORS

Nicholas C. Burckel, University of Wisconsin, Parkside
Edgar C. Duin, Falls Church, Virginia
Ralph D. Gray, Indiana University, Indianapolis
John Healy, Washington, D.C.
Willard Carl Klunder, Indiana University, Indianapolis
Arthur McClure, Central Missouri State University
Marie Marmo Mullaney, Caldwell College

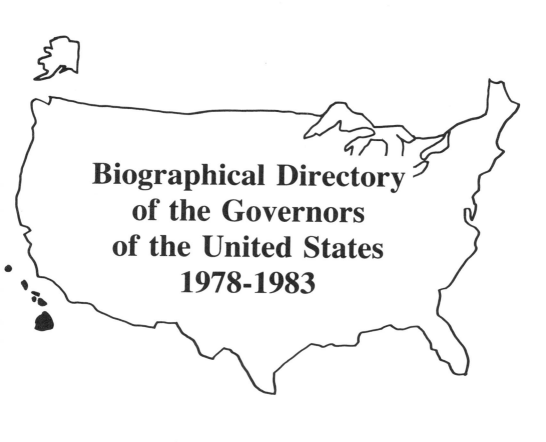

Biographical Directory
of the Governors
of the United States
1978-1983

George Corley Wallace (Credit: Governor's Office, Alabama)

ALABAMA

WALLACE, George Corley, 1963-1967, 1971-1972, 1972-1979, 1983-

Born on August 25, 1919 in Clio, Alabama, the son of George C., a farmer, and Mozell (Smith) Wallace. A Methodist, Wallace is the brother of Jack, Gerald, and Marianne. He married Lurleen Burns on May 23, 1943, who died on May 7, 1968. Wallace married a second time to Cornelia Ellis Snively on January 4, 1971. Following his divorce in 1978, he married a third time to Lisa Taylor, the daughter of a wealthy Alabama coal mine operator, on September 9, 1981. Almost 30 years his junior, Taylor, along with her sister, had a country singing act that entertained prospective Wallace voters at rallies during the late 1960s. Wallace is the father of Bobbie Jo, Peggy Sue, George Corley Jr., and Janie Lee by his first wife.

After attending Barbour County, Alabama High School, Wallace received an LL.B. from the University of Alabama in 1942. He was admitted to the Alabama bar that same year. Wallace served in the United States Army Air Force from 1942 to 1945, achieving the rank of Flight Sergeant. Alabama's Assistant Attorney General from 1946 to 1947, he was also a member of the Alabama House of Representatives from 1947 to 1953. Wallace was a Judge for the Third Judicial District of Alabama between 1953 and 1958, and had a private law practice in Clayton, Alabama from 1958 to 1962. He is a member of the American Legion, the Veterans of Foreign Wars, the Disabled American Veterans, the Masons, the Moose, the Elks, and the Modern Woodmen of the World.

Following an unsuccessful campaign for Governor in 1958 as a racial moderate, Wallace became a staunch segregationist and won the governorship in 1962. He defeated Jim Folsom to win the Democratic nomination, and received 303,987 votes in the uncontested general election. Wallace was sworn into office on January 14, 1963. During his first administration Wallace barred the enrollment of blacks at the University of Alabama, promising to preserve "segregation forever." President John F. Kennedy then ordered the Alabama National Guard to active duty, and forced state officials to comply with federal court orders dealing with integration. Wallace eventually became known as the nation's premier foe of integration.

Constitutionally prohibited from succeeding himself in office, Wallace attempted to amend the Alabama constitution to allow him to do so. His efforts failed, and he left office on January 16, 1967. Nevertheless, Wallace's wife Lurleen had been elected Governor in November 1966, and her husband served as a $1.00-a-year Special Assistant, an arrangement which allowed him to make most of the important executive decisions. When she died in office on May 7, 1968, Lurleen Wallace was succeeded by Alabama's Lieutenant Governor, Albert P. Brewer.

Wallace was the unsuccessful American Independent Party candidate for President in 1968, although he won 13.6 percent of the vote nationally, the strongest third party candidacy since 1924. In the 1970 Alabama Democratic gubernatorial primary election, Wallace trailed the incumbent Brewer; however, he captured the runoff primary, and was elected to a second gubernatorial term in the general election on November 3, 1970. Wallace received 634,046 votes, compared with National Democratic Party of Alabama candidate John L. Cashin's 125,491 and Independent A.C. Shelton's 75,679. He was inaugurated on January 18, 1971.

As a candidate for the 1972 Democratic Presidential nomination, Wallace had received more popular votes in the primaries than anyone else at the time he was gunned down in a Maryland shopping center in May. The assassination attempt by Arthur Bremer, Jr. left Wallace permanently paralyzed from the waist down. As a result of his wounds, he relinquished his duties as chief executive to Lieutenant Governor Jere L. Beasley on June 4, 1972; by July 7, however, he had recovered sufficiently to reassume the office. Because of a 1968 amendment to the Alabama Constitution which allowed governors to succeed themselves, Wallace was eligible to run for re-election in 1974. He won 83 percent of the vote in the general election on November 5, 1974, receiving 497,574 votes against Republican Elvin McCary's 88,381.

Barred by law from seeking a third consecutive term in 1978, Wallace considered running for the Senate seat being vacated by Alabama's retiring veteran Senator John Sparkman. To that end, the Legislature even passed a bill guaranteeing him police protection after he left the Statehouse. Wallace's surprise decision not to seek the Senate, confirmed in June 1978 after a second seat became available with the death of Alabama's other Senator, James B. Allen, moved political commentators to write his political obituary. Both supporters and opponents interpreted his action as being tantamount to permanent retirement from electoral politics.

In retirement, Wallace worked for the University of Alabama in Birmingham as a Director of Development for Rehabilitative Services. There was also some discussion concerning the possibility of endowing a chair at one of the state universities, to enable him to teach law, political science, or government.

Yet the man who has been called a compulsive campaigner ultimately found political life irresistible, and in May 1982 he announced his candidacy for an unprecedented fourth term as Governor of Alabama. Running on a tax-cutting platform, he directed his campaign toward "the little man" in a state suffering from a 14.5 percent unemployment rate. Wallace's opponents for the Democratic nomination were Lieutenant Governor George McMillan, who perceived himself as Alabama's best hope for a progressive, "New South" image, and Joe McCorquodale, Speaker of the Alabama House for eight years, who was supported by farmers, bankers, big business, big land owners, and timber and forest product interests. Since no candidate received 50 percent of the vote as required by state law (Wallace polled 44 percent to McMillan's nearly 30 percent and McCorquodale's 25 percent), Wallace and McMillan took part in a runoff election.

The runoff campaign tested not only political alignments, but also cultural styles and social classes. McMillan, a liberal lawyer from Mountain Brook, Birmingham's richest white suburb, depicted himself as a New South progressive. Claiming that Wallace represented the "politics of the past," he charged that poor leadership when either George or Lurleen Wallace controlled state government for all but six of the last 20 years had caused Alabama to miss much of the Sun Belt prosperity experienced by other states in the Southeast. Essentially, McMillan attempted to put together an urban coalition of blacks and middle and upper class whites, a novel political approach in Alabama.

Wallace, on the other hand, made much of his experience, and attacked McMillan's liberal views on some issues. He called for victims' rights in criminal cases, including monetary restitution by those convicted, and condemned "tax loopholes for the rich." Adopting a populist theme, he characterized the election as a battle between the "little people" and the wealthy. Pledging to combat a national economic trend in which "the rich get richer and the poor get poorer," Wallace campaigned heavily in blue-collar neighborhoods and towns where steel mills and auto plants had closed. In a stunning about-face that drew nationwide publicity, Wallace openly courted the black vote, which constituted about 25 percent of the electorate. In actions viewed skeptically by many, he also repudiated his former racist sentiments, acts, and statements, saying that his attacks had never been against blacks directly but against interference by the federal government in state affairs.

Wallace won the runoff by a margin of 51.5 percent to 48.5 percent, in a showing that demonstrated the strong rural-urban cleavages in Alabama politics. He captured both his usual rural strongholds in predominantly white counties and several counties in which blacks represented the majority. The former segregationist even got up to 40 percent of the vote in urban black precincts in Montgomery. Indeed, black leaders conceded that he received minority votes because blacks were helped by education and job programs Wallace has sponsored before he left office in 1978.

In the general election Wallace played an unfamiliar role as a liberal versus the ultraconservative Emory Folmar, the Republican mayor of Montgomery. A millionaire shopping center developer, Folmar advocated tough police tactics and supported the tenets of the "Moral Majority." The outcome was never in doubt. Wallace forged a populist coalition of blacks, labor unions, and poor whites. Speaking out for children, the jobless, the elderly and infirm, he attacked public utilities, banks, and "rich Republicans." Promising an era of economic growth by arguing that his international stature could attract business to the state, Wallace won 58 percent of the vote.

A persistent Presidential candidate, Wallace has said that he might have had a good chance of becoming President has it not been for the injuries he suffered in 1972. He has also expressed the belief that his dark horse Presidential campaigns in 1968, 1972, and 1976 created the climate that made it possible for Jimmy Carter, a fellow Southerner, to be elected President. As a national spokesman for the social, political, and economic discontent of working class whites in many eastern and midwestern states, he believes that he has made a unique contribution to American politics by allowing himself to be the people's "instrument" in bringing about "much of the change in American political thought."

Bibliography: Lester A. Sobel, ed., *Facts on File Yearbook, 1963* (New York, 1964); Lester A. Sobel, ed., *Facts on File Yearbook, 1972* (New York, 1973); "Democrats: Who's Almost Who," *Newsweek* (October 7, 1974); Congressional Quarterly, Inc., *Guide to U.S. Elections* (Washington, D.C., 1975); Roy Glashan, *American Governors and Gubernatorial Elections,1775-1975* (Stillwater, Minn., 1975); *New York Times*, April 22 and June 19, 1977, April 21, May 17-18, and June 22, 1978, January 16, 1979, September 10, 1981, May 23, September 3, September 8, September 26, September 29-30, October 3, and November 3, 1982; Michael Barone *et al.*, eds., *The Almanac of American Politics, 1978-84* (New York and Washington, D.C., 1977-83); "Fresh Faces in the Mansions," *Time* (November 15, 1982). MMM

Forrest Hood James, Jr. (Credit: Alabama Department of Archives and History)

JAMES, Forrest Hood, Jr. ("Fob"), 1979-1983

Born in Lanett, Alabama on September 15, 1934, the son of Forrest Hood and Rebecca (Ellington) James. An Episcopalian, James received a B.S.C.E. from Auburn University in 1955; on August 20 of that year he married Bobbie May Mooney. They have three children—Forrest Hood III, Timothy E., and Patrick F.

An All-America football halfback at Auburn, James played professionally for the Montreal Alouettes in the Canadian Football League in 1956 and 1957. At about the same time he served as a Lieutenant in the United States Army Corps of Engineers. In 1958 James quit football and was a construction superintendent in Alabama until 1962, when he founded Diversified Products Corporation of Opelika, Alabama, a company he ran until 1978. Diversified makes barbells and ping-pong tables. A minor official in the Republican Party, James switched to the Democratic Party in 1977 and sought the nomination for Governor in 1978. It appeared for a time that the chief challenger in that election would be Cornelia Wallace, the wife of incumbent Governor George C. Wallace, who could not succeed himself. When Mrs. Wallace decided not to run, James met State Attorney General Bill Baxley in a runoff. Although endorsed by George Wallace, Baxley's campaign was handicapped by a relative lack of television money and rumors that he owed large gambling debts. James took the runoff by about 100,000 votes and faced Republican nominee Guy Hunt in the general election, which James won easily by 551,886 votes to 196,963.

During James' term Alabama received federal disaster aid after Hurricane Frederic caused $1 billion in damage to the Mobile, Alabama area, destroying the historic district of that city. There was also a mass arrest of Ku Klux Klansmen in Montgomery after the Klansmen marched without a permit. In 1981 the federal Justice Department sued the city of Mobile, claiming that the at-large system of elections for city commissioners resulted in racial bias. The state also established a Health Planning and Development Agency, and Alabama's drug criminal statutes were revised.

George Wallace was elected to a fourth term as Governor of Alabama in 1982. To win the nomination, Wallace had run as a populist and sought the support of black voters.

Bibliography: *Birmingham Journal*, September 27, November 5, and November 9, 1978; *Who's Who in America* (Chicago, 1981); *Washington Post*, May 16, 1981. Certain of James' papers are at the Alabama Department of Archives and History in Montgomery. JH

Jay Sterner Hammond (Credit: Secretary of State, Alaska)

ALASKA

HAMMOND, Jay Sterner, 1974-1982

Born on July 21, 1922 in Troy, New York, the son of a Protestant minister. A Protestant, he and his wife Bella Gardiner have two daughters, Heidi and Dana.

Hammond lived for a time in southern Vermont and Pennsylvania before World War II interrupted his studies in petroleum engineering at Penn State University. During the war he enlisted in the United States Navy, serving as a Marine fighter pilot before his honorable discharge as Captain in 1946. Hammond came to Alaska that year, graduating from the University of Alaska, Fairbanks, with a degree in biological science in 1948. Before seeking his first political office in the late 1950s, he worked for the United States Fish and Wildlife Service, established an air taxi service, worked as a registered game guide and commercial fisherman, and built a sportsman's lodge on Lake Clark and a fishing lodge on Wood River Lakes.

A Republican, Hammond was first elected to the Alaska House of Representatives in 1959, completing three terms in all, and serving as Chairman of the Resources Committee, Minority Whip, and Majority Whip. From 1965 to 1967 he was Manager of Bristol Bay Borough, the first borough in Alaska. (Boroughs in Alaska are much like counties in other states.) He served that borough again between 1972 and 1974, this time as Mayor. In the intervening years, 1967 to 1972, he was elected to the Alaska Senate, serving as Majority Whip, Majority Leader, Chairman of the Rules Committee, and President of the Senate.

To win election as Governor in 1974, Hammond had to defeat every former chief executive Alaska ever had. In the Republican primary he beat Walter Hickel and the man who had succeeded him, Keith Miller. He then proceeded to win the general election by defeating William Egan, who had been the Democratic gubernatorial candidate in every election since statehood. Hammond won 48 percent of the vote, compared to Egan's 47 percent. Although Egan charged that Hammond would "lock up Alaska's resources in an icebox," Hammond's emphasis on environmental protection appealed to enough voters to gain him the narrow victory.

Philosophically, Hammond is known as an individual who does not believe unequivocally in growth and development, who has argued against federal interference with Alaskan land use policy, who favors increasing taxes on oil companies, and who has expressed doubts as to whether the state ought to be spending all its oil wealth so rapidly. His chief political asset, commentators believe, is his open and informal style.

In his 1978 campaign for re-election, Hammond again faced a challenge from former Governor Hickel in the Republican primary, who attacked Hammond's program of controlled growth as one that amounted to "no growth at all." Although Hammond defeated Hickel by a mere 98 votes to gain the Republican nomination, the former Nixon Interior Secretary mounted a write-in campaign that attracted 26 percent of the vote in the general election. Hammond won his bid for a second term, but with a plurality of only 39 percent of the vote against three challengers. The campaign in 1978 was also marked by one moment of high drama, when Hammond, a former bush pilot, rescued a group of people from their downed plane. During his second term as governor, Alaska abolished its state income tax, and the Legislature passed a controversial bill returning surplus oil revenues to residents, with those who had lived longer in the state getting more.

Hammond retired from politics in 1982, choosing not to run for a third term. A sometime doggerel writer, he has published several articles on outdoors topics, as well as one book of verse.

Bibliography: Evangeline Atwood and Robert N. DeArmond, *Who's Who in Alaskan Politics* (Portland, 1975); Michael Barone *et al.*, eds., *The Almanac of American Politics, 1978-80* (New York, 1977-79); *The Alaska Almanac: Facts About Alaska* (Anchorage, 1978); biographical information, Governor's Office, Alaska. MMM

William Jennings Sheffield

SHEFFIELD, William Jennings, 1982-

Born on June 26, 1928 in Spokane, Washington, Sheffield moved to Alaska in 1953. A Presbyterian, he is a widower with one daughter, Deborah.

Trained as a radio broadcast engineer at DeForest Training School in Chicago and a member of the United States Army Air Corps from 1946 to 1949, Sheffield is founder and Chairman of the Board of Sheffield Enterprises, a hotel management firm that owns ten hotels in Alaska and Canada's Yukon Territory. Combining his business talents with a sense of civic involvement, he has been President of the Alaska Visitors Association and that state's Chamber of Commerce; he is also a former National Director of the United States Jaycees. Sheffield was Chairman of the state March of Dimes, the state Cancer Society, the Easter Seal Telethon, and the St. Jude's Children's Hospital Telethon. His political activities include membership on the Anchorage City Planning Commission (1960-63) and the Anchorage Charter Commission (1976), service to the Foundation Board of the University of Alaska, chairmanship of the Alaska State Parole Board, and election as a Delegate to local, state, and national Democratic Party conventions.

Sheffield's business ventures had made him a millionaire, and in seeking the Alaska governorship in 1982 he broke all state records by spending more than $1 million, much of it his own money, to win the Democratic nomination against a field of five other candidates. Nevertheless, his primary victory was a narrow one. Sheffield defeated his closest challenger, Fairbanks lawyer Steve Cowper, by only 600 votes.

In the general election Sheffield's opponent was insurance agent Tom Fink, an outspoken conservative and former Speaker of the Alaska House of Representatives, who had won the Republican nomination by defeating the favored candidate, Lieutenant Governor Terry Miller. Campaigning in the remote bush country, Sheffield picked up much support in small villages usually ignored by politicians. Alaska's voters were also impressed by his business experience. Most important to his victory was his popular stand on two hotly contested political issues: a proposal to spend $2.8 billion to move the state capital from Juneau to Willow, 580 miles away, and an attempt to repeal a law that allowed rural Alaskans to take fish and game for subsistence. The attempt to move the capital aroused considerable opposition in southeastern Alaska, while the debate on hunting and fishing rights took on racial overtones, since residents of the Alaska bush were more likely to be Alaska natives. Sheffield opposed both measures, while Fink did not.

Bibliography: *New York Times*, July 6 and November 4, 1982; "Where the GOP Will Hold Its Own," *U.S. News and World Report* (October 4, 1982); National Governors' Association, *Governors of the American States, Commonwealths, and Territories* (Washington, D.C., 1983); biographical information, Governor's Office, Alaska. MMM

Wesley H. Bolin

ARIZONA

BOLIN, Wesley H., 1977-1978

Born in Butler, Missouri on July 1, 1908, the son of Don Strother and Margaret (Combs) Bolin. A Congregationalist, Bolin was twice married. He was survived by his wife, Marion Knappenberger, whom he married on August 14, 1967, and by five sons—Wesley, Bill, Thomas, Bruce, and Steven.

Bolin moved with his family to Phoenix, Arizona in 1917. After attending Phoenix Junior College from 1928 to 1929, he completed the LaSalle Extension School course in law, in preparation for a career in law enforcement. Bolin was proprietor of a dry cleaning business before his involvement with the Young Democrats led to his election as Constable of the West Phoenix Precinct, a post he held from 1938 to 1942. In 1942 he was appointed Justice of the Peace for the West Phoenix Precinct, to complete the term of Nat T. McKee. Serving in that position until 1948, he helped to organize the Arizona Justices of the Peace and Constables Association, and became that organization's first Secretary-Treasurer. First elected Secretary of State in 1948, Bolin served for ten consecutive terms, winning even in those election years when Republicans captured most of the offices in the state. He was called a "pinto" Democrat, to use the Arizona term, because of his practice of hiring conservative Republicans as his chief advisers; Bolin's victories were attributed in part to this tendency to make bipartisan commitments and appointments. Active in the National Association of Secretaries of State, he served as its President from 1952 to 1953, and was Chairman of the Arizona Code Commission in 1956.

In 1973 Bolin attracted national attention in connection with an attempt to recall from office Governor Jack Williams, a Republican. A coalition of United Farm Workers, environmentalists, women's rights groups, and other liberal organizations sought the recall after Williams refused to veto a law prohibiting secondary boycotts and strikes during harvests and limiting the power of the United Farm Workers to organize in the fields. Bolin, as Secretary of State, ruled against recall, claiming that the petition had too few valid signatures. Recall leaders viewed his scrupulous attention to the signature verification process as a deliberate delay, but Bolin continued to insist that he was simply "following procedures" and acting on the Attorney General's advice.

As Secretary of State for almost three decades, Bolin served as Acting Governor in the absence of the chief executive. Thus, he had some experience in the post when the unpopular Governor Raul H. Castro resigned to become United

States Ambassador to Argentina. Bolin was sworn in as Arizona's fifteenth governor on October 21, 1977.

Consistent with his earlier bipartisan approach, one of Bolin's first acts as chief executive was to appoint two Republicans with business backgrounds as his top staff aides. A fiscal conservative, he appealed to the Legislature to hire no new personnel in state agencies and to enact no budget increases. Still, his administration had not really developed a consistent philosophy or any specific policies when Bolin died of a sudden heart attack in his Phoenix home on March 4, 1978, less than five months after taking office. He had just completed a tour of flood damaged areas of Arizona and written an appeal to President Jimmy Carter, seeking designation of the state as a disaster area. Bolin had announced his intention to run for election to the governor's office that year. Had he lived, he would have faced a primary fight against a former aide of Raul Castro, Dino DeConcini, the brother of Arizona's United States Senator Dennis DeConcini. DeConcini had already entered the race, and received Castro's endorsement.

Bolin was succeeded in office by Attorney General Bruce Babbitt. House Minority Leader, Representative John J. Rhodes of Arizona, eulogized him as "one of the finest public servants." Bolin had been an active supporter of the Boy Scouts and Boys Clubs, and in 1976 was named Man of the Year by the Boys Club of Phoenix.

Bibliography: New York Times, April 2, 1973, October 21, 1977; *Facts on File, 1977; New York Times Biographical Service*, March 5, 1978; Robert Sobel and John W. Raimo, eds., *Biographical Directory of the Governors of the United States, 1789-1978*, 4 vols. (Westport, Conn., 1978); Michael Barone *et al.*, eds., *The Almanac of American Politics, 1980* (New York, 1979). MMM

Bruce Edward Babbitt (Credit: Markow Photography)

BABBITT, Bruce Edward, 1978-

Born on June 27, 1938, Babbitt is the son of a patrician family who came to Arizona when it was still a frontier and became wealthy by operating Indian trading posts near Flagstaff and then expanding to other interests. A Roman Catholic, he left Arizona to attend the University of Notre Dame, where he was elected student body President. Hoping to capitalize on the great mineral wealth of Arizona, Babbitt majored in geology and went on to receive an M.A. in geophysics at the University of Newcastle in England. He and his wife Hattie, who is a trial lawyer, have two children.

A mining trip to Bolivia quickly changed Babbitt's career ambitions. As he explained to a reporter, "I saw so much misery, such human deprivation while in Bolivia that I thought, how can I live in an ivory tower filled with such people problems?" While earning his law degree at Harvard, he took time off to take part in the civil rights marches in Selma, Alabama; after graduating in 1965, he joined the Johnson administration's anti-poverty drive as a civil rights lawyer. Babbitt was also Special Assistant to the Director of VISTA from 1965 to 1967. He returned to Arizona in 1967 and became a member of the Phoenix law firm of Brown and Bain.

Babbitt entered state politics in 1974, and was elected Attorney General on a platform promising to deal vigorously with land fraud, securities and insurance irregularities, bribery in business regulation, and other white collar crime. His crusading prosecution of price-fixing and other anti-trust activity reportedly endangered his life. According to court testimony, a murder contract was placed on his life by the same people who in June 1976 murdered *Arizona Republic* reporter Don Bolles, who had been investigating land fraud in Arizona. Babbitt won fame for prosecuting that case, and for winning consumer refunds in suits against companies that engaged in price-fixing practices.

Babbitt became Arizona's chief executive through a partly accidental, partly tragic sequence of events. In 1977, when Democratic incumbent Raul Castro was appointed United States Ambassador to Argentina, Secretary of State Wesley Bolin succeeded to the governorship. But when Bolin suddenly died in March 1978, after less than five months in office, Attorney General Babbitt found himself Arizona's third governor within five months.

Because the Republican Party had grown considerably stronger in Arizona by 1978, Babbitt did not have an especially easy time of it when he sought election to his own term that year. In the general election he narrowly defeated the Republican challenger, automobile dealer and former State Senator Evan Meacham, by winning just 52 percent of the vote. As governor, Babbitt sought to place some environmental controls on the state's growth and advocated modest increases in state government services. He acquired something of a national reputation when he was named by President Jimmy Carter to serve on a commission investigating the Three Mile Island nuclear plant accident. Drawing on his own background as an engineering student, he helped to draft a report that was widely accepted as responsible and fair. Although he began his political career as a liberal, Babbitt has recently come to question orthodox liberal approaches to issues, especially by criticizing federal programs which require too much paperwork and give too much control to Washington. When the Reagan administration announced its program of budget cuts early in 1981, Babbitt alone among America's governors suggested an alternative.

In his 1982 campaign for re-election, Babbitt won an easy victory over Arizona's Senate President, the Republican Leo Corbet. Babbitt won 62 percent of the vote in an election widely believed to have enhanced his reputation as a rising star in national Democratic politics. He has been mentioned as a possible candidate for the United State Senate when Barry Goldwater's term expires in 1986. Presently, Babbitt serves as Chairman of the National Governors' Association Subcommittee on Water Management.

Babbitt's family spends a good deal of time backpacking in and around the Grand Canyon and other parts of the state, and the governor has published two books reflecting his affinity for the great outdoors: *Color and Light: The Southwest Canvases of Louis Akin* (1973), and *Grand Canyon: An Anthology* (1978).

Bibliography: Michael Barone *et al.*, eds., *The Almanac of American Politics, 1978-82* (New York and Washington, D.C., 1977-81); "New Governor for Arizona," *New York Times*, March 8, 1978; "Where the GOP Will Hold Its Own," *U.S. News and World Report* (October 4, 1982); National Governors' Association, *Governors of the American States, Commonwealths, and Territories* (Washington, D.C., 1983); biographical information, Western Governors' Conference. MMM

.

David Hampton Pryor

ARKANSAS

PRYOR, David Hampton, 1975-1979

Born on August 29, 1934 in Camden, Arkansas, the son of Edgar and Susie (Newton) Pryor. A Presbyterian, Pryor is married to the former Barbara Jean Lunsford of Fayetteville, Arkansas. They have three sons—David Jr., Mark, and Scott.

Pryor attended public schools in Camden and was graduated from Camden High School in 1952. He attended Henderson State University in Arkadelphia, Arkansas between 1952 and 1953, and in 1957 received a B.A. from the University of Arkansas, Fayetteville. Pryor earned his LL.B. from the University of Arkansas Law School in 1964.

The founder and publisher between 1957 and 1961 of the *Ouachita Citizen*, a Camden newspaper, Pryor was also in private practice with a Camden law firm when he began his political career. A populist Democrat with moderate to liberal views on many issues, he was first elected to the Arkansas State House of Representatives as a Delegate from Ouachita County in 1960, and re-elected in 1962 and 1964. In November 1966 he was chosen to fill the unexpired term of Congressman Oren Harris, who had resigned to take a federal judgeship, and for whom Pryor had served as a page in the early 1950s. Pryor was a United States Congressman from Arkansas between 1966 and 1973, gaining national attention as a spokesman for the elderly. During his second House term he worked in a Washington area nursing home without identifying himself, in order to investigate and expose abuses in that area. When he was unable to get the House to set up a special committee on the problems of the elderly, he formed his own committee in a trailer parked at a nearby gas station.

In 1972 Pryor took on a challenge that virtually every politician in the state told him he couldn't win: he decided to challenge the state's senior Senator, the venerable John L. McClellan, for the Democratic nomination (tantamount to election in Democratic Arkansas). Campaigning intensely all over the state for months, and making much of the fact that McClellan was 76 years old, Pryor forced a runoff by holding his opponent to 44 percent of the vote in their initial contest—itself a startling feat in the eyes of political observers. Pryor lost the runoff by 18,000 votes, after a surprisingly vigorous comeback by McClellan and a campaign that seized on Pryor's labor support to argue that union bosses wanted to get even with McClellan for his past investigations into union practices. McClellan also made the most of standard conservative issues—busing, gun control, and school prayer.

Pryor then returned to Little Rock to practice law, but in 1974 incumbent Governor Dale Bumpers' sudden decision to run for the United States Senate gave Pryor an opportunity to run for chief executive. His most serious challenge came from a fellow Democrat, the former Governor and legendary segregationist Orval E. Faubus, who was making a comeback attempt. Although Faubus concentrated heavily on the busing issue, Pryor won a majority in the three-man primary, and thereby avoided a runoff. He went on to defeat Republican Ken Coon in the general election by a vote of 358,018 to 187,872. Pryor was re-elected virtually without opposition two years later, easily defeating Republican Leon Griffith, by capturing 83 percent of the vote.

During Pryor's administration an Advisory Board on Law Enforcement Standards was organized, and four new state agencies were created—an Arkansas Office on Drug Abuse Prevention, a State Printing Board, a State Health Planning Agency, and a Statewide Health Coordinating Council. Pryor followed the example of other Democratic state executives in Arkansas by endorsing conservative fiscal policies. He placed a moratorium on state hiring, reduced out-of-state travel by half, and proposed a controversial program for reducing state income taxes by 25 percent. Critics immediately accused Pryor of using the tax package to promote his candidacy in the 1978 United States Senate race, a charge he denied.

Nonetheless, Pryor was indeed a candidate in the 1978 race to succeed the late Senator John L. McClellan. He faced strong opposition from two opponents: Congressman Jim Guy Tucker, a Harvard-educated lawyer who had also served two terms as State Attorney General; and three-term Congressman Ray Thornton, a Yale-educated lawyer who had become prominent as a member of the House Judiciary Committee that considered the impeachment of Richard Nixon, and who waged a highly effective and well-financed media campaign. The race attracted what political observers considered the most outstanding contenders in any single race in the modern history of Arkansas. Although Pryor received fewer votes than had been predicted in public opinion polls, he finished first in the three-way race with 35 percent of the vote, compared with Tucker's 32 percent, and then went on to defeat Tucker, by winning 55 percent of the vote in the runoff election. Pryor trounced Republican political novice and former Peace Corps volunteer Tom Kelly in the general election, 76 percent to 16 percent. (Independent John Black drew seven percent of the vote.)

Because Arkansas has been in the habit of choosing its senators young and then re-electing them for years (e.g., J. William Fulbright served for 30 years and McClellan for 35), observers expect the young and energetic Pryor to have a long and promising career. Indeed, in November 1984 he won re-election to the Senate by a convincing margin of 57 percent to 43 percent over the Republican Ed Bethune. Pryor is a member of the Senate Committee on Agriculture, Nutrition, and Forestry; the Senate Finance Committee; the Special Committee on Aging; and the Select Committee on Ethics. Before his election to the prestigious Senate Finance Committee in January 1983, he served on the Senate Governmental Affairs Committee. He is also a member of the Democratic Steering

Committee in the Senate. In 1979 Pryor was one of a group of senators who visited the Soviet Union to discuss terms of a strategic arms limitation treaty with the United States. He has also been instrumental in outlining "serious, pervasive problems" of waste and mismanagement in the government's practice of hiring private consultants, and has held joint House-Senate hearings on the practice of issuing consulting contracts.

Bibliography: "Arkansas: Home Rule?," *Newsweek* (December 20, 1976); Michael Barone *et al.*, eds., *The Almanac of American Politics, 1978-82* (New York and Washington, D.C., 1977-81); *New York Times*, May 14, June 1, June 10, and June 14, 1978, August 31 and September 6, 1979, March 21, 1980, May 14, 1981, November 8, 1984; *Who's Who in American Politics, 1981-82* (New York, 1981); Alan Ehrenhalt, ed., *Politics in America, 1982* (Washington, D.C., 1981); biographical information, U.S. Senate Office. MMM

Bill Clinton

CLINTON, Bill, 1979-1981, 1983-

Born in Hope, Arkansas on August 19, 1946. A Baptist, Clinton is married to the former Hillary Rodham. They have a daughter, Chelsea.

Educated in the public schools of Hot Springs, Arkansas, Clinton received a degree in international affairs from the Georgetown University School of Foreign Service in 1968. He attended the University of Oxford as a Rhodes Scholar, and received a degree from Yale Law School in 1973. Joining the staff of the University of Arkansas Law School, he also practiced law in Fayetteville before making his first run for public office in 1974. In that Watergate year he was narrowly defeated for Congress in the Third District, holding incumbent John Paul Hammerschmidt, a Republican, to 52 percent of the vote. Afterwards, he continued to teach law; he also taught in the Criminal Justice Program at the University of Arkansas at Little Rock.

Elected Arkansas Attorney General in 1976, Clinton sued to hold down utility rates, fought against 25 cent pay phone calls, and ended bans on liquor and eyeglass advertising. Having established a reputation as an energetic and activist politician—indeed, one reporter noted that Clinton "worked like a madman"—he was elected the nation's youngest Governor in 1978. After gaining 60 percent of the vote against four other candidates to win the Democratic nomination without a runoff, he went on to defeat Republican State Chairman A. Lynn Lowe in the general election by capturing 63 percent of the vote compared with Lowe's 37 percent. The campaign received national publicity. At 32, Clinton became the youngest man to be chosen chief executive of any state since Harold Stassen carried Minnesota in 1938 at the age of 31.

Boyishly handsome and charismatic, Clinton also had a rather unorthodox background for a rising politician from the deep South. He had worked as the Texas State Coordinator for George McGovern's ill-fated 1972 Presidential race, and had been a staff attorney for the House Judiciary Committee before the Nixon impeachment hearings. A supporter of the Equal Rights Amendment, Clinton also seemed an anomaly because his wife Hillary, herself a lawyer, was a strong feminist who campaigned for her husband while using her maiden name. Clinton also managed to campaign successfully against a rising "Proposition 13" sentiment to cut state taxes. Instead of promising to cut taxes, he asked for new highway taxes and a $132 million spending increase to upgrade the state's school system, which was ranked 49th in quality nation-wide. Explaining that he believed the citizens of Arkansas were tired of being ranked last or next to last according to major indices of social and economic welfare, he sought to accelerate the state's economic growth and to make permanent improvements in the quality of life for its residents.

During his first term Clinton established a strong record in bringing jobs to Arkansas and in selling the state's products abroad. He held down utility rates and curbed utility costs, while working vigorously to improve the state's educational system with programs to test students in basic skills, to increase opportunities for gifted children, to advance vocational education, and to increase teachers' salaries. Clinton also initiated tax cuts for senior citizens by removing the sales tax from medicine and increasing the homestead property tax exemption for the elderly. He worked to eliminate waste in government, and sponsored one of the nation's first "workfare" programs, which required that people requesting food stamps also register to work. This requirement has eliminated several thousand ineligible people from food stamp rolls. Clinton also led the way in calling for the appointment of women and minorities to Cabinet-level jobs. With his activist programs and leadership style, Clinton was able to regain power for the governor's office that had been usurped by the Legislature under previous administrations. For all these achievements, *Time* magazine honored Clinton in 1979, listing him as one of America's outstanding young leaders and counting him among the "50 faces to watch" in the future.

Nevertheless, Clinton had his critics. He was sometimes lampooned in political cartoons as a brat furiously pedalling a tricycle. Many thought he was more interested in national than in state politics. Conservative opponents tried to use his wife's feminism against him, and assailed him for his liberal views by charging him with support for gun control, the Panama Canal treaties, and the decriminalization of marijuana. Most of all, however, Clinton's political stature was damaged by his handling of the Cuban refugee situation. Thousands of Cuban refugees who had left or been expelled from Cuba during Fidel Castro's celebrated maneuvers of 1980 were housed at Fort Chaffee, Arkansas, and Clinton was hurt politically by his inability to force the White House to have other states shoulder some of the burden and costs. His 1980 defeat by Republican Frank White, a businessman and political novice, was widely viewed as a simple case of voter backlash against the Democratic Party on both the state and national levels. White won that election by attracting 52 percent of the vote compared with Clinton's 48 percent.

After leaving office, Clinton joined the Little Rock law firm of Wright, Lindsey, and Jennings, but astute observers knew that his political career was far from over. Indeed, he returned to the governor's mansion two years later, defeating White in his bid for re-election and becoming the first person in the state's history to be elected to a second, non-consecutive term as chief executive. This time, however, he encountered a strong challenge from members of his own party to win the Democratic gubernatorial nomination. Facing former Congressman Jim Guy Tucker and former Lieutenant Governor Joe Purcell in the primary, he was forced into a runoff when no one earned a majority in the first contest. In the second contest he defeated Purcell, 54 percent to 46 percent, to gain the Democratic nomination and the chance to run against White again.

Clinton spent much of his campaign apologizing for the mistakes of his first term. He also sought to reassure voters that, contrary to rumors, he had no national political ambitions. In terms of substantive issues, the election hinged on a record $227 million in utility rate increases approved during White's term.

Public opinion surveys had consistently demonstrated that Arkansas Power and Light was one of the most unpopular institutions in the state, and Clinton capitalized on voter displeasure both with the rate increases and with White's failure to tame the "monster." The race generated an astonishingly high voter turnout (72 percent), and this time Clinton won by a margin of 55 percent to 45 percent. He has identified his top priority during his second term to be putting the unemployed back to work.

In November 1984 Clinton became the first Arkansas chief executive to win a third term since Orval Faubus, when he defeated Republican newcomer Elwood Freeman by a margin of 62 percent to 38 percent.

Bibliography: "Money, Money, Money," *Time* (November 20, 1978); *New York Times Biographical Service*, 9 (November 1978), 1019; *New York Times*, December 14, 1978, February 25, 1979, August 5 and November 12, 1980, January 4, May 24, May 26-27, June 8-9, and October 28, 1982, January 12, 1983, November 8, 1984; "50 Faces for America's Future," *Time* (August 6, 1979); Michael Barone *et al.*, eds., *The Almanac of American Politics, 1980-82* (New York and Washington, D.C., 1979-81); *Who's Who in American Politics, 1981-82* (New York, 1981); Alan Ehrenhalt, ed., *Politics in America, 1982* (Washington, D.C., 1981); "Southern Star Rising Again," *Time* (September 20, 1982); "Fresh Faces in the Mansions," *Time* (November 15, 1982); National Governors' Association, *Governors of the American States, Commonwealths, and Territories* (Washington, D.C., 1983); biographical information, Governor's Office, Arkansas. MMM

Frank White (Credit: ©Larry Obsitnik)

WHITE, Frank, 1981-1983

Born in Texarkana, Arkansas on June 4, 1933, the son of Loftin E. and Ida (Clark) White. A member of the Fellowship Bible Church, White is married to the former Gay Daniels.

After graduating in 1956 from the United States Naval Academy with a B.S. in engineering, White served in the Air Force from 1957 to 1961, and was stationed in the United States, Greenland, and Europe. He was a senior account executive with Merrill, Lynch, Pierce, Fenner, and Smith from 1961 to 1973; he also served as Vice President of the Commercial National Bank of Little Rock between 1973 and 1975, and as President and Chief Executive Officer of Capitol Savings and Loan Association from 1977 to 1980.

In spite of being a political novice, White defeated Marshall Chrisman by winning 72 percent of the vote, compared with Chrisman's 28 percent, to gain the Republican gubernatorial nomination in 1980. Bolting the Democratic Party to run as a Republican, he was seen as a "sacrificial" candidate, given little chance of defeating incumbent Bill Clinton. Consequently, his upset victory by a narrow margin came as a stunning surprise. White's success was attributed to several factors. He managed to portray Clinton as the candidate of the privileged, out of touch with state voters. He also capitalized on certain identifiable and admitted mistakes Clinton had made in office, such as his highly unpopular hike in auto license fees. Most important, he profited from voter displeasure with Clinton, President Jimmy Carter, and Democrats in general for their handling (or mishandling) of the Cuban refugee situation. Many of the Cubans who came to America following Fidel Castro's celebrated "gaol delivery" in 1980 were housed at Fort Chaffee, a rarely used army installation near Arkansas' western border. In May 1980 riots erupted in the crowded compound, a situation that White turned to his advantage. Using TV commercials showing rioting Cubans, White charged that Clinton had not "stood up" to the White House as he had promised, and condemned the fact that Arkansas was being asked to carry the refugee burden without other parts of the country doing their share.

White won the general election by attracting 52 percent of the vote compared with Clinton's 48 percent, and thus became only the second Republican governor in Arkansas history. While political observers were surprised by White's breakthrough, they recognized that Arkansas shared many of the demographic ingredients that had helped Republicans elsewhere in the South in recent years: an increasing suburban vote, general population growth, and an influx of corporate business.

Once in office, White immediately faced some thorny problems. Republicans were displeased by his appointment of an overwhelmingly Democratic Cabinet, and criticized the Legislature's formulation of a re-districting plan following the 1980 census that reduced the largely Republican Third District of the state. (White eventually allowed this plan to become law without his signature.) He also attracted widespread attention as a religious fundamentalist targeted by the American Civil Liberties Union. A member of a small evangelical Bible sect which the day after his election had announced that White's victory "was a victory for the Lord," the governor signed and praised a bill that would require Arkansas schools to give balanced treatment to theories of evolution and scientific creationism. With its passage, Arkansas became the first state in which such a bill had been passed by both houses of the Legislature, and the ACLU immediately announced plans to challenge the law in the federal courts.

Although White's election drive had been aided by members of the "Moral Majority" and other religious-fundamentalist groups, he angered even his own supporters by failing to assist such groups with their legislative goals, especially a bill to discourage abortions. White's image was further sullied by the disclosure that, at the request of his office, lobbyists had been supplying liquor for him to serve to legislators at social functions in the governor's mansion. This solicitation of favors from lobbyists offended religionists less than the fact that the governor's home had been used as a bar, and White found himself denounced by the Arkansas Christian Civic Foundation. Finally, while White had once been a strong backer of Ronald Reagan's "New Federalism," in 1982 he parted company with the President over the administration's latest round of budget cuts. While White argued that unemployment was already a serious problem in the state, and that proposed reductions in federal aid would likely force a dramatic increase in state taxes, his views served once again to isolate him from state Republicans.

Because of such problems, political analysts predicted early on that White would face strong Democratic opposition should he seek re-election in 1982. White hoped that voters would remember his attempts to seek tighter controls over the regulatory process, his firm stand on the death penalty, his reorganization of the state's vocational education system, and his efforts to expand the Arkansas Republican Party, but he faced criticism from a variety of groups. Consumers across the state charged that he let utility companies gouge them with rate increases; Republicans complained that he had not delivered patronage jobs and lamented some of his unfortunate appointments (*e.g.*, his selection of segregationist Orval E. Faubus as Director of the state's Veterans' Affairs Office); state lawmakers of both parties bemoaned his lack of leadership; and blacks decried his overall conservatism, general support of Reagan administration policies, and aggressive support of the death penalty. Well-financed nonetheless, White easily won renomination with about 80 percent of the vote against two challengers, Marshall Chrisman and Connie Voll. In the general election his opponent once again was the Democrat Bill Clinton, who spent much of the campaign apologizing for the errors of his first term and claiming that he had learned from his mistakes. Political observers considered the race to be the "most negative campaign in the state's recent history," since neither man was particularly popular with the voters, and both had blemishes on their records as governor. Nonetheless, the contest generated an astonishingly high voter turnout. While White portrayed Clinton as a "tax and spend" man, an ambitious liberal with his eyes on national rather than state politics, Clinton hammered away at utility rate increases during White's term, and hinted that White's business connections put him in close contact with the very groups against whom he was supposed to protect consumers. It seemed less than coincidental to some voters that White was a stockholder in one utility holding company and a board member of a utility before becoming governor. Indeed, rising utility rates and White's ties to utilities became the central issue in the campaign. He lost his bid for re-election, with Clinton gaining 55 percent of the vote to the incumbent's 45 percent.

Named Outstanding Young Man in Arkansas by the state's Jaycees in 1975, White is a member of the Rotary and American Legion. Upon his defeat, he retired to his banking and business interests.

Bibliography: *New York Times*, March 18, March 22, and December 6, 1981, March 2, May 24, May 27, and October 28, 1982; *Who's Who in American Politics, 1981-82* (New York, 1981); Michael Barone and Grant Ujifusa, eds., *The Almanac of American Politics, 1982* (Washington, D.C., 1981); Alan Ehrenhalt, ed., *Politics in America, 1982* (Washington, D.C., 1981); "Southern Star Rising Again," *Time* (September 20, 1982). MMM

Edmund Gerald Brown, Jr. (Credit: California State Library)

CALIFORNIA

BROWN, Edmund Gerald, Jr., 1975-1983

The second member of his family to occupy the California Statehouse in recent years, "Jerry" Brown is the son of former California Governor Edmund "Pat" Brown, who served as chief executive from 1959 to 1967, and Bernice (Layne) Brown. Born in San Francisco on April 7, 1938, the younger Brown received national attention and attained a public prominence that his father never did.

Brown did not immediately choose a political career but, as a Roman Catholic, decided instead to enter the Jesuits' Sacred Heart Novitiate in Los Gatos, California in August 1956. Increasingly dissatisfied with the life of detachment and solitude, however, he left in January 1960, six years before he would have been ordained. Brown later told an interviewer, "I decided I wanted to get into the world." He majored in classics at the University of California, Berkeley, and was graduated in 1961; he then enrolled in Yale Law School. In 1962 he spent some time in Mississippi doing legal work for the civil rights movement.

After graduating from Yale in 1964, Brown clerked for California Supreme Court Justice Matthew O. Tobriner. He then travelled extensively throughout Central and South America, before joining a prestigious Los Angeles law firm. Disgusted with the United States' involvement in Vietnam, he first entered the political arena when he joined the California Democratic Council in 1967 and helped to organize that group's peace campaign. In 1968 Brown was an Alternate Delegate to the Democratic National Convention in Chicago, and served as Southern California Vice Chairman and Treasurer for the McCarthy campaign. After he marched with Cesar Chavez and his agricultural workers in Coachella Valley in 1969, he made his first bid for elective office, defeating 132 other candidates for a seat on the Board of Trustees of Los Angeles Community College (1969-70). Brown was elected California Secretary of State in 1970, and promised to tame the "special interests" who were "running amok" in the state. One of the first of the nation's Democratic officeholders to call for Richard Nixon's resignation, he also made a vigorous attempt to reform California's campaign contribution practices. He endeared himself to the voters by filing suit against individual candidates and suing three oil companies for allegedly making illegal contributions. When Brown announced his candidacy for Governor in January 1974, critics pointed to his youth, inexperience, and reformist leanings, but he nevertheless won the Democratic nomination with 38 percent of the primary vote. An individualist who took surprising positions on issues, liberal on some, conservative on others, Brown, who was at the time only 36 years old, defeated Republican State Comptroller Houston I. Flournoy in the general election by gaining 50 percent of the vote to Flournoy's 47 percent.

Once in office, Brown changed the face of state government by appointing to state agencies a racially mixed group of young technocrats, poverty lawyers, environmentalists, and former consumer advocates. He also involved women and minorities in state government in record numbers. Calling for a balanced budget and no new spending programs, he attracted national media attention for his ascetic lifestyle, and for working late, riding in unobtrusive cars, and living in a bachelor's apartment rather than the governor's mansion. Brown's "less is more" philosophy, his commitment to reform politics, and his almost missionary zeal fascinated young voters, and he soon announced that he would be a favorite son candidate for the Democratic Presidential nomination in 1976. As one of the rising stars of national Democratic politics, he defeated frontrunner Jimmy Carter in four primaries (Maryland, New Jersey, California, and Nevada), and even finished just behind him as a write-in candidate in Oregon.

One of the major legislative achievements of Brown's first term was a bill providing farm laborers with the right to choose their own union in a secret ballot election, legislation which solved a problem that had haunted California for years. He also eliminated privileged tax shelters and took strong measures to reduce air pollution in the Los Angeles basin and other urban areas.

In Brown's 1978 campaign for re-election, his opponent was the rather bland Republican Evelle Younger, described by one observer as "as dull as a mashed potato sandwich." Although Brown won 61 percent of the two-party vote, a higher figure than either his predecessor Ronald Reagan or his father had ever had, his star was already beginning to dim, for he found himself on the wrong side of three issues important to Californians: nuclear power and capital punishment (both of which he strongly opposed) and California's now somewhat infamous "Proposition 13" referendum, a measure to reduce property taxes and state spending. When 65 percent of the electorate voted in favor of Proposition 13, Brown reversed his earlier position and earned a reputation among some as an opportunist. He also began to develop the image of being rather "flaky," and critics termed him "Governor Moonbeam" after he suggested that the state launch its own satellite. His on-again, off-again relationship with pop singer Linda Ronstadt raised eyebrows in some quarters, and he was sharply attacked for his judicial appointments and quixotic Presidential ambitions. In contrast to his 1976 flirtation with Presidential politics, Brown failed badly in 1980. In what has been called a "disastrous" run for his party's nomination, he ran a poor third to both Jimmy Carter and Edward Kennedy in the primaries. Brown's most damaging *contretemps* was his cautious handling of the Mediterranean fruit fly infestation that threatened to wipe out the state's multibillion dollar agribusiness income in 1981. While no one ever proved that aerial spraying was effective or that humans weren't endangered by it, his go-slow approach to the problem was widely criticized.

Brown chose not to run for a third term as governor in 1982, but tried instead for the United States Senate seat being vacated by S.I. Hayakawa. His campaign ads urged voters "to take another look," and heralded the number of jobs the state had gained while he was governor. His advocates also praised Brown's liberal stands on the environment, nuclear power, and affirmative action. Yet even one of his own advisers admitted that "in eight years as governor he has managed to offend every segment of the population at one time or another," and pollster Mervin D. Field concluded that "we have not seen a politician in California as disliked as Jerry Brown." In the general election he was defeated by San Diego's Republican Mayor Peter Wilson in one of the most expensive Senate contests in state history. Although his supporters would always remember him as scrupulously honest, original, compassionate, and refreshing, Californians had obviously tired of his activist brand of politics.

Succeeded as governor by traditional Republican George Deukmejian, Brown left office with a $1.5 billion deficit, caused both by the recession and by the state aid he was forced to give to maintain city and county services after Proposition 13 had curtailed property tax revenues. Brown eventually retired to his Laurel Canyon, Los Angeles home to read, write, and learn to operate the Apple III computer given him by his staff. He frankly admits that he still has political ambitions.

Bibliography: Current Biography, 1975; *California Blue Book*, 1975; J. D. Lorenz, *Jerry Brown: The Man on the White Horse* (Boston, 1978); Michael Barone *et al.*, eds., *The Almanac of American Politics, 1980* (New York, 1979); "California's Jerry Brown Runs for the Senate—And Away From His Flaky Image," *People* (November 9, 1981); "Duel for the Senate Comes Down To Who Is Disliked the Least," *U.S. News and World Report* (October 4, 1982); "The Battle for the Senate," *Newsweek* (October 11, 1982); *New York Times*, November 3, 1982; "Jerry Brown: I Shall Return," *Newsweek* (November 15, 1982); "New Governor, New Style," *Time* (January 17, 1983). Brown's papers are housed in the University Library at UCLA. MMM

Richard David Lamm (Credit: William Thach)

COLORADO

LAMM, Richard David, 1975-

Born on August 3, 1935 in Madison, Wisconsin, the son of A.E. and Mary (Townsend) Lamm. A Unitarian, Lamm married the former Dorothy Vennard on May 11, 1963; the couple have two children, Heather and Scott Hunter.

Lamm received a B.A. in business administration from the University of Wisconsin in 1957 and a law degree from the University of California (Boalt Hall) in 1961. In 1960 he qualified as a certified public accountant. A First Lieutenant in the United States Army from 1957 to 1958, he has worked as an accountant, a tax clerk with the California Franchise Tax Board, an attorney with the Colorado Antidiscrimination Commission, and an attorney in private practice with the Denver firm of Jones, Meiklejohn, Kilroy, Kehl, and Lyons. Lamm was also Associate Professor of Law at the University of Denver from 1969 to 1974.

President of the Denver Young Democrats in 1963 and Vice President of the Colorado Young Democrats in 1964, Lamm began his political career as a member of the Colorado House of Representatives, serving from 1967 to 1975; he was Assistant Minority Leader of that body from 1971 to 1975. Lamm first came to state-wide attention as a leader in the environmental movement that emerged in Colorado during the 1970s. With Sam Brown and David Mixner, he was one of the organizers of the so-called "anti-Olympics movement," a referendum to deny state funding for the 1976 Winter Olympics on the grounds that the Games would be too expensive, would destroy much of Colorado's environment, and would benefit only a handful of big businessmen and real estate developers. Colorado's voters agreed, and the 1976 Winter Olympic Games were held in Innsbruck, Austria. Earlier, Lamm had come to national attention as the sponsor of a liberalized state abortion law that was passed before the United States Supreme Court's *Roe v. Wade* decision dictated uniform national standards in this area.

Lamm became the leading gubernatorial contender in Colorado as the 1974 election approached. After Mark Hogan, the Democratic gubernatorial candidate in 1970, stepped out of the race, Lamm defeated the moderate state legislator Tom Farley in the primary by a margin of 59 percent to 41 percent, for the chance to face incumbent Republican John Vanderhoof in the general election. Vanderhoof, who had succeeded to the governorship when Governor John Love took a Ford administration appointment, attacked Lamm as an outsider who would stop economic growth so suddenly that massive unemployment would result. Lamm responded that he only wanted to see limits placed on growth, and emphasized the damage that the federal government's unrestricted exploitation of surface coal and oil-bearing shale was doing to the state's environment. In the general election Lamm defeated Vanderhoof soundly, gaining 54 percent of the vote to Vanderhoof's 46 percent.

Despite his great promise, however (*Time* magazine had included him among America's top 200 leaders in 1974), Lamm's first two years in office were described as disastrous by many political observers. He was unable to get his programs through the Legislature, feuded with the press, and alienated many with his somewhat abrasive personality. When the Republicans won control of both houses of the State Legislature in 1976, Lamm grew more conciliatory, and began to develop the programs and policies for which he has become well known. Despite predictions that he might have trouble winning re-election in 1978, he defeated Republican Ted Strickland rather convincingly, winning 59 percent of the vote compared with Strickland's 39 percent. Having cut taxes and reduced welfare rolls during his first term, Lamm was able to pre-empt standard Republican issues, and Strickland was reduced to complaining that Lamm had appointed too many out-of-staters to top jobs. Differences of style between the two men also proved significant. As the Texas-born owner of a successful oil-related business and an occasional Baptist preacher, Strickland appealed less to Colorado voters than the well-educated, affluent, and liberal Lamm. By the end of his second term, Lamm seemed more popular and less controversial than ever, and he had little trouble winning a third term in 1982. Able to balance the requirements of economic growth with environmental protection, he trounced Republican John Fuhr, a former Speaker of the Colorado House, by gaining 67 percent of the vote to Fuhr's 33 percent.

During his three terms in office, Lamm has sought to administer an efficient and effective state government that is responsive to Colorado's citizens, preserve and enhance the state's infrastructure, establish a diversified economic base, improve the state's environment, and cooperate with the Western Governors' Policy Office to ensure that western states are considered in developing federal policies. He has also tried to implement a comprehensive energy conservation program, improve the state's educational system, restore a meaningful executive budget through sound fiscal management, decrease crime, and improve the quality of life for all state citizens. Believing that the best interests of the state are served by a policy of limited growth, Lamm favors attracting clean, high-tech industries to Colorado, and has promised to combat tough economic times with a combination of austerity, hard work, and imagination. He has opened his administration by recruiting professional managers from other parts of the country to run various departments of state, has increased assistance to the elderly and to dependent children, cracked down on shoddy nursing homes, humanized the prison system, and stopped spending to promote tourism—which, he said, was growing to unmanageable and potentially damaging proportions.

Lamm has also emerged as a nationally known figure, by defending and presenting the needs and interests of western states. A book he co-authored with Denver historian Michael McCarthy, *The Angry West: A Vulnerable Land and Its Future* (Houghton Mifflin, 1982), details the region's history of exploitation by both eastern companies and the federal government. A co-founder of the Western Governors' Policy Office and its Chairman from 1977 to 1978, Lamm headed the Democratic Party's platform committee on energy and the environment at its 1984 Convention. Governor Lamm has also been Chairman of the National Governors' Association Committee on Human Resources and a member of its Committee on Energy and the Environment.

Having worked with Ted Kennedy and John Anderson to unseat Jimmy Carter in 1980, Lamm has admitted to at least a literary interest in Presidential politics. He is presently working on a novel about a third-party candidate who nearly wins the Presidential election. Political observers feel that Richard Lamm is one of the rising stars in national Democratic politics.

Bibliography: "200 Faces for the Future," *Time* (July 15, 1974); "Colorado's Lonely Long-Distance Runner," *Economist*, 264 (September 17, 1977), 55; Michael Barone *et al.*, eds., *The Almanac of American Politics, 1978-82* (New York and Washington, D.C., 1977-81); Alan Ehrenhalt, ed., *Politics in America, 1982* (Washington, D.C., 1981); *Who's Who in American Politics, 1981-82* (New York, 1981); *New York Times*, March 7, June 22, and July 12, 1981, February 18, September 16, November 23, and November 28, 1982, January 12 and April 16, 1983; "A White-Water Governor," *Newsweek* (July 19, 1982); National Governors' Association, *Governors of the American States, Commonwealths, and Territories* (Washington, D.C., 1983); biographical information, Governor's Office, Colorado. MMM

Ella Tambussi Grasso (Credit: Library of Congress, Congressional Collections)

CONNECTICUT

GRASSO, Ella Tambussi, 1975-1980

Born on May 10, 1919 in Windsor Locks, Connecticut, the daughter of Giacomo, a baker from the Italian Piedmont, and Maria (Olivia) Tambussi. A Catholic, she married Thomas Grasso, a retired school principal, on August 31, 1942; she was the mother of two children, James and Suzanne.

Ella Grasso attended parochial school in Windsor Locks, the Chaffee School in nearby Windsor, and Mount Holyoke College in South Hadley, Massachusetts, graduating from Mount Holyoke with a B.A. in 1940 and an M.A. in 1942. She was employed during World War II as Assistant Director of Research in Connecticut for the War Manpower Commission. A Democrat, Grasso began working for her party in 1943 as a speech writer and campaign supporter. She was elected to the Connecticut House of Representatives in 1952 and 1954, serving from 1953 to 1957. She was also Connecticut's Secretary of State from 1959 to 1971. Elected to the United States Congress in 1970 and re-elected in 1972, Grasso served in the House of Representatives from 1971 to 1975. She was nominated by the state Democratic Party to run for Governor in 1974, and faced Republican Robert H. Steele. In the election Grasso received 643,490 votes, a majority of 58.4 percent, while Steele received 440,169 votes and minor candidates drew 19,054 votes.

After her inauguration on January 8, 1975, Grasso immediately proposed a record budget of $1.43 billion. To raise needed revenue she called for a one percent hike in the sales tax. She also supported a program of social and economic reform but, at the same time, sought to economize wherever possible. Grasso tried to reject a personal salary increase, and when told she could not constitutionally do so, she accepted the raise and then returned it to Connecticut's Treasury in the form of a gift. Promising an "open government," she asked the Legislature for a "right to know" statute which would open government records and meetings to the public. In her first term Grasso also made proposals to solve the problem of rising public utility rates. Heeding the complaints of utility executives who said that they lacked the money for capital improvements, she asked the Legislature to pass laws which would enable the state to borrow money for utility construction programs.

In 1978 Grasso engaged in a tough primary fight for renomination against Lieutenant Governor Robert K. Killian, whom she defeated by 137,904 votes to 66,924. In the general election she defeated United States Representative Ronald Sarasin by 613,109 votes to 422,316. Grasso won every Connecticut county in that election, and did particularly well in the Hartford area. During the campaign she reminded voters that Sarasin had voted in 1970 for a state personal income tax, a tax which she continued to oppose during her second term. In 1979 Grasso called the Legislature into special session to deal with energy matters. Early in 1980 the Legislature struggled to approve a budget for the state, a process made more difficult by Connecticut's large debt and low revenue. Shortly after the budget was passed, Grasso revealed that she had had a cancerous cyst removed. On December 4, she announced that she would resign from office on New Year's Eve because she did not have the stamina to endure another legislative session. Lieutenant Governor William A. O'Neill was sworn in on that day as her successor. Grasso died on February 5, 1981 in Hartford, and was buried at Windsor Locks, Connecticut.

Bibliography: Hope Chamberlin, *A Minority of Members: Women in the United States Congress* (New York, 1973); *Christian Science Monitor*, July 26, 1974; Herbert F. Janick, *A Diverse People: Connecticut, 1914 to the Present* (Chester, Conn., *c.* 1975); Roy Glashan, *American Governors and Gubernatorial Elections, 1775-1975* (Stillwater, Minn., 1975); Congressional Quarterly, Inc., *Guide to U.S. Elections* (Washington, D.C., 1975); *Boston Globe*, November 8, 1978; *New York Times*, December 5, 1980 and February 5-10, 1981; Warren J. Mitofsky, ed., *Campaign '78* (New York, 1980); *Connecticut Register and Manual* (Hartford, 1981). Mrs. Grasso's papers are at the Archives, History and Genealogy Unit of the Connecticut State Library in Hartford. JH

William Atchinson O'Neill (Credit: Office of the Governor, Connecticut)

O'NEILL, William Atchinson, 1980-

Born in Hartford, Connecticut on August 11, 1930 to Frances and Joseph O'Neill. His father was a private chauffeur. William O'Neill married Natalie Scott Damon in 1962, a fifth-grade teacher in East Hampton, Connecticut; they have no children.

Early in O'Neill's life his family moved to East Hampton, where he attended the local schools and was graduated from East Hampton High School. He later attended New Britain Teacher's College and the University of Hartford. A combat flier with the United States Air Force from 1950 to 1953, he returned to East Hampton after the war. His father owned a tavern there; the son still owns ''O'Neill's Restaurant.'' O'Neill served on the East Hampton Democratic Town Committee from 1954 to 1980. After two unsuccessful bids, he was elected to the Connecticut House of Representatives as a Democrat in 1966; he was Assistant Majority Leader for the 1971 and 1972 sessions, Assistant Minority Leader for the next two sessions, and Majority Leader from 1975 through 1978. O'Neill strongly supported Governor Grasso in the 1974 election, and when John M. Bailey, the Connecticut State Democratic Chairman and former Democratic National Chairman, died the next year, Governor Grasso at first nominated O'Neill to the vacancy. O'Neill accepted, but Grasso later withdrew her support. Relations between the two were strained after that incident, and he was elected Lieutenant Governor in November 1978, despite Grasso's unwillingness to endorse a candidate in the primary. A conservative, O'Neill stated the view as lieutenant governor that Connecticut should not enact a state income tax.

When Grasso resigned from office on December 31, 1980 due to ill health, O'Neill assumed the governorship the same day. He steered the Legislature through two special sessions, one concerning the budget and the other flood relief. O'Neill also approved an unpopular tax on incorporated businesses.

There was no Democratic primary in 1982, and O'Neill defeated former State Senate Majority Leader Lewis B. Rome in the general election by 578,264 votes to 497,773. O'Neill campaigned on the theme that Connecticut had been relatively prosperous during the recession. Rome drew strong support from normally Republican Fairfield County, but he was unable to overcome the incumbent's advantage in the rest of the state. In 1983 O'Neill led a number of governors in resisting federal attempts to force the states to permit tandem trailers on certain highways. O'Neill received the Connecticut Firefighters Association Certificate of Appreciation in 1972, and has been active in veterans' affairs. His term will expire in 1987.

Bibliography: New York Times, December 5, 1980 and November 3, 1982; *Connecticut Register and Manual* (Hartford, 1981). JH

Pierre Samuel du Pont, IV (Credit: ©1984 Dennis Brack, Black Star)

DELAWARE

Du PONT, Pierre Samuel, IV, 1977-

Born on January 22, 1935 in Wilmington, Delaware, the son of Pierre Samuel du Pont, III, an industrialist, and Jane (Holcomb) du Pont. An Episcopalian, du Pont is the brother of Jane de Doliete and Michele Wainwright. He married Elsie Ravenel Wood on May 4, 1957, by whom he is the father of Elsie Ravenel, Pierre S., Benjamin Franklin, and Eleuthere Irenee.

Du Pont was graduated from Phillips Exeter Academy in 1952, and received a B.S.E. in 1956 from Princeton University. He entered the United States Navy as an Ensign in 1957, and obtained his discharge in 1960 with the rank of Lieutenant. Following his military service he attended Harvard Law School, receiving an LL.B. in 1963.

In 1968 du Pont, a Republican, was elected to the Delaware House of Representatives, where he served until 1970. Elected to the United States House of Representatives in 1970, he was a member of that body until 1977. Du Pont also acted as technical representative for Du Pont Nemours and Company from 1963 to 1970. On November 2, 1976, he defeated Sherman W. Tribbitt, a Democrat, by a vote of 130,531 to 97,480 to become Governor of Delaware. He took the oath of office on January 18, 1977.

Early in du Pont's administration, despite the governor's opposition to the action, a federal judge ordered the Wilmington, Delaware school district merged with eleven other districts in New Castle County in order to achieve racial integration. In 1979 Delaware, which authorizes hanging in capital cases, nearly sold its gallows to satisfy a debt the state owed the Delaware Legal Aid Society. Though unsold, the gallows also remained unused during du Pont's tenure.

In 1980 du Pont achieved an easy victory in Delaware's gubernatorial contest, defeating William J. Goody, a Democratic legislator, by a vote of 159,004 to 64,217. He thus became the first chief executive of the state in 24 years to be elected to consecutive terms. Du Pont has sought to create a favorable business climate in Delaware, which had earlier developed a reputation as anti-business. During his tenure the state's constitution was amended to limit spending to 98 percent of the estimated revenue. Personal income taxes were also lowered by 10 percent. Another constitutional change made it necessary to obtain a three-fifths vote of both legislative chambers before a new tax could be imposed. Under du Pont banking and credit laws were loosened, and the state worked to broaden its economic base. (Chemicals and autos, highly cyclical industries, were the first and second largest employers in Delaware in 1981.)

Du Pont's current term ends in 1985. He reportedly turned down an opportunity to run for the United States Senate in 1984.

In November 1984 du Pont's *protégé*, Republican Lieutenant Governor Michael N. Castle, won Delaware's gubernatorial contest by defeating his Democratic opponent, former State Supreme Court Justice William T. Quillen. Castle captured that election by a margin of 133,892 votes to 107,736.

Bibliography: Gerard Colby Zilg, *Du Pont: Behind the Nylon Curtain* (Englewood Cliffs, N.J., 1974); Congressional Quarterly, Inc., *Guide to U.S. Elections* (Washington, D.C., 1975); Bob Hollingsworth, ed., *Facts on File Yearbook, 1976* (New York, 1977); *New York Times*, January 19, 1977 and November 8, 1984; *Philadelphia Inquirer*, November 5, 1980; *Washington Post*, January 10 and March 10, 1981; Richard M. Scammon and Alice V. McGillivray, *America Votes*, 14 (Washington, D.C., 1981). JH

Reubin O'Donovan Askew (Courtesy: Reubin O'Donovan Askew)

FLORIDA

Born on September 11, 1928 in Muskogee, Oklahoma, the son of Leo Goldberg Askew and Alberta O'Donovan. A Presbyterian, Askew is the brother of Leo Jr., Roy, John, Bonnie Buchanan, and Molly Stewart. His father, an itinerant carpenter, left the family shortly after Reubin's birth, and his mother supported the family by working as a maid and seamstress. Askew was a Sergeant and paratrooper in the United States Army in 1946, and a Captain in the Air Force from 1951 to 1953, during the Korean conflict. He married Donna Lou Harper in 1956, and is the father of Angela Adair and Kevin O'Donovan.

Askew received a B.S. in public administration from Florida State University in 1951, and a law degree from the University of Florida in 1956; he also served as President of the student body at both schools. He began his career in public service as Assistant County Solicitor of Escambia County from 1956 to 1958. Elected to the Florida House of Representatives from Escambia County in 1958, he was chosen to serve in the State Senate in 1962.

As a relatively unknown state senator from Pensacola, Askew upset the favorite in the 1970 Democratic gubernatorial primary, and went on to beat incumbent Republican Governor Claude Kirk in the general election by winning 57 percent of the vote. By 1974, Askew was to go into his campaign for re-election with—in the words of one political observer—"accomplishments virtually no other governor in the nation could match." Defeating three candidates in the Democratic primary—Ben Hill Griffin, Jr., Tom Adams, and Norman Bie—he won renomination with 69 percent of the vote. In the general election he defeated Democrat-turned Republican Jerry Thomas, a former State Senate President who contended that Askew was spending too much of the taxpayers' money. Despite such charges, Askew captured 61 percent of the vote, thus becoming the first governor in Florida history to be elected to a second consecutive four-year term.

Askew received high praise from various quarters during his tenure as chief executive. A liberal, he was hailed as one of the progressives of the "New South," and numbered among the "200 Leaders of the Future" by *Time* magazine in 1974. The keynote speaker at the 1972 Democratic National Convention, Askew was, in the view of one media analyst, "on practically everybody's list as a Vice-Presidential possibility in 1976." He was Chairman of the National Governors' Association from 1976 to 1977. In a presentation made to the Southern Political Science Association in November 1981, Askew was named in a listing of the "ten outstanding governors of the twentieth century." Governors included in this select group were considered to have "made a difference not only in their states but also on behalf of states in the federal system, those who were successful at home and influential beyond."

First elected on a tax reform theme in 1970, Askew began his governorship by urging the adoption of a corporate income tax. Despite intense opposition from the business community, the measure was approved by the Legislature and submitted to the voters as a constitutional referendum. It won overwhelming approval, due in large part to Askew's campaign effort, and thus became the first such tax in the state's history. This victory was followed by the repeal of consumer taxes on household utilities and apartment rentals. Additional state revenues were shared with schools and other units of local government to ease the burden of local property taxes on homeowners. With Askew's urging, the Legislature increased the homestead exemption from $5,000 to $10,000 for senior citizens and the disabled. He also supported a decrease in local school taxes and the exemption of the first $20,000 in intangibles from state taxes.

Askew also supported "government in the sunshine," or disclosure by public officials of their income. He advocated stricter conservation laws, including the planning and regulation of lands and water, the provision of $200 million for the purchase of endangered lands, and the establishment of a Department of Natural Resources. Askew urged the Legislature to reconsider the death penalty and to reduce job discrimination against ex-convicts. To aid the poor, he raised the financial limit on the family assistance program. He also created a state-wide grand jury to investigate organized crime in Florida, and opposed a 1978 referendum to allow casino gambling in Miami Beach.

Askew is believed to have made his biggest mark as governor in the civil rights area. He worked to ease tensions after the desegregation of Florida's public schools, fought legislative efforts to close the schools, and put his prestige on the line when he campaigned in 1972 against a state-wide referendum supporting an anti-busing amendment to the United States Constitution. Askew encouraged the employment of more blacks in state government. He named the first black to the Florida Supreme Court since Reconstruction, appointed the first black as a member of the Cabinet in 100 years, and named blacks to state regulatory boards and agencies. As a result of such efforts, he received various awards: the John F. Kennedy "Profiles in Courage" Award from B'nai B'rith in 1973, the William Booth Award of the Salvation Army, the 1973 Herbert H. Lehman Ethics Medal for applying personal religious and ethical values to public life, and the Human Relations Award from the National Conference of Christians and Jews in 1976.

Askew's popularity remained high in Florida throughout his eight years in office, despite his unpopular stands on some issues (like busing and right to work laws) and his support of proposals to raise taxes. Constitutionally ineligible to seek a third term, he became the object of much speculation concerning his future political ambitions. Despite his retirement from state government, he remained very much in the public eye. President Jimmy Carter appointed Askew to several posts: Chairman of the President's Advisory Committee on Ambassadorial Appointments, Chairman of the Select Commission on Immigration and Refugee Policy, and United States Trade Representative with the rank of Ambassador Extraordinary and Plenipotentiary (a Cabinet-level position). In 1980 Askew was being considered as a possible Vice-Presidential running mate by Edward Kennedy in the Massachusetts Senator's bid to wrest the Democratic Presidential nomination from Jimmy Carter. In 1981 Askew was named to the board of a new lobbying group call "Trade Net," committed to the promotion of open and expanded world trade.

As the "most underdog of underdogs," Askew was one of the earliest entrants in the race for the 1984 Democratic Presidential nomination. His campaign deviated from the standard Democratic line on various issues, and urged Democrats "to reach out to the business community and give it a reason for voting Democratic." Askew remained outspoken on environmental protection, and insisted it was a more important national issue than most politicians were aware. His bid for the White House never caught on, however, and he withdrew from the Presidential race on March 1, 1984, after having received only one percent of the vote in the New Hampshire primary. After his withdrawal, Askew returned to the Miami law firm of Greenberg, Traurig, Askew, Hoffman, Lipoff, Rosen, and Quentel, where he is a partner.

Bibliography: Jon Nordheimer, "Florida's 'Supersquare'—A Man to Watch," *New York Times Magazine* (March 5, 1972); Robert Sherrill, "Best the South Has To Offer This Year," *Saturday Review* (June 17, 1972); "200 Faces for the Future," *Time* (July 15, 1974); "Six Others for '76—And More To Come," *Time* (February 17, 1975); *New York Times*, September 10, 1977, March 25 and August 9, 1979, August 10, 1980, November 23, 1981, January 10 and November 15, 1982, March 2, 1984; Michael Barone *et al.*, eds., *The Almanac of American Politics, 1978-80, 1984* (New York and Washington, D.C., 1977-79, 1983); Allen Morris, *The Florida Handbook, 1983-1984*; "Reubin Askew's Lonely Run for President," *U.S. News and World Report* (September 26, 1983). MMM

Robert Graham (Credit: Office of the Governor, Florida)

GRAHAM, Robert (Bob), 1979-

Born in Coral Gables, Florida on November 9, 1936. Graham is the son of Ernest and Hilda (Simmons) Graham, a distant cousin of former President Jimmy Carter, and brother-in-law of Katherine Graham, the publisher of the *Washington Post*. A member of the United Church of Christ, he is married to the former Adele Khoury, by whom he is the father of Gwendolyn Patricia, Glynn Adele, Suzanne, and Kendall Elizabeth.

Graham received a B.A. from the University of Florida in 1959 and an LL.B. from Harvard University in 1962. He is a cattle and dairy farmer and Chairman of the Board of Sangra Development Corporation, a real estate development firm. Graham is also an attorney and a member of the Florida bar. In 1966 he became a member of the Florida House of Representatives. He was named by the Florida Jaycees as one of the five most outstanding young men in Florida in 1971; the same year he became a member of the State Senate, and in 1972 he was chosen the outstanding first-term member of that body. Graham received an award in 1973 as the most valuable member of the Senate, and an award as the second most effective senator in 1976. In 1978 he entered a field of eight Democratic hopefuls for the gubernatorial nomination. Graham took part in a runoff election against Robert L. Shevin, whose identification as a Jew from Miami hurt him in the rest of the state. After winning the primary with 54 percent of the vote, Graham faced Republican Jack Eckerd in the general election. The campaign became an expensive battle of millionaires (Eckerd owns a large retail drug chain), and Graham had to overcome the handicap of hailing from South Florida, which had never seen a local citizen become chief executive. In the end, he carried most of the counties in the state, beat Eckerd narrowly in Duval County (Jacksonville), and won by an overwhelming margin in Miami's Dade County. The final count was 1,406,580 votes for Graham and 1,123,888 votes for Eckerd.

Graham assumed office on January 2, 1979, succeeding Reubin Askew. On May 18, 1979, he signed the death warrant of John Arthur Spenkelink, who became the first person to be executed against his will since a United States Supreme Court decision had temporarily halted all executions. Graham later ordered an investigation, when it was charged that the prisoner had been abused before his electrocution. The next year Graham called out the National Guard to quell a major riot in Miami. The governor also made an effort to work one day a month at jobs ranging from teacher and television newsman to sponge fisher and cook. This policy reportedly gave Graham a good image with the working class in Florida, and contributed to his electoral success. The beginning of America's space shuttle program returned Florida's Cape Canaveral missile complex to national prominence in 1981. The following year Graham approved a recodification of Florida's insurance laws, which had been enacted during a special legislative session.

In the 1982 gubernatorial primary Graham defeated two weak opponents, one of whom was an advocate of homosexual rights. In November he overwhelmed L.A. (Skip) Bafalis, a ten-year veteran of the United States House of Representatives. Graham enjoyed an easier victory than in 1978, taking even most northern Florida counties convincingly. He received 1,739,553 votes, while Bafalis received only 949,013. At the same time, voters enacted a measure endorsed by Graham that gave judges the power to deny bail to certain defendants. In 1983 Graham, noted for his wing-tip shoes and pin-stripe suits in the land of bermuda shorts and bikinis, was named one of the best dressed men of the year.

Bibliography: *Miami Herald*, November 8, 1978 and November 3, 1982; *Washington Post*, May 19 and August 11, 1979; Michael Barone and Grant Ujifusa, eds., *The Almanac of American Politics, 1982* (New York, 1981); *Who's Who in America* (Chicago, 1982). JH

George Dekle Busbee (Credit: Georgia Department of Archives and History)

GEORGIA

BUSBEE, George Dekle, 1975-1983

Born on August 7, 1927 in Vienna, Georgia, the son of Perry Green Busbee, a mule trader, and Nell (Dekle) Busbee. A Baptist, Busbee married Mary Elizabeth Talbot on September 5, 1949, by whom he is the father of Beth Talbot, Busbee Wiggins, Jan Guest Curtis, George Dekle, and Jeff Talbot.

Busbee served in the United States Naval Reserve during World War II. He received a B.B.A. from the University of Georgia in 1949, and an LL.B. from that institution in 1952. Busbee was admitted to the Georgia bar in 1952, and began his law practice in Albany, Georgia. He served as a member of the Georgia House of Representatives from 1957 to 1974, holding the positions of Assistant Administration Floor Leader from 1963 to 1965, Administration Floor Leader in 1966, and House Majority Leader from 1967 to 1974. As the Democratic gubernatorial candidate, Busbee was elected Governor of Georgia on November 5, 1974, defeating the Republican candidate, Ronnie Thompson, by a vote of 646,777 to 289,113. He was inaugurated on January 14, 1975.

During Busbee's first term the federal Equal Rights Amendment was rejected by the Georgia Legislature; new revenue sources, including the option of imposing local sales taxes and hotel-motel taxes, were approved for local governments; and an investigation was begun by the governor into allegations of massive overcharging by some of Georgia's doctors. Tuition to the state's colleges and universities increased by an average of 15 percent, and the Georgia Supreme Court ruled that zoning decisions by local governments were subject to court review. The Georgia Supreme Court also decreed that the state law requiring open meetings of state agencies did not apply to committee meetings of the Georgia House and Senate.

Busbee was eligible to run again in 1978 because of a recent constitutional amendment which allowed a chief executive to succeed himself. He easily defeated a large field of candidates led by Roscoe E. Dean, Jr. in the 1978 Democratic primary, and faced Rodney Cook in the general election. Cook accused Busbee of being insensitive to the need for lower taxes, and he criticized the chief executive for the prison riots at Reidsville. Cook also complained of the poor performance of Georgia's school system. Busbee responded by ordering state agencies to slash their budgets sharply. On election day Busbee won every county in the state, defeating Cook by 534,572 votes to 128,139.

During his second term in office Busbee was particularly interested in attracting foreign export trade, making frequent visits throughout the world for that purpose.

He also urged Congress to remove certain export restrictions. Atlanta was plagued by a series of murders of black children during these years. It was widely presumed that the killings were racially motivated, but Wayne Williams, a black man, was eventually arrested and convicted for two of the murders. The state's sunshine law was revised while Busbee was in office, and the Governor supported consumer protection for public utilities customers. Busbee suffered throughout his administration from difficult relations with former Governor and President Jimmy Carter, whose supporters he defeated in the 1974 primary. Busbee was succeeded as chief executive in 1983 by Joe Frank Harris.

Bibliography: *New York Times*, November 6, 1974; Congressional Quarterly, Inc., *Guide to U.S. Elections* (Washington, D.C., 1975); Roy Glashan, *American Governors and Gubernatorial Elections, 1775-1975* (Stillwater, Minn., 1975); *Atlanta Constitution*, October 23 and November 8, 1978, March 12 and April 1, 1979; Michael Barone *et al.*, eds., *The Almanac of American Politics, 1980* (New York, 1979); Warren J. Mitofsky, *Campaign '78* (New York, 1980). Busbee's papers are at the Georgia Department of Archives and History in Atlanta. JH

George Ryoichi Ariyoshi (Credit: Governor's Office, Hawaii)

HAWAII

ARIYOSHI, George Ryoichi, 1974-

The son of a sumo wrestler, Ariyoshi was born on March 12, 1926 over a soybean curd shop in the Japanese section of Honolulu. He is the first American of Japanese ancestry to be elected governor of a state and the third chief executive of Hawaii since it gained statehood. His parents, Ryozo and Mitsue (Yoshikawa) Ariyoshi, operated a dry cleaning shop after coming to Hawaii. The President of his senior class at McKinley High in Honolulu, Ariyoshi served as an interpreter with the United States Army's Military Intelligence Service in Japan at the end of World War II. After returning to Hawaii, he attended the University of Hawaii and then transferred to Michigan State University, where he received a B.A. in history and political science in 1949 and a J.D. in 1952.

A practicing attorney, Ariyoshi entered politics as part of the Democratic machine established following World War II by former Governor John A. Burns. He was elected to the Territorial House of Representatives in 1954, and served for four years before his election to the Territorial Senate in 1958. After Hawaii achieved statehood he remained in the State Senate, serving as Chairman of the Health and Welfare Committee in 1959, Chairman of the Ways and Means Committee from 1962 to 1964, Majority Leader from 1965 to 1966, and Majority Floor Leader from 1969 to 1970. In 1962 Ariyoshi was selected as one of the top ten legislators in Hawaii by the Kiwanis Club.

Ariyoshi was elected Lieutenant Governor in 1970, thus becoming the first Japanese-American to hold that position in any American state. When Governor Burns fell ill, Ariyoshi served as Acting Governor from October 1973 until the end of Burns' term. Upon his mentor's resignation due to cancer of the colon, Ariyoshi sought election to his own term as Governor in 1974. He won his party's nomination after a stiff challenge from Honolulu Mayor Frank Fasi, a savage critic of the Burns organization and a controversial public figure. The candidate of the Democratic establishment, Ariyoshi promised to bring more dollars into Hawaii. He went on to defeat Republican Randolph Crossley, a Honolulu businessman, by attracting 55 percent of the vote in the general election. Ariyoshi compiled his heaviest margins in the so-called Neighbor Islands, where the Democratic organization had strong support from heavily unionized agricultural workers and dockers.

Although Ariyoshi has the distinction of never having lost an election, and was re-elected to the governorship in 1978 (defeating Republican John Leopold, 55 percent to 44 percent) and again in 1982, his victories have not been without difficulty. In particular, the Fasi-Ariyoshi rivalry is a classic one in Hawaiian politics, and Ariyoshi's sometimes abrasive contests with the three-term mayor of Honolulu have opened wounds in the state's Democratic Party. Fasi again challenged Ariyoshi in the 1978 gubernatorial primary, gaining 49 percent of the vote to the governor's 51 percent, and also in the 1982 general election, when he established his own Independent Democratic Party to confront the incumbent.

The two men have disagreed on several issues. In 1975 Fasi condemned salary increases voted for high state officials, including the governor, and a pension bill that the legislators voted for themselves. Hoping to capitalize on the discontent of voters and taxpayers on that instance, he had his own problems two years later when he was accused of arranging a bribe of $500,000 from a real estate developer and then collecting part of it himself. Asserting his innocence (the accusations were later dropped), Fasi accused Ariyoshi of arranging to have the charges brought to spoil his rival's chances of winning the Democratic gubernatorial nomination in 1978. The two have also been on a collision course over Ariyoshi's efforts to control Hawaii's rising population. While Fasi has argued that development is good, Ariyoshi is a strong believer in population control, and once proposed limiting the number of people who could move to the islands. In 1977 Ariyoshi was criticized by Fasi when he signed a bill establishing a one-year residency requirement for most state and county jobs. Although Fasi claimed the measure was unconstitutional, it was endorsed by the public employee unions which have repeatedly given Ariyoshi their electoral support. There are also contrasts in character and style between the two men. While Fasi is flamboyant and dynamic, the non-charismatic Ariyoshi has frankly admitted that he is not an "image person." Documentary campaign films routinely feature little footage of him speaking, and in 1978 his campaign slogan was "quiet but effective."

Many political observers believe that the general public is disappointed with both men. There have even been signs of resentment within the governor's own ethnic constituency. Some feel that he has become "just another *haole* at heart," a pejorative term applied to whites from the mainland. In 1982 Ariyoshi narrowly won his bid for a third term, gaining 45 percent of the vote in a three-man race against Fasi and Republican State Senator D.G. Anderson. Even more humiliating was the bitter primary contest, in which his leadership ability was attacked by six members of his own party, including his own lieutenant governor, Jean Sadako King. Ariyoshi polled 53.3 percent of the vote in that election.

Ariyoshi is one of America's senior governors in terms of service. In 1977 he received national publicity for ordering search and destroy missions against Hawaii's marijuana growing areas. Approximately $15 million worth of marijuana was destroyed. A Delegate to the Democratic National Convention in 1976 and 1980, he served as Chairman of the Western Governors' Conference from 1977 to 1978, and was President of the Pacific Basin Development Council between 1980 and 1981. Currently, he is Vice Chairman of the Committee on

Legal Affairs and Chairman of the task forces on Tourism and Public Retirement Systems of the National Governors' Association.

Ariyoshi has been awarded honorary degrees by the University of the Philippines at Quezon City (1975), the University of Guam at Agana (1975), the University of the Visayas in the Philippines (1977), and Michigan State University (1979). He has also received distinguished alumni awards from Michigan State University and the University of Hawaii (1975). Throughout his long career in public service, he has been a member of the YMCA Board of Managers (1955-57) and the American Bar Association House of Delegates (1969). He is Past President of the Hawaii Bar Association, the Hawaii Bar Foundation, and the Military Intelligence Service Veterans Club. A Protestant, Ariyoshi and his wife, Jean Miya Hayashi, have three children—Lynn Miye, Todd Ryozo, and Donn Ryoji.

Bibliography: *New York Times*, April 20 and October 7, 1974, June 23, 1975, June 3, June 28, and December 18, 1977; "The AJA's: Fast Rising Sons," *Time* (October 20, 1975); Michael Barone *et al.*, eds., *The Almanac of American Politics, 1978, 1982* (New York and Washington, D.C., 1977, 1981); National Governors' Association, *Governors of the American States, Commonwealths, and Territories* (Washington, D.C., 1983); biographical information, Western Governors' Conference; biographical information, Governor's Office, Hawaii.
MMM

John Victor Evans

IDAHO

A Democrat and former Lieutenant Governor of Idaho, Evans first succeeded to the governorship in January 1977, when President Jimmy Carter selected then Governor Cecil Andrus to be his Secretary of the Interior. The son of David Lloyd and Margaret (Thomas) Evans, Evans was born on January 18, 1925 in Malad City, a small town in the heavily Mormon southeast corner of the state.

Evans attended Idaho State University and was graduated from Stanford University with a degree in business and economics. He also spent 18 months overseas as an Army infantryman during World War II. He first entered public service at age 27, choosing to follow in his grandfather's footsteps, and acquired extensive experience in state government. A member of the Idaho State Senate from 1953 to 1957 and again from 1967 to 1974, he was Majority Leader from 1957 to 1959 and Minority Leader from 1969 to 1974. Evans also served as Mayor of his native Malad City from 1960 to 1966, during the break in his senatorial career. While in the State Senate, he was a member of the National Legislative Committee on Natural Resources; in recognition of his performance, he received the Distinguished Service Award from the Association of Idaho Cities in 1974.

First elected Lieutenant Governor of Idaho in 1974, Evans was elected to the Executive Board of the National Conference of Lieutenant Governors in August 1975. After succeeding to the governorship, he emphasized a long-standing interest in environmentalism and assumed a leadership role among the nation's chief executives. Elected Vice Chairman of the Western Governors' Conference in September 1977 and Chairman in June 1978, Evans, a rancher by trade, was named Chairman of the National Governors' Association Agricultural Subcommittee on Rangeland Management in September 1979.

Although political observers at first believed that he lacked former Governor Andrus' political style, Evans managed state affairs well enough to win election to his own term as chief executive in 1978, soundly defeating Republican legislative leader Allen Larsen with 59 percent of the vote. The contest marked the third time in a row that the Democrats had captured the Statehouse in this increasingly Republican state, and the second time in the state's history that the voters had chosen a Mormon as governor. Helping Evans in 1978 was the decidedly unpopular position taken by Larsen on one key issue. Although both candidates were Mormons, Evans did not believe that the state should legislate Mormon rules of morality. Larsen's proposals to restrict liquor sales stirred intense opposition in a state where more than 70 percent of the voters are not Mormons. Capitalizing on a widespread fear that the Mormons "were trying to take over the state," Evans did especially well in the largely non-Mormon Idaho panhandle.

Rather conservative for a Democrat, Evans has nevertheless retained protection of the environment as an important item on his agenda. One of his major controversies in office early on was a dispute with Idaho Attorney General Wayne Kidwell over whether to sue the state of Washington for seeding clouds which might otherwise drop moisture over Idaho. In his 1982 campaign for re-election, Evans faced a strong challenge from Republican Lieutenant Governor Philip Batt, a wealthy farmer, who criticized Evans for his support of budget cuts and a four-day work week for state employees. A folksy campaigner, the incumbent won, but with only 51 percent of the vote.

Currently, Governor Evans is Chairman of the National Governors' Association Subcommittee on Nuclear Power. He is married to Lola Daniels and has five children—David, John, Martha, Susan, and Thomas.

Bibliography: Michael Barone *et al.*, eds., *The Almanac of American Politics, 1978, 1982* (New York and Washington, D.C., 1977, 1981); *Idaho Blue Book*, 1981-82; National Governors' Association, *Governors of the American States, Commonwealths, and Territories* (Washington, D.C., 1983). The file of John V. Evans is located at the Idaho Historical Society in Boise, Idaho. MMM

James R. Thompson (Credit: Office of the Governor, Illinois)

ILLINOIS

THOMPSON, James R., 1977-

Born in Chicago, Illinois on May 8, 1936, the first child of J[ames] Robert, a Chicago pathologist, and Agnes (Swanson) Thompson, of Dekalb, Illinois. Thompson was raised in the Presbyterian faith. He has three siblings—Donald, Larry, and Karen.

After attending local grammar and secondary schools, Thompson enrolled in 1953 at the University of Illinois, Navy Pier, Chicago. Two years later he resided temporarily with his family in St. Louis and attended Washington University. Without receiving his undergraduate degree, Thompson entered Northwestern University Law School in 1956. He served as student Editor-in-Chief of the *Journal of Criminal Law, Criminology, and Police Science*, and received a law degree in 1959. After his admission to the Illinois bar, he served from 1959 to 1964 as Assistant State's Attorney for Cook County under Republican Benjamin Adamowski and, following the 1960 election, the Democrat Daniel Ward. Thompson argued more than 200 cases before the Illinois Supreme Court, and took the lead in prosecuting pornography cases (although he lost the Lenny Bruce case on appeal). In 1964 he presented the state's arguments before the United States Supreme Court in the case of *Escobedo v. Illinois*. By a five to four vote, the Court ruled in favor of Escobedo, thereby broadening the concept of the civil rights of suspects during police interrogations.

Thompson returned to Northwestern University as an Assistant Professor of Law later in 1964. He co-authored three criminal casebooks with his former mentor—Fred Inbau—and others, and was promoted to Associate Professor. While at Northwestern, Thompson in 1966 joined Inbau and former Chicago Police Superintendent O. W. Wilson in founding Americans for Effective Law Enforcement (AELE). Thompson served as Vice President of this organization, which has often acted as *amicus curiae* for police and prosecutors. He was a member of the committee that revised the Illinois criminal code from 1959 to 1963, and of the President's task force on crime in 1967.

Thompson left Northwestern in 1969 to accept a post under William J. Scott as Assistant State Attorney General for Illinois. The following year he was named Chief of the Department of Law Enforcement and Public Protection, and soon thereafter he became Assistant United States Attorney for the Northern District of Illinois. In November 1971 Thompson was appointed United States Attorney, and during his almost four years in that office he earned a reputation as a prosecutor of corrupt public officials. Under his leadership, some 300 individuals were convicted of various charges of professional misconduct.

Thompson received the Republican nomination for Governor in 1976, and easily defeated his Democratic opponent—Michael J. Howlett—by a vote of 3,000,395 to 1,610,258. His margin of victory was the largest in Illinois history. Thompson took time during the campaign to marry Jayne Ann Carr, a lawyer, on June 19, 1976. During his unique two-year first term, Thompson was instrumental in securing passage of a "Class X" crime law. This provides a mandatory six-year minimum sentence for those convicted of specified violent crimes; three convictions brings a mandatory life sentence.

Illinois in 1978 began holding gubernatorial elections in non-Presidential election years, and Thompson defeated Michael Bakalis by a vote of 1,859,684 to 1,263,134. The nearly 600,000 vote margin was a record for an incumbent chief executive in Illinois. Thompson's popularity also was demonstrated during the re-election campaign by the many personal gifts he and his wife received following the birth of their first child, Samantha Jayne, on August 3, 1978. During his second term he continued to balance the state budget, despite having no general tax increases with which to work.

Nevertheless, Thompson faced a fierce challenge from Adlai Stevenson in his third election campaign in 1982. His margin of victory—5,074 votes—was the smallest in state history (1,816,101 to 1,811,027). The outcome was not officially recognized until the Illinois Supreme Court ruled against Stevenson's request for a state-wide recount. Thompson considers his three consecutive terms in office, unprecedented in the history of Illinois, to be his "biggest political accomplishment." His greatest disappointment has been the repeated failure of the State Legislature to ratify the Equal Rights Amendment. Thompson was named Chairman of the National Governors' Conference in 1983.

Bibliography: *Illinois Issues*; *Chicago Tribune*; Robert E. Hartley, *Big Jim Thompson of Illinois* (Chicago, 1979); James R. Thompson to Willard Carl Klunder, April 7, 1983 (quoted). WCK

Otis R. Bowen (Credit: Indiana Republican State Central Committee)

INDIANA

BOWEN, Otis R., 1973-1981

Born at Richland Center, near Rochester, Indiana, on February 26, 1918, the son of Vernie, a school teacher, and Pearl (Wright) Bowen. The brother of Esther B. Bremer, Evelyn B. Ambacher, Richard Bowen, and Sarah B. Marvin, Bowen is a Lutheran. He married Elizabeth A. Steinmann on February 25, 1939; they had four children: Richard, Judith, Timothy, and Robert.

After attending school in Kewanna, Fulton, and Francesville, Bowen was graduated from Francesville High School in 1935. He received a B.A. degree in chemistry from Indiana University in Bloomington in 1939, and earned an M.D. degree from the university's School of Medicine in Indianapolis in 1942. Upon completing his medical training in 1942, Bowen was commissioned a First Lieutenant in the United States Army Medical Corps, and rose to Captain while serving in the Pacific theater of operations. In 1946 he established a family medical practice in Bremen, Indiana, and served on the medical staffs of hospitals in Bremen, Plymouth, Mishawaka, and South Bend.

From 1952 to 1956 Bowen was Marshall County Coroner, and in 1956 he was elected to the Indiana General Assembly. He served in the House of Representatives for one term, but was defeated for re-election by four votes. He was returned to the Legislature in 1960, however, and remained through 1972; he was Republican Minority Leader in the House during its 1965 session. Subsequently, Bowen served as Speaker of the House during the next three legislative terms (from 1967 through 1972). Defeated in his first try for the Republican gubernatorial nomination in 1968, he overcame his image among factionalized party leaders as an outsider to win the nomination in 1972. Bowen had the support of rank-and-file party members, particularly in areas away from the capital city, and had a basic program to put forward—property tax relief coupled with controls on local government spending.

His opponent in the general election was former Indiana Governor Matthew E. Welsh, whom Bowen defeated by 300,000 votes. Bowen was re-elected in 1976 over Secretary of State Larry A. Conrad by slightly more than 300,000 votes. The key to his re-election (Bowen was the first chief executive of Indiana eligible to succeed himself since the 1851 constitutional prohibition on consecutive terms was repealed in 1972) was the successful implementation in 1973 of his property tax relief proposal. The plan not only reduced individual property taxes by 25 percent through the creation of a fund from which deficiencies were paid, but it included controls against other uses of the dedicated revenues as well as special benefits to elderly, disabled, and low income individuals and families. Bowen's first term was also identified with a significant expansion of the state's recreational facilities—parks, forests, reservoirs, and historical sites and memorials—under a revitalized Department of Natural Resources. Moreover, the governor's low-key personality and his perception by the public as a hard-working, trustworthy public servant—the family doctor image of one who listened, learned, and responded to needs—contributed to his re-election.

Bowen's second term featured continued efforts to protect his fiscal reforms, avoid new taxes (indeed, personal income taxes were lowered by five percent in 1978), keep government expenses at a minimum, and respond to crises as they arose. The latter included a number of natural disasters (blizzards in 1977 and 1978 and severe flooding in 1979) and a prolonged coal miners' strike in 1977-78. Earlier, he had faced similar problems with a particularly devastating tornado in 1974, two prison guard hostage situations, and the threatened collapse of the state's rail transportation system following bankruptcy of the Penn-Central Company, which operated 47 percent of Indiana's track mileage. Bowen's calm but firm responses in all of these situations proved effective. His administration also instituted a state government personnel reclassification system designed to reduce inefficiencies and inequities, brought to an early completion Indiana's portion of the interstate highway system, pushed through the Legislature a model law limiting medical malpractice awards, and supported the state's ratification of the Equal Rights Amendment in 1977.

Increasingly during his second term, Bowen provided leadership to regional and national organizations. He was Chairman of the Midwestern Governors' Conference, the Republican Governors' Association, and the National Governors' Association, and he was appointed by President Gerald Ford to the Commission on Federal Paperwork. Bowen's final year in office was marred by the lingering illness of his wife, for whom the governor-physician provided much of the medical care personally. Mrs. Bowen died on January 1, 1981, twelve days before the governor's second term ended. Upon leaving office, Bowen accepted a professorship in the family practice unit of the Indiana University School of Medicine in Indianapolis, and in the fall of 1981 he married the recently widowed Rose M. Hochstetler of Bremen. In 1981 President Ronald Reagan named Bowen to a new commission on federalism, and in 1983 he appointed him Chairman of an Advisory Council on health care financing through Social Security programs.

Bibliography: Hubert H. Hawkins and Robert R. McClarren, eds., *Indiana Lives* (Hopkinsville, Ky., 1967); Vernie Bowen, "Bowen Family," in *Fulton County Folks*, ed. Shirley Willard (Rochester, Ind., 1974), I, 108-15; William J. Watt, *Bowen: The Years as Governor* (1981); "Indiana Governors" file, Indiana Division, Indiana State Library, Indianapolis. The papers of the Bowen administration are in the Archives Division of the Commission on Public Records in the Indiana State Library. RDG

Robert D. Orr (Credit: Indiana Republican State Central Committee)

ORR, Robert D., 1981-

Born in Ann Arbor, Michigan on November 17, 1917, of parents who were lifelong residents of Evansville, Indiana, Robert D. Orr is the son of Samuel L., an industrialist, and Louise (Dunkerson) Orr. A Presbyterian, he is the brother of Samuel and Kendrick Orr. The Orr family has resided in Indiana since 1835 (since 1806 on Governor Orr's maternal side) when Samuel Orr, a Scotch-Irish immigrant to the United States in 1833, moved to Evansville to establish a mercantile and iron manufacturing business in that Ohio River town. The Orr Iron Company in Evansville continued to be operated by the family until 1974, when it was acquired by the Shelby Steel Company.

Robert Orr grew up in Evansville, attending school there and at the Hotchkiss School in Connecticut, from which he was graduated in 1936. His education also included occasional trips abroad, one of which (in 1935) is delightfully described in James L. Clifford, *From Puzzles to Portraits: Problems of a Literary Biographer* (1970). In 1940 Orr received a B.A. degree in history from Yale University; he then attended the Harvard University Graduate School of Business Administration. Following America's entry into World War II, Orr enlisted in the United States Army, attending Officers Candidate School, and subsequently served on the Quartermaster General's staff in the Pacific. He left the service in 1946 as a Major and with a Legion of Merit decoration. In 1944 Orr married Joanne ("Josie") Wallace of Springfield, Massachusetts, who was also in the military during World War II as a Ferry Command pilot with the Women's Air Force Service Pilots. The Orrs have three children—a son, Robert D., and twin daughters, Susan and Robbin.

Following their military service, the Orrs took up residence in Evansville and joined in the management of the Orr Iron Company which, after 1948, was headed by Orr's older brother, Samuel. During the next few years Robert Orr became active in a number of other businesses in the Evansville community, specializing (with others) in the economic development of the region by buying vacant factories, refurbishing them if necessary, and then finding new owners and industrial uses for the plants. Orr was also Chairman of the board of Indian Industries, a manufacturer of recreational products, and a member of the board of several other companies, including Hahn, Sign Crafters, Erie Investments, Sterling Brewers, Evansville Metal Products, and Product Analysis and Research Industries, all of Evansville, and Dixson, Inc., of Grand Junction, Colorado. He played an important role in local civic affairs, serving as Deacon and Elder in the First Presbyterian Church of Evansville. Orr was also a member of Rotary Club, active in the Evansville YMCA, a Director of the Willard Library, Vice President of Evansville's Future, Inc., and President of the Buffalo Trace Council of the Boy Scouts of America. Subsequently, Orr served as a Director of the Indiana Manufacturers Association for eight years; he is a Trustee of Hanover College. In 1953, when named the Jaycees' Young Man of the Year and given its Distinguished Service Award, he was an officer in 13 service organizations and a Director of 12 companies.

Orr began his political career in a modest way, serving first as a member and then Chairman of the Center Township Advisory Board in Vanderburgh County (1950-54), and then as Republican Precinct Committeeman from 1954 to 1962; from 1958 to 1960, he was Treasurer of the Eighth District Republican Committee. In 1965 Orr was elected Chairman of the Vanderburgh County Republican Central Committee, a position he held for six years. During this time he also launched a legislative career, winning election to the Indiana State Senate in 1968. Before his four-year term ended, however, he was named to the Republican state ticket in 1972 as Otis R. Bowen's running mate, and elected Lieutenant Governor of Indiana in 1972. Both Bowen and Orr were re-elected in 1976.

As lieutenant governor, Orr presided over the State Senate and frequently had to cast tie-breaking votes, particularly when the state tax system was restructured in 1973. He also had primary responsibility, since Indiana's lieutenant governor also serves as Commissioner of Agriculture and Director of the Indiana Department of Commerce, for promoting state economic development and for fostering tourism programs. Orr participated regularly (not a traditional role for lieutenant governors) in Governor Bowen's staff meetings and policy discussions, and received high marks for his loyalty to the governor's programs. Endorsed by the popular Bowen to be his successor, Orr easily won the party's nomination in 1980. His campaign stressed the Bowen connection—"Let's Keep a Good Thing Going"—and resulted in a victory over Democratic candidate John Hillenbrand, II by the largest plurality in the history of the state.

Despite this auspicious beginning, Orr's first year as governor was marked by difficulties. Not only was the state in the midst of a recession, which turned what had been a comfortable surplus into a large deficit during 1982, but pent-up demands among various groups of state employees for improved wages and working conditions, unmet by Governor Bowen's property tax relief and budget austerity programs, boiled over. In addition, Orr's leadership style contrasted sharply with his predecessor's, whose departure from office was made even more poignant by the death of his wife shortly before the term ended. Moreover, his major recommendations to the Indiana General Assembly in 1981 against any tax increases (which also meant minimal increases for state workers and for public education) and for a jobs creation and general economic development program, while popular with the general public, irritated most of the 27,000 state employees and disappointed public school teachers. The generally poor economic conditions of the early 1980s, highlighted by unemployment rates which exceeded 20 percent in such automotive-related manufacturing centers as Anderson, Kokomo, and Muncie, and which reached 14 percent state-wide, exacerbated the traditional needs of the state for improved mental health and correctional facilities, and for additional educational and highway maintenance and construction funding.

In 1982, following the fall general elections which resulted in continued

Republican majorities in both houses of the Legislature, Governor Orr confirmed Democratic charges that the projected state deficit for 1983 was in excess of $450 million. After he called the Legislature into special session in December to deal with the problem, the state income tax was increased from 1.9 to three percent and the state sales tax from four to five percent. When the regular session of the Legislature convened in January 1983, it appeared that the taxation issue had already been handled, but difficult new issues emerged, particularly utility reform legislation. The governor, in his 1983 state of the state message, had stressed the need for educational reforms, especially through additional instruction in mathematics, science, and the use of computers, and announced a "Decade of Excellence in Education" program. His second priority related to his long-standing interest in jobs creation and general economic development. Budget restrictions, however, meant that little could be done to deal with these problems in a decisive way.

The most explosive issue in 1983 concerned the huge increase in utility rates, particularly natural gas rates which had climbed 40 to 50 percent within the year. The utility reform bill which emerged in 1983, given Governor Orr's firm opposition to any "construction work in progress" (CWIP) expenses being passed along to consumers, contained no reference to CWIP. It did, however, expand the number of members on the state regulatory agency (the Public Service Commission) and limited the size and frequency of allowable rate increases. As Governor Orr testified before the United States Senate Committee on Energy and Natural Resources in March 1983, the state had only limited ability to deal with the issue; Congress was the responsible body in this area, and he urged prompt action.

Only the second governor constitutionally able to succeed himself since Indiana's 1851 Constitution was amended in 1972, Governor Orr defeated his Democratic challenger, Wayne Townsend, by just over 100,000 votes out of about 2.1 million ballots cast in Indiana's 1984 gubernatorial contest.

Bibliography: "Indiana Governors" file, Indiana Division, Indiana State Library, Indianapolis; Indianapolis *News*, Indianapolis *Star*, 1980-83; William J. Watt, *Bowen: The Years as Governor* (1981); Margaret McKinney, "The Orrs," in *Evansville's Founding Families* (1982); *New York Times*, November 8, 1984.
RDG

Robert D. Ray (Credit: Office of the Governor, Iowa)

IOWA

RAY, Robert D., 1969-1983

Born on September 26, 1928 in Des Moines, Iowa, the son of Clark and Mildred (Dolph) Ray. A Disciple of Christ, Ray married Billie Lee Hornberger on December 21, 1951; he is the father of Randi Sue, LuAnn, and Vicki Jo.

After serving in the United States Army from 1946 to 1948, Ray was graduated from Drake University in 1952; he received his law degree from the same institution in 1954, and established a private law practice. Chairman of Iowa's Republican Party from 1963 to 1968, he was first elected Governor of Iowa in 1968 when he defeated the Democratic candidate, Paul Franzenburg, by a vote of 614,328 to 521,216. In 1970 Ray won a second term, beating Robert D. Fulton, a former Iowa Lieutenant and Acting Governor, by a vote of 403,394 to 368,911. In 1972 he won a third term when he again won over Franzenburg, this time by a count of 707,177 to 487,282. In 1974 Ray won an unprecedented fourth term, defeating James F. Schaben by a vote of 534,518 to 377,553. Finally, in 1978 Ray faced Jerome Fitzgerald, the Majority Leader of the Iowa House, and polled 491,713 votes compared with Fitzgerald's 345,519.

Ray first assumed office on January 16, 1969. During his administration a tuition grant program for private college students was established, the Legislature was reduced in size from 185 to 150 members, a three percent service tax on construction and advertising was repealed, and direct state aid to hard-pressed Iowa cities was begun. Other developments during Ray's fourteen-year tenure included the establishment of a long-range bonding program to construct new buildings on state university campuses, the repeal of Iowa's sales tax refund, the passage of a "no fault" divorce law, the reduction from 21 to 18 of the age limit at which individuals could participate in political affairs, the establishment of a state Department of Environmental Quality and a state Department of Transportation, and the reform of Iowa's county system of government and its judicial system. Ray's governorship also saw Iowa gain a favorable opinion in the United States Supreme Court over a suit filed by the Omaha Indian Tribe concerning title to land along the Missouri River.

In the 1978 gubernatorial race Jerome Fitzgerald contended that Ray had been in office too long, and tried to make an issue out of an investigation into the Iowa National Guard. Nevertheless, Ray demonstrated that his political appeal had not diminished by taking all but seven of the state's counties in that election. In 1980 Ray criticized President Jimmy Carter's decision to cancel shipments of grain to the Soviet Union in retaliation for the occupation of Afghanistan by

Soviet forces. Ray described the state's economy that year as as "flat as Iowa's best farmland." He was also reportedly disturbed by the state's budget problems in the face of continuing recession. Citing personal reasons, Ray did not seek re-election in 1982.

At the time of his retirement, Ray was the senior governor in terms of length of continuous service in the United States. He was succeeded by Lieutenant Governor Terry Branstad. Ray is now with an insurance company in Cedar Rapids, Iowa.

Bibliography: Frank T. Nye, "The 63rd General Assembly of Iowa," *The Palimpsest*, 50 (October 1969), 545-608; Leland L. Sage, *A History of Iowa* (Ames, 1974); Roy Glashan, *American Governors and Gubernatorial Elections, 1775-1975* (Stillwater, Minn., 1975); Secretary of State, *Iowa Official Register, 1975-1976* (Des Moines, 1976); *Des Moines Register*, November 8-9, 1978; *Wilson v. Omaha Indian Tribe*, 422 U.S. 653 (1979); Warren J. Mitofsky, ed., *Campaign '78* (New York, 1980); *New York Times*, March 5 and May 3, 1982. Former Governor Ray controls access to his papers, which are on deposit at the Iowa State Historical Department, Division of Historical Museum and Archives, Des Moines. JH

Robert Frederick Bennett

KANSAS

BENNETT, Robert Frederick, 1975-1979

Born on May 23, 1927 in Kansas City, Missouri, the son of Otto Francis Bennett, a Johnson County farmer, and Dorothy Bass (Dodds) Bennett. A Protestant, Bennett married the former Mildred Joan Gregory on June 10, 1949. He is the father of Robert Frederick Jr., Virginia Lee, Cathleen Kay, and Patricia Ann. Following a divorce from his first wife, he married Olivia Fisher of Norfolk, England on July 16, 1971.

A Marine Corps veteran of the Pacific theater during World War II, Bennett received an A.B. from the University of Kansas in 1950. He was recalled to active duty with the Marines during the Korean War, but completed his formal education in 1952 when he received an LL.B. from the University of Kansas. Bennett has been a practicing attorney in Johnson County, Kansas since 1952, and was a founding partner of the law firm of Bennett, Lytle, Wetzler, and Winn. He was also Director and Secretary of the Kansas State Bank from 1962 to 1968.

Bennett held a variety of political posts before becoming Governor of Kansas in 1975. A Councilman in Prairie Village, Kansas between 1955 and 1957, he also served as Mayor of that community for eight years (1957-65) and President of the Kansas League of Municipalities in 1959. He was first elected as a Republican to the Kansas State Senate in 1964, and re-elected to two additional four-year terms; he acted as Senate President from 1972 to 1975. During his ten-year Senate career, Bennett was Chairman of the committees on Interstate Cooperation, Commercial and Financial Institutions, Claims and Accounts, and Organization, Calendar, and Rules. He also served as Chairman of the Legislative Coordinating Council, and the joint committees on Consumer Protection and Metropolitan Law Enforcement. Bennett was Vice Chairman of the Senate Assessment and Taxation Committee, and Chairman of the Legislative Budget Committee. His service on various other Senate committees included those on Banks and Banking, Corporations, Judiciary, Education, Post Audit, Legislative Services, and Facilities. A member of several special committees studying school finance and the state's tax structure, he devoted much of his legislative career to educational matters, especially a major revision of the school finance formula in Kansas. As President of the Senate, he was active in promoting legislative reform, and authored several major bills on education, taxation, and consumer affairs.

Bennett won a four-man primary in 1974 to gain the Republican gubernatorial nomination. His closest rival was Donald Concannon, whom he defeated by a very narrow margin. In the general election against Democrat Vern Miller, Bennett again achieved a narrow victory, this time by a margin of only 3,677 votes. The 1974 general election was the first in Kansas for a four-year gubernatorial term, and major issues included "law and order," wise use of tax dollars, and more efficient use of state resources. Miller had established a strong record as Sedgwick County Sheriff, and ran as a law and order man and a staunch opponent of student dissent. His tough line may have hurt him, however, for it was in Douglass County, home of the University of Kansas, and Riley County, home of Kansas State University, that Bennett compiled a 12,000 vote margin. Also important to Bennett's victory was his strength in the well-to-do Kansas City suburbs in Johnson County, just across the Missouri line, that traditionally voted Republican by a large majority.

During his term in office Bennett emphasized education, the agricultural economy, government efficiency, and a cautious approach to state spending. A hiring freeze was placed on many state agencies. His administration increased support for local schools and higher education, expanded homestead property tax relief for senior citizens, reorganized the departments of Transportation, Economic Development, and Human Resources, expanded options for financing local governments, and created a state energy office. Under Bennett Kansas also increased support for community mental health programs, reformed the judiciary, expanded minority participation on state boards and commissions, embarked on an expanded program to repair, rebuild, and resurface state highways, and increased support for welfare programs. Bennett was an active governor who demonstrated his interest in all areas of the state by participating personally in budget hearings and making on-site inspections of major state institutions. Nationally, he served as Vice Chairman of the National Republican Governors' Association, Chairman of the National Governors' Conference Committee on Urban and Rural Development, and Chairman of the National Committee on Child Abuse and Neglect of the Education Commission of the States. He also served on the Executive Committee of the National Governors' Conference, and was a Delegate to the Republican National Convention in Kansas City in 1976.

During his tenure as chief executive, Bennett was a Trustee of Baker University, a member of the Board of Governors of the University of Kansas Law School, a member of the Board of Nominators for the American Institute for Public Service, Honorary Chairman of the Kansas 4-H Foundation, Honorary Chairman of the All-Kansas Tax Council, a member of the Selection Committee of the Fort Leavenworth Hall of Fame, and an honorary member of Alpha Kappa Psi (the National Professional Business Administration fraternity). He was named an honorary member of Omicron Delta Kappa at the University of Kansas, holds the 32nd Scottish Rite Degree, and was elected in 1976 to the Demolay Legion of Honor. In 1975 Bennett was presented the Outstanding Citizen Award by the Kansas Engineering Society and was named Kansan of the Year by the *Topeka Daily Capital*.

Political observers expected Bennett to win re-election in 1978. In their opinion, he had proven to be a "reasonably competent executive" who had kept taxes down and expanded state aid to various programs and agencies. Although Kansas Democrats had attacked spending increases during his term, that growth had been managed without tax increases, and state aid to localities had helped to curb property tax increases. Bennett's greatest weakness, however, proved to be not his record but his manner. His beard and his white shoes left some Kansans muttering that he did not seem like a governor. Hailing from the Kansas suburbs of Kansas City, Missouri, he did not have roots in the rural part of the state. Indeed, he was considered distant and aloof, even arrogant and stand-offish by some voters. Although Kansas is a traditionally Republican state, Bennett had never been truly popular there. His narrow defeat by Democrat John Carlin, the first Democratic Speaker of the Kansas House since 1912, hinged more on style than substance. As a dairy farmer, Carlin appealed to rural voters in this historically agricultural state and, since he had beaten a more liberal opponent, Bert Chaney, in the Democratic primary, he could not be depicted as a big spender. Carlin won the general election with 51 percent of the vote.

After his defeat, Bennett returned to private law practice. He is a member of the Missouri Bar Association, the Bar Association of the State of Kansas, the Kansas League of Municipalities, the University of Kansas Alumni Association, and Prairie Village Optimist Club.

Bibliography: Michael Barone *et al.*, eds., *The Almanac of American Politics, 1978-80* (New York, 1977-79); *New York Times*, July 29 and August 6, 1978; *Who's Who in American Politics, 1981-82* (New York, 1981); biographical information, Governor's Office, State of Kansas. MMM

John W. Carlin

CARLIN, John W., 1979-

Born on August 3, 1940 in Salina, Kansas, the son of John William and Hazel (Johnson) Carlin. A Lutheran, Carlin married Ramona Lenore Hawkinson in 1962. They had two children, David and Lisa, before divorcing. In 1981 Carlin married Karen Bigsby Hurley, a former member of his political staff.

A lifelong Kansan, Carlin attended high school in Lindsborg and was graduated from Kansas State University at Manhattan, where he earned a B.S. in dairy science, with honors, in 1962. While attending Kansas State, he was a member of Farm House fraternity, Phi Kappa Phi, and Blue Key.

After an unsuccessful campaign in 1968, Carlin was first elected to public office in 1970 as a Democratic member of the Kansas House of Representatives; he was re-elected in 1972, 1974, and 1976. He served as Minority Leader from 1975 to 1977, and as Speaker of the House from 1977 to 1979, thereby becoming the first Democrat to serve in the latter position since 1912. In the House, Carlin served on the Agriculture and Livestock Committee, the Education Committee, the Ways and Means Committee, and the Commission on Higher Education. A member of the State Finance Council, he was also Chairman of the Legislative Coordinating Council, the Legislative Budget Committee, and the Rural Development Committee of the National Conference of State Legislatures. Carlin was a Delegate to the Democratic National Convention in 1976, and to the Democratic Mid-Term Convention in 1978.

In November 1978 Carlin was elected Governor of Kansas at age 38, a victory considered an upset by most political observers. Due to the unpopularity of the incumbent Republican governor, Robert F. Bennett, there was a serious contest for the Democratic nomination, with Carlin defeating liberal Bert Chaney and former American Legion National Commander Harry Wiles to gain his party's nomination. The three men received 55 percent, 26 percent, and 18 percent of the vote, respectively. Although the Democrats hammered away at increases in spending during Bennett's term, the incumbent had managed that growth without tax increases, and political observers believed him to be a reasonably competent administrator. Carlin's victory surprised political pundits even more since Kansas is a traditionally Republican state. Nonetheless, in an election that hinged more on style than substance, Carlin's image proved more to the liking of Kansas voters. A dairy farmer and cattle sales manager from a rural county, he seemed to embody Kansas values more than the suburbanite Bennett, a lawyer from the affluent Kansas City suburbs. Carlin won by the narrow margin of only about 16,000 votes.

Once in office, Carlin immediately reneged on a campaign promise to sign a death penalty bill. Several technical reasons for rejecting the bill existed, but Carlin, in what he called "one of the toughest decisions he had to face," vetoed the bill as a matter of conscience. Rather than angering voters, however, some commentators thought his action aroused sympathy because it had demonstrated moral courage. Carlin went on to veto two other death penalty bills in the next three years.

Observers feel that Carlin has grown in office after facing some early organizational problems. He achieved his greatest national attention when he came out against the binding rule sought by his fellow Carter supporters at the 1980 Democratic National Convention. One of the most controversial issues of his first term was his attempt to push a tax bill through the Legislature that would take eight percent of the revenue on oil and gas produced in the state. Clyde Reed, editor of the *Parsons Sun*, called the episode "the political sensation of the decade—and longer—in Kansas." Once before, in 1957, such a severance tax was voted and promptly challenged by the courts because of a drafting error. As funds for local spending diminished, however, teachers and members of labor unions backing the severance tax were pitted against drillers and energy operating companies. Carlin supported the severance tax as a means to provide increased funding for government and proper financing for public schools, but opponents accused him of exploiting the issue for political gain. Said one critic, "He thinks that's the way to get ahead because everyone hates big oil."

In 1982 Carlin easily won the Democratic nomination for a second term, his only challenge coming from Jimmy D. Montgomery, a disc jockey. In the general election he defeated Republican Sam Hardage, a Wichita businessman, by gaining 54 percent of the vote to Hardage's 45 percent. He is the first governor of Kansas to be inaugurated to a second consecutive four-year term.

As his second term began, Carlin was forced to offer the Republican-controlled Legislature a $51 million package of spending cuts, combined with steps to speed tax collections and others to delay aid payments to local governments. Also under consideration were taxes on oil and gas production, more taxes on gasoline, liquor, and cigarettes, and cancellation of general assistance for 4,400 able-bodied state residents, one-third of the total enrolled.

Governor Carlin is a member of the Executive Committee of the National Governors' Association and Past Chairman of the NGA Committee on Agriculture. He also serves as Chairman of the NGA Task Force on Agriculture Exports and the Subcommittee on the Environment. He is Past Chairman of the Midwestern Governors' Conference and Past Chairman of the six-state High Plains Study Council.

Active in civic and community affairs, especially the 4-H program, Carlin formerly served as a member of the Board of Directors of the First National Bank and Trust Company of Salina. He owns and maintains an interest in an 800-acre dairy farm near Smolan, Kansas, which was homesteaded by his family four generations ago. A member of the Kansas Holstein Association and the Holstein Association of America, he is especially interested in the farm's Holstein operation, which at one time was one of the most successful and productive herds in Kansas.

Bibliography: *New York Times*, July 29, 1978, February 22, March 22, and June 1, 1981, August 3, 1982, March 5, 1983; Michael Barone and Grant Ujifusa, eds., *The Almanac of American Politics, 1982* (Washington, D.C., 1981); Alan Ehrenhalt, ed., *Politics in America, 1982* (Washington, D.C., 1981); *Who's Who in American Politics, 1981-82* (New York, 1981); National Governors' Association, *Governors of the American States, Commonwealths, and Territories* (Washington, D.C., 1983); biographical information, Governor's Office, State of Kansas. MMM

Julian Morton Carroll (Credit: Kentucky Department of the Arts)

KENTUCKY

CARROLL, Julian Morton, 1974-1979

Born on April 16, 1931 in Paducah, Kentucky, the son of Elvie B. and Eva (Heady) Carroll. A Protestant, Carroll married Chariann Harting on July 22, 1951; he is the father of Kenneth Morton, Iva Patrice, Bradley Harting, and Ellyn Kriston.

Carroll received an A.A. degree from Paducah Junior College in 1952, an A.B. degree from the University of Kentucky in 1954, and an LL.B. in 1956 from Kentucky. Admitted to the Kentucky bar in 1956, he has been a member of the Paducah law firm of Reed, Scent, Reed, and Walton since 1960. Carroll was a member of the Kentucky House of Representatives from 1962 to 1971, serving as Speaker of that body from 1968 to 1971. He was elected Lieutenant Governor of Kentucky in 1971.

On December 28, 1974, Governor Wendell Ford resigned as Kentucky's chief executive to accept an appointment to the United States Senate, and Lieutenant Governor Carroll was sworn in the same day. On November 4, 1975, the Democrat Carroll was elected Governor of Kentucky, receiving 470,159 votes to Republican Robert E. Gable's 277,998. During his administration eleven counties in western and southern Kentucky were declared disaster areas in 1975, federal desegregation was ordered in the Louisville public schools, a record $1.67 billion was appropriated by the 1976 Legislature, and highway and other construction was funded by an increase in the gasoline tax. Other features of Carroll's tenure included passage of an increase in the state's minimum salary, provision of tax relief for new business construction, approval of a law for the protection of mental patients, enactment of medical malpractice regulations, and replacement of the State Labor Department with the Department of Human Resources.

Late in his gubernatorial term, Carroll faced a peculiar problem. While absent from the state to serve as Chairman of the National Governors' Association, Thelma Stovall, the Lieutenant Governor, called the State Legislature into special session to cut taxes. During Carroll's absence from Kentucky on other occasions, she ordered an investigation of the state's financial records, and vetoed a bill that would have rescinded ratification of the Equal Rights Amendment by the Legislature. Stovall claimed that she vetoed the amendment with Carroll's consent, but the governor was clearly more concerned about her decision to call a special session. When the state capital was hit by a severe flood on December 11, 1978, the day designated by Stovall for the special session to begin, Carroll postponed the session for a month and used the time to organize his supporters.

Under Kentucky's constitution, Carroll could not succeed himself in office.

Bibliography: *New York Times*, December 29, 1974 and November 5, 1975; Roy Glashan, *American Governors and Gubernatorial Elections, 1775-1975* (Stillwater, Minn., 1975); Congressional Quarterly, Inc., *Guide to U.S. Elections* (Washington, D.C., 1975); *Washington Post*, December 23, 1978. JH

John Young Brown, Jr. (Credit: Office of the Governor, Kentucky)

BROWN, John Young, Jr., 1979-1983

Born in Lexington, Kentucky on December 28, 1933, the son of John Y. Sr., a noted Kentucky political figure and often-defeated candidate for the United States Senate, and Dorothy (Inman) Brown. A Baptist, Brown has three children by a previous marriage—John Y. III, Eleanor Farris, and Sandra Bennett. In 1979 he married Phyllis George of Denton, Texas, who was Miss America of 1971 and currently serves as a national television commentator on professional football. Brown has one son, Lincoln Tyler, by his second marriage.

Brown received his B.A. from the University of Kentucky in 1957, and was graduated from the University of Kentucky Law School in 1960. He later became President of Kentucky Fried Chicken and, together with the chain's founder, Colonel Harland Sanders, earned a fortune in one of the first and most successful fast-food businesses. In 1971 Brown became owner of Ollie's Trolley, Inc., of Louisville, Kentucky, a fast-food business that operated from mockups of trolleys. In 1972 and 1973 he first experienced politics as Chairman of the Democratic Party's National Telethon. Brown was briefly a part-owner of the Boston Celtics professional basketball franchise in 1978, during a lackluster period in that illustrious team's history. He had previously owned the Buffalo Braves of the National Basketball Association.

In 1979 Brown entered Kentucky's gubernatorial race and defeated Harvey Sloane in the Democratic primary. Financing the campaign with the aid of his estimated $20 million fortune, Brown faced former Governor Louis B. Nunn in the general election. The campaign was personal and bitter. Brown attacked Nunn for enacting a two-cent sales tax measure while chief executive. Nunn retaliated by conducting "Operation Undercover," which attempted to link Brown to Las Vegas gambling, organized crime, and a former employee who had been convicted of smuggling marijuana. In the end, Brown carried most of the state, losing only in the heavily Republican southcentral region. The final vote was 558,088 for Brown and 381,278 for Nunn.

Brown's flamboyant lifestyle came into question soon after he took office. He was criticized for holding expensive parties, including one aboard a yacht moored off Manhattan during the 1980 Democratic National Convention. Shortly after Brown was inaugurated, the state lost a suit in the United States Supreme Court over the location of its boundary with Ohio. Later in his administration Brown sought unsuccessfully to revise Kentucky's constitution to permit consecutive gubernatorial terms. Although he admitted that he was not likely to be re-elected, two of his Cabinet members underwrote a $150,000 bank loan to finance an advertising campaign. In 1982 Kentucky drastically revised its strip-mining law and enacted a provision limiting late, non-therapeutic abortions to hospitals. The latter piece of legislation was declared partly unconstitutional by a federal court.

In 1983 Brown again produced a Democratic telethon, which was marred by "dirty tricks" attributed to followers of the ultra-conservative "Moral Majority."

That same year he underwent open heart surgery. During his recuperation Lieutenant Governor Martha Layne Collins, who claimed that she had been unable to obtain sufficiently detailed medical information from Brown's physicians, unilaterally took over the duties of the governor's office. She eventually won the governorship in her own right, defeating the Republican James Bunning, a former major league baseball pitcher, by a vote of 554,439 to 448,360.

Bibliography: *The Courier-Journal* (Louisville), May 30 and November 7, 1979; *Washington Post*, April 3, 1981; Richard M. Scammon and Alice V. McGillivray, eds., *America Votes*, 14 (Washington, D.C., 1981); *Who's Who in America* (Chicago, 1982); *Congressional Quarterly Weekly Report* (November 12, 1983). JH

Edwin Washington Edwards

LOUISIANA

EDWARDS, Edwin Washington, 1972-1980, 1984-

Born in Marksville, Louisiana on August 7, 1927, the son of Clarence W. and Agnes (Brouillette) Edwards, who were French-speaking sharecroppers. A Roman Catholic, Edwards married Elaine Schwartzenburg on April 5, 1949. He is the father of Anna Edwards Hensgens, Victoria Elaine, Stephen Randolph, and David Edwin.

After serving in the Naval Air Corps during World War II, Edwards received an LL.B. from Louisiana State University School of Law in 1949. In private practice with a Crowley, Louisiana law firm from 1949 to 1964, he first entered public service when he was elected as a Democrat to the Crowley City Council in 1954. He was re-elected to a second term in 1958. Edwards first captured state-wide attention when he ran for the State Senate in 1963. Surprising the experts, he defeated the president *pro tem* of the Senate, an incumbent of 20 years. As a floor leader in the Senate, Edwards played an active part in the passage of key legislation. Following the death of Seventh District Congressman T.A. Thompson in an auto accident in 1965, Edwards defeated four other candidates to win election to the United States House of Representatives. He remained in Congress for almost seven years, winning re-election in 1966, 1968, and 1970. Edwards served on the Public Works, Judiciary, and Internal Security committees. The Democratic Whip for the Louisiana and Mississippi delegations for four years, he played a key role in increasing United States exports of Louisiana farm products. He was also considered by experts to have a rather liberal voting record for a Congressman from the Deep South.

Edwards bested 17 other candidates to win the Democratic nomination for Governor in 1971, and narrowly defeated State Senator J. Bennett Johnston of Shreveport in the primary runoff by a vote of 584,262 to 579,774. In February 1972 he defeated Republican David Treen in the general election, gaining 57 percent of the vote to Treen's 43 percent. As a French-speaking Cajun, Edwards won by an especially wide margin in the "Cajun country" along the Gulf of Mexico, outside New Orleans in the bayou country south of Alexandria, and west of the Mississippi River. He also gained a majority of the black vote.

Inaugurated on May 9, 1972, Edwards became Louisiana's first French-speaking chief executive in more than a century, and one of the state's few public officials to have served at the city, state, and national levels. He was fortunate to inherit a state that had put racial issues behind it, a state ready to reap the benefits of economic prosperity as the price of oil rose. In 1973 Edwards called a special "energy crisis session" of the Louisiana Legislature, which doubled the severance tax on natural gas and changed the levy on oil from a volume to a value basis, thus adding $169 million a year to the Treasury. He also received a measure of national attention as a spokesman for the oil industry. Graced with a special ability to dominate the Legislature, Edwards was considered to be a highly successful administrator in his first term and had little trouble winning re-election in 1975. That election was the first to be conducted under a new open primary law which the governor himself had engineered. The new system required candidates from all parties to enter an October primary. If any candidate polled 50 percent of all votes cast for the office, that candidate was elected; if not, the top two candidates faced each other in a runoff election. Thus, Edwards faced five primary opponents in 1975, all Democrats—Robert G. Jones, Wade O. Martin, Jr., Ken Lewis, A. Roswell Thompson, and Cecil M. Pizzi. He gained 62 percent of the vote to Jones' 24 percent and Martin's 12 percent. The other candidates split the remaining two percent.

Edwards eventually came to dominate state politics as had no governor since the legendary Huey Long. Major achievements of his administration included the calling of a state constitutional convention and an addition to the natural gas tax to finance health, education, and prison improvement. His tenure was also marked by the creation of a plan to simplify state aid to local governments, the establishment of tough policies to fight crime and to aid law enforcement, and the construction of an intrastate highway connecting north and south Louisiana. Edwards represented the state on numerous multi-state commissions and committees. Chairman of the Interstate Oil Compact Commission and State Co-Chairman of the Ozarks Regional Commission, he was host governor for the 1975 National Governors' Conference held in New Orleans. A member of the Energy Committee of the Southern Governors' Conference, Edwards also served on the Committee on Natural Resources and Environmental Management of the National Governors' Conference. He was a member of the National Governors' Conference Task Force on Foreign Trade and Tourism, and has served on the NGC's Rural and Urban Development Committee.

One of the most colorful governors Louisiana has ever had, Edwards won widespread popularity because of his ability to appeal to and to work well with various social groups. His popularity stood him in good stead when charges of scandal surfaced in 1976, charges that as a member of Congress he had received gifts from Korean government agent Tongsun Park. Later, in 1980, he was one of thirteen Louisiana public officials subpoenaed to appear before a federal grand jury investigating allegations of bribery in connection with a major federal undercover investigation in the Southwest. Despite such problems, however, political observers consider Edwards to have been one of the most popular and strongest chief executives in state history, and during his years in office he received national attention as a spokesman for the New South. He nominated Jerry Brown for President at the 1976 Democratic Convention, and there were even rumors that he might be offered the Vice-Presidential nomination that year.

Political observers predicted that he could easily have won a third term had he been constitutionally eligible to run again in 1979. Indeed, he proved his appeal in October 1983 by overwhelming the incumbent Republican Governor David C. Treen by a margin of 62 percent to 36 percent, thereby becoming the state's first chief executive to be elected to three terms.

Edwards was the Louisiana State Chairman for Jimmy Carter's re-election campaign in 1980. An ex-pilot, he retains an interest in aviation. He is a member of the Lions and the American Legion.

Bibliography: Anita Schrodt, ''Three Days in the Life of That 'Cajun Fella,'' *Biography News*, 1 (April 1974), 398-99; Michael Barone *et al.*, eds., *The Almanac of American Politics, 1978-82* (New York and Washington, D.C., 1977-81); *New York Times*, May 16, 1979, February 11, 14-15, 17 and November 2, 1980; Alan Ehrenhalt, ed., *Politics in America, 1982* (Washington, D.C., 1981); *Who's Who in American Politics, 1981-82* (New York, 1981); *Congressional Quarterly Weekly Report* (October 29, 1983); biographical information, Governor's Office, State of Louisiana. MMM

David C. Treen (Credit: Executive Department, Louisiana)

TREEN, David C., 1980-1984

Born on July 16, 1928 in Baton Rouge, Louisiana, the son of Joseph Paul and Elizabeth (Speir) Treen. A Methodist, Treen married the former Dolores ("Dodie") Brisbi of Metairie, Louisiana in May 1951. They have three children— Jennifer Treen Neville, David Conner Treen, Jr., and Cynthia Treen Lunceford.

Educated in the public schools of East Baton Rouge, Jefferson, and Orleans parishes, Treen was graduated from Fortier High School in New Orleans in 1945. He majored in history and political science at Tulane University, where he was President of his freshman class and a member of the Honor Board; he received a B.A. in 1948. In 1950 Treen was graduated with honors from Tulane University Law School. There he was a member of ODK (a national leadership fraternity), Phi Delta (a legal fraternity), and the Order of the Coif (a legal scholastic fraternity). He was also the winner of a Junior-Senior Moot Court competition. After a short stint from 1950 to 1951 as an associate attorney with the New Orleans firm of Deutsch, Kerrigan, and Stiles, Treen served two years of active duty as a First Lieutenant with the United States Air Force. Stationed in Wichita Falls, Texas, and London, England, he also acted as a defense counsel and a prosecuting counsel while in the Air Force. Treen then resumed his legal career as Vice President and Legal Counsel of the Simplex Manufacturing Corporation in New Orleans from 1952 to 1957. He was also an associate attorney with Beard, Blue, and Schmitt, and subsequently a partner in the firm of Beard, Blue, Schmitt, and Treen from 1957 to 1972.

Chairman of the Republican Executive Committee of Jefferson Parish between 1963 and 1967, Treen made unsuccessful runs for the United States Congress in 1962, 1964, and 1968, each time against the long-time incumbent Democrat Hale Boggs. His percentage of the popular vote increased each time, from 32 percent to 44 percent to 49 percent respectively, as Boggs' support of civil rights legislation weakened his popularity among Louisiana voters. Treen also made an unsuccessful gubernatorial race in 1972, losing to Democrat Edwin Edwards, who polled 57 percent of the vote to Treen's 43 percent. Although Treen did well in Jefferson Parish and in the predominantly Protestant northern part of the state, Edwards won large enough majorities in so-called "Cajun country" and among the state's black voters to secure his election. Treen, however, was elected to the United States Congress later that same year, defeating J. Louis Watkins by polling 54 percent of the vote. The first Republican elected to Congress from Louisiana in the twentieth century, Treen drew his greatest support from Metairie, the high-income suburb in Jefferson Parish just west of New Orleans. He was re-elected to subsequent terms in 1974, 1976, and 1978, defeating Charles Brisbaum in 1974 with 59 percent of the vote and David Scheuerman in 1976 with 73 percent of the vote. He ran unopposed in 1978.

In Congress, Treen was Chairman of the Republican Study Committee and a member of the Executive Committee of the Republican Congressional Campaign

Committee. He was also a member of the House Select Committee on Intelligence, the Ad Hoc Select Committee on the Outer Continental Shelf, the Merchant Marine and Fisheries Committee, and the Armed Services Committee. He served on subcommittees on military personnel, investigations, the coast guard and navigation, the merchant marine, and oceanography. Treen had a conservative voting record in Congress.

Political observers knew that Treen had long had his eyes on the Louisiana governorship. In 1979 he led a field of nine candidates (all Democrats except himself) in the open primary held to determine a successor to the popular outgoing Governor Edwin Edwards, who was constitutionally ineligible to seek a third term. The hotly contested, $20 million race attracted the largest voter turnout in Louisiana's history, and was considered by experts to be the most expensive non-Presidential campaign in American history. Treen led all candidates with 22 percent of the vote. His rivals (all Democrats) were Public Service Commissioner Louis Lambert (21 percent), Lieutenant Governor James E. Fitzmorris (20 percent), Secretary of State Paul Hardy (17 percent), House Speaker E. L. ("Bubba") Henry (10 percent), and State Senator Edgar G. Mouton, Jr. (nine percent). Three others shared one percent of the vote. According to Louisiana's election law, the two top vote-getters in the primary, regardless of their party affiliation, were eligible to face each other in the general election. Here Treen was helped by in-fighting among his Democratic opponents. Observers had predicted that Lieutenant Governor Fitzmorris would face Treen in the general election, but when Lambert pulled ahead by a few thousand votes, Fitzmorris charged voter fraud and election irregularities. The integrity of the free-spending Lambert was attacked by members of his own party. As a candidate he had little potential for unifying state Democrats, and most of the other Democrats originally in the race, even those with decidedly liberal reputations, endorsed Treen in the general election.

In the runoff between Treen and Lambert, the vote divided sharply along racial and economic lines. Lambert, who tried to portray his opponent as the candidate of the "silk-stockinged" and privileged, presented himself as a modern-day Harry Truman, and drew strength from a state-wide Democratic coalition of blacks, rural populists, and organized labor. Treen, on the other hand, ran as a conservative, pledging to veto any effort to repeal Louisiana's "right to work" law, which outlaws the union shop. Others were wary of Treen because of his membership during the early 1960s in the Louisiana States' Rights Party, which included some avowed segregationists in its ranks. Nonetheless, Treen's reputation for honesty and integrity appealed to many voters. He promised to give the state a politically independent "elections integrity commission" and proposed campaign spending laws. His decision to disclose his own personal finances had few precedents in the state.

Despite President Jimmy Carter's last-minute support of Lambert, the election was a cliffhanger. Treen won by a margin of only 9,871 votes out of the nearly 1.4 million votes cast. He drew his greatest support in the affluent white suburban parishes and in the other sizable towns of the state. Treen's election in a state where Democrats outnumber Republicans 18-1 drew national attention, and seemed to be a harbinger of growing Republican strength in the once solidly Democratic South. With his victory, Treen became the first Republican chief executive of Louisiana in the twentieth century. (Louisiana's last Republican governor had been William Pitt Kellogg, a carpetbagger from Vermont, who held office from 1873 to 1877.)

Once in power, Treen announced that the way had been cleared for an out-of-court settlement of a seven-year-old federal integration lawsuit against Louisiana's 17 public colleges and universities. He also supported the budget-cutting efforts of the Reagan administration, signed a bill that requires students in Louisiana public schools be taught both Biblical and scientific explanations of human evolution, approved legislation that gave Louisiana $35 million to fight the erosion of almost 50 square miles of its coast each year, and began the search for a solution to the state's environmental ills. Treen's administration is credited with being more aggressive on environmental protection matters than that of his predecessor. He served as Chairman of the National Governors' Association Subcommittee on Oil and Gas, and is immediate Past Chairman of the Interstate Oil Compact Commission.

Treen had the misfortune of facing the popular former Governor Edwin W. Edwards in Louisiana's 1983 gubernatorial contest. He lost that election by a margin of 62 percent to 36 percent, failing to carry even those parts of the state which were usually Republican strongholds.

Bibliography: Michael Barone *et al.*, eds., *The Almanac of American Politics, 1978-82* (New York and Washington, D.C., 1977-81); *New York Times*, October 29, November 1, December 8-10, 12-14, 1979, October 10, 1980, April 18, July 22, August 22, 26, November 22, 27, 1981, April 18, August 10, and November 28, 1982; Alan Ehrenhalt, ed., *Politics in America, 1982* (Washington, D.C., 1981); *Who's Who in American Politics, 1981-82* (New York, 1981); National Governors' Association, *Governors of the American States, Commonwealths, and Territories* (Washington, D.C., 1983); *Congressional Quarterly Weekly Report* (October 29, 1983); biographical information, Governor's Office, State of Louisiana. MMM

James Bernard Longley (Courtesy: James B. Longley, Jr.)

MAINE

Born on April 22, 1924 in Lewiston, Maine, the son of Wallace, a streetcar conductor, and Nancy (Brown) Longley. A Roman Catholic, Longley married Helen Walsh; he is the father of five children—Jim, Sue, Kathy, Steve, and Nancy.

After attending the public schools in Lewiston, Longley studied at Baldwin College in 1947, and received an LL.B. from the University of Maine, Orono, in 1957. He was then admitted to the bar. He served with the United States Army Air Corps during World War II and, upon his return home, entered the insurance business as an executive with Longley Associates. Very much a self-made man, Longley became a millionaire through the business and won additional prestige as President of the insurance industry's "Million Dollar Roundtable."

Longley never held a political office before his election as Governor of Maine in 1974. A registered Democrat, he served Governor Kenneth M. Curtis as Chairman of the Maine Management and Cost Survey Commission, where he was charged with recommending possible savings in state government. The result was a final report showing how the state could save $23.8 million a year. While involved with the Commission, Longley grew increasingly disgusted with what he termed the ineptitude and inefficiency of "professional politicians."

The Maine Legislature's apparent indifference and failure to act upon the Commission's recommendations spurred Longley's gubernatorial candidacy. Urged into politics by two friends, Common Cause Chairman John Gardner and Canadian Prime Minister Lester Pearson, he formed his own party, "Longley for Maine." Longley campaigned as an outsider and non-politician in 1974, the post-Watergate year when such qualities proved highly attractive to voters. Longley's rags-to-riches success story also had great appeal. As a youth he was required to work to help support his widowed mother, who had six children. He had also been a textile worker before achieving success in business, and went to the Statehouse calling himself "just an average guy."

Longley conducted his campaign with the same hard-driving efficiency that marked his business ventures. Substantial financial support came from associates in the insurance business, while the recruitment of dozens of young volunteers gave his campaign a populist image. In a state suffering the largest deficit in its history, Longley campaigned on a promise to reduce Maine's $705 million budget by $24 million without cutting services. He also pledged to solve Maine's chronic economic backwardness by skillful budget paring and by attracting new business to the state.

In an upset that shocked national political analysts, Longley defeated two candidates, Democrat George J. Mitchell, a Muskie *protégé*, and Republican James S. Erwin, who had only narrowly lost to outgoing Governor Kenneth Curtis four years before. The vote totals were 40 percent, 37 percent, and 23 percent, respectively. Not only had Longley made inroads in mill towns like Lewiston, but he had also cut heavily into what was left of the traditionally Republican Yankee vote. There was also a bigger than usual turnout on election day. With his victory, Longley became the first independent to capture a governorship since 1937, and the first independent ever to win the chief executive's office in Maine.

Although Longley claimed his victory on election night by announcing "I'm still a Democrat," in office he faced numerous problems on account of his frequently expressed contempt for politicians and his independent stance. In particular, he often became embroiled in battles with the Legislature over his outspoken views. For example, he infuriated members of both parties when he referred to one legislator as a "common pimp," called opponents "criminals," and declared that "it is the professional politicians who prostitute the system." Political observers felt such tactics impaired his cost-cutting efforts.

Governor Longley attacked waste at the state university, reducing its budget request sharply, causing its chancellor to resign, and alienating its board of trustees. He presided over a series of austere state budgets that included no new taxes, but no new spending programs either. Public employees were denied pay increases, while Longley sharply trimmed the budget requests of every government department and asked the Legislature to consolidate several top administrative jobs. Just after he was inaugurated, he initiated a highly publicized "closed door policy." Locking every door leading to his office except one, he hoped to make the point that lobbyists with big-spending notions were no longer welcome. Through such measures, Longley presided over the first tax cut in the history of the state.

Under Longley's direction, the Legislature considered education, mental health, the aged, and conservation of Maine's timber, mineral, water, fishing, and farm land resources. Improvements were made in the highway and penal systems. A $30 million deficit in spending for education was wiped out, and two huge cuts were made in welfare spending. The aim of his administration, Longley maintained, was to run state government like a successful business.

Though Longley called himself a liberal, he was criticized by some liberals once he was in office. He was an outspoken opponent of feminism, asserting that it would undermine motherhood. In 1975 he called for a return of prayer to the public schools, and in 1977, when America's governors voted 31-4 in support of Jimmy Carter's welfare reforms, he joined three conservative Republicans in opposition. Longley's relations with the Carter administration worsened in February 1978 after he condemned the proposal of a White House study group that suggested the state put up $1.7 million annually for 15 years as part of a $30 million land compensation settlement with the Penobscot and Passamaquoddy Indians.

Longley's voter popularity in Maine increased throughout his term, however, as he became involved in battles with the Legislature, teachers' unions, and virtually every other organized pressure group. While he alienated almost every influential group in Maine, he acquired a popularity rating almost unparalleled in state history. He chose, however, not to run for a second term in 1978, keeping a promise he had made when elected and hoping that his continued status as a "non-politician" would improve his chances for accomplishment. Although many of his supporters urged him to reconsider, and polls indicated that he could beat any challenger by at least a two to one margin, Longley drew satisfaction from the fact that he was keeping his word to the people of Maine. He was widely hailed in the national press as the "Governor who kept his promises." Proof of Longley's popularity was that, after his announced retirement, every gubernatorial candidate in 1978 tried to emulate his style.

Longley left office in January 1979, after having halved unemployment and used a $40 million state surplus to provide tax rebates. On leaving office, he returned to his insurance business. His only political activity was to serve as Co-Chairman of the National Taxpayers Union drive for a constitutional amendment that would compel Congress to balance the federal budget. A rumored run for the United States Senate never materialized, perhaps due to ill health. One year after leaving office, Longley publicly disclosed that he had cancer. He died at his home in Lewiston, Maine on August 16, 1980, at the age of 56.

Bibliography: "Architect of the Biggest Upset," *Time* (November 18, 1974); Roy Glashan, *American Governors and Gubernatorial Elections, 1775-1975* (Stillwater, Minn., 1975); Congressional Quarterly, Inc., *Guide to U.S. Elections* (Washington, D.C., 1975); "Maine: In Hot Blood," *Newsweek* (April 7, 1975); "No More Wine and Roses," *Time* (April 14, 1975); "Yankee Who Tames Bureaucrats," *U.S. News and World Report* (August 7, 1978); Vernon Louviere, "The Governor Who Kept His Promises," *Nation's Business* (October 1978); Michael Barone *et al.*, eds., *The Almanac of American Politics, 1978-80* (New York, 1977-79); Eugene H. Methvin, "The Governor Who Kept His Word," *Reader's Digest* (December 1979); "Former Gov. Longley of Maine Is Dead," *New York Times Biographical Service*, 11 (August 1980), 1137. MMM

Joseph Edward Brennan (Credit: Office of the Governor, Maine)

BRENNAN, Joseph Edward, 1979-

Born on November 2, 1934 in Portland, Maine, the son of John J. and Katherine (Mulkerin) Brennan. A Roman Catholic, Brennan is divorced. He has two children—Joseph E. and Tara E.

Brennan served in the United States Army from 1953 to 1955. He received a B.S. degree from Boston College in 1958, and an LL.B. from the University of Maine in 1963. Admitted to the Maine bar in that year, he began a private law practice in Portland. Brennan was elected to the Maine House of Representatives in 1965, and in 1967 he served as Assistant Minority Leader. He became Attorney for Cumberland County in 1971. In 1973 he served in the Maine Senate, acting as Minority Leader of that body. He was appointed Attorney General of Maine in 1975. Brennan became nationally prominent when he took a hard line in opposing the damage claims of the Penobscot and Passamaquoddy Indian tribes, who asserted that Maine had taken 12.5 million acres of land from them without the approval of the United States Congress. Brennan sought to make the federal government pay the claims.

While the Indian claims were still pending, Brennan was a candidate in the 1978 Democratic gubernatorial primary and defeated Phillip L. Merrill by about 12,000 votes. Richard S. Carey placed third in that race. During the campaign United States Attorney General Griffin Bell threatened to sue the state, unless a settlement was reached with the Indians. Brennan won the general election easily, defeating Linwood Palmer, the Republican candidate, by 176,493 votes to 126,862. (Incumbent Governor James B. Longley, an independent, had withdrawn from the election to honor his pledge that he would run for only one term.) Brennan easily carried the state, with the major issues being the Indian claims and Palmer's call for a mandatory limit on state spending.

During his first term Brennan vetoed a bill banning smoking in all public places. He also sought an injunction to force striking state employees to return to work, and appointed George Mitchell to succeed Edmund Muskie as United States Senator when the latter resigned to become United States Secretary of State. In 1979 an energy assistance bill for Maine was enacted at the governor's request. Brennan finally reached an out-of-court settlement in 1980 with the Indian tribes for $81.5 million, a settlement which the federal government quickly approved. Maine later received some federal compensation.

Brennan ran unopposed in the 1982 gubernatorial primary, and easily defeated Charles L. Cragin in the general election by a margin of 281,066 votes to 172,949. In 1983 Governor Brennan was seeking a hospital cost containment bill.

Bibliography: New York Times, March 24, 1978; *Boston Globe*, November 5, 1978; Warren J. Mitofsky, ed., *Campaign '78* (New York, 1980); *Who's Who in America* (Chicago, 1982); *USA Today*, March 30, 1983. JH

Blair Lee, III (Credit: Maryland State Archives)

MARYLAND

LEE, Blair, III, 1977-1979

Born on May 19, 1916 in Silver Spring, Maryland, the son of Colonel E. Brooke and Elizabeth (Wilson) Lee. An Episcopalian, Lee is the descendant of Richard Lee, Richard Henry Lee, Francis Lightfoot Lee, Zachary Taylor, Montgomery Blair, and Blair Lee (Maryland's first elected United States Senator). He was married to Mathilde Boal on July 6, 1944, and is the father of Blair IV, Pierre Boal Lee, Joseph W., Christopher G., Frederick B., Philip L., John F., and Jeanne M. Lee.

Lee received an A.B. from Princeton University in 1938. He rose to the rank of Lieutenant Commander in the United States Naval Reserve, and was on active duty from 1941 to 1945. Lee served as editor of the *Maryland News* (Silver Spring) from 1945 to 1949, and as President of the Silver Spring Board of Trade between 1948 and 1949. He became a member of the Maryland Press Association in 1949, and served as Vice Chairman and Park Commissioner of the Maryland National Capital Park and Planning Commission from 1949 to 1951. Lee was engaged in private planning and zoning construction from 1954 to 1959, and in property management from 1969. A Democrat, he entered the Maryland House of Delegates in 1955, serving until 1962. In 1962 he made an unsuccessful bid for nomination to the United States Senate. He was a Delegate to the Democratic national conventions of 1948, 1960, 1964, and 1972, and acted as an Alternate Delegate in 1968. Lee was Montgomery County (Maryland) Campaign Manager for John F. Kennedy in 1960, and Regional Coordinator of the Middle Atlantic States for the Johnson-Humphrey Presidential campaign of 1964. In 1966 he was elected to the Maryland Senate, where he was Vice Chairman of the Senate Finance Committee and a member of the Legislative Council. He served in the Senate until 1969. In 1970 Lee was selected by Governor Marvin Mandel to serve as Secretary of State. Mandel announced that Lee would assume the functions of a lieutenant governor, since Maryland had none at that time. The General Assembly subsequently enacted a constitutional amendment which created the office. Voters ratified this amendment in November 1970, and at the same time chose Lee to fill the new office.

Lieutenant Governor Lee was appointed by Governor Mandel as Acting Governor in June 1977, at the start of Mandel's federal corruption trial. He continued in that role after Mandel was legally suspended from office on October 7, 1977, upon his sentencing to four years in federal prison for his conviction on charges of bribery and mail fraud.

However, Lee's hold on the governorship was weakened by Mandel's refusal to resign formally from office at the time of his sentencing. Maryland's attorney general ruled that, barring Mandel's own resignation, Lee could not assume the title of governor because Mandel could reclaim the office if he were vindicated on appeal. Mandel's suspension gave Lee complete authority, though still not with the title of governor.

Lee ultimately was unable to define his own goals and accomplishments. Although he attempted to divorce himself from Mandel by pledging a more open administration, he remained politically vulnerable because of his link with the tainted administration and because of his reputation as Mandel's hand-picked successor. Lee also offended many Democrats by choosing integrity over loyalty in his appointments. In particular, his refusal to give a Mandel-promised Cabinet appointment to State Senator Roy N. Staten hurt him politically. Lee was faced with the difficult problem of distancing himself just enough from the Mandel administration to assure citizens of his own integrity, while simultaneously struggling to avoid offending Mandel's strong political machine in Baltimore, whose money and organization he needed to enhance his future political prospects. In the end, he could not pull off this difficult balancing act.

Lee's vulnerability manifested itself in his race for the Democratic gubernatorial nomination in 1978. Entering the September primary as a favorite with the advantage of incumbency and with ''integrity in government'' as his theme, he was upset by a relative political unknown, Harry R. Hughes. A former Maryland Secretary of Transportation who had resigned from Mandel's Cabinet after charging that the administration had tampered with a $24 million bid on a contract to begin construction of Baltimore's subway system, Hughes was aided at the polls by this publicized break from the corruption-ridden regime. Having a competent record in state government, first in the Legislature and then in Mandel's Cabinet, Hughes was also helped by a surprise endorsement from the *Baltimore Sun*. Apparently eager for an alternative to Lee, Maryland's voters gave Hughes 37 percent of the vote in a four-man race. Lee came in second with 34 percent.

Although he had been expected to serve out the remainder of Mandel's second term (due to expire on January 17, 1979), Lee suddenly lost his position early that month. On January 11, 1979, when a federal appeals court overturned Mandel's conviction because of legal and technical flaws in the trial, he was legally empowered to assume the governorship for the final six days of his term. Mandel formally reclaimed his office on January 15, 1979. In a letter written that day, he withdrew the June 1977 letter by which Blair had become acting chief executive.

Lee has been described as a ''patrician liberal and old-line aristocrat'' who was ''the polar opposite of his patron.'' A man whose personal wealth is in the range of $2.5 million, his political record has been termed ''unblemished'' by political observers.

Bibliography: *New York Times*, November 4, 1970, June 5, August 25-26,

August 28, and October 8, 1977, September 14 and November 9, 1978, January 12-13 and January 16, 1979; Bob Hollingsworth, ed., *Facts on File Yearbook, 1976* (New York, 1977); "Maryland's Acting Governor," *New York Times Biographical Service*, 8 (October 1977), 1421-22; Michael Barone *et al.*, eds., *The Almanac of American Politics, 1980, 1984* (New York and Washington, D.C., 1979, 1983); biographical information on Blair Lee, III, Hall of Records, Annapolis, Maryland. MMM

Marvin Mandel (Credit: Maryland State Archives)

MANDEL, Marvin, 1969-1977, 1979

Born on April 19, 1920 in Baltimore, Maryland, the son of Harry, a clothing cutter, and Rebecca (Cohen) Mandel. A Jew, Mandel married Barbara Oberfeld on June 8, 1941; he is the father of Gary and Ellen. Following his divorce in 1973, he married Jeanne Dorsey in 1974.

Educated in Baltimore's schools, Mandel was graduated from City College in 1937. He later attended the University of Maryland, and was graduated from that institution's law school in 1942. Mandel was appointed Justice of the Peace of Baltimore City in 1950, and served in the Maryland House of Delegates from 1952 until he assumed the governor's office. As a member of the House, he was Chairman of its powerful Ways and Means Committee. In 1963 Mandel was elected Speaker, a post he held until he became Governor. When Spiro T. Agnew resigned the governorship to become Vice President of the United States, Mandel was selected by the Maryland Legislature to fill the post. He assumed office on January 7, 1969.

A Democrat, Mandel was elected Governor in his own right on November 3, 1970, when he defeated Republican C. Stanley Blair with 67 percent of the vote. His margin of victory was the largest ever recorded by a gubernatorial candidate in the history of the state to that time. Capturing 66 percent of the vote in the 1974 Democratic gubernatorial primary against three other candidates, Mandel went on to defeat Republican Louise Gore to win re-election on November 5, 1974. In that election Mandel polled 602,648 votes (63 percent) to Gore's 356,449.

Mandel was regarded as an efficient, competent chief executive, and received praise for his ability to hold down taxes and at the same time establish innovative programs. During his term in office, he restored persons to Medicaid rolls who had been removed during the Agnew administration, created a Drug Abuse Authority and a State Housing Authority, supported the passage of eight constitutional amendments in 1969, and secured the reorganization of the Executive Department. More of the costs of education were assumed by the state during Mandel's years in office, and gasoline and alcohol taxes were increased to improve Maryland's transportation system.

Other significant legislative achievements of the Mandel administration include: increasing the state's contribution to community colleges; enactment of a prevailing wage law; strengthening of Maryland's Human Relations Commission; creation of the Maryland Council of Economic Advisors (only the second in the nation on the state level); and passage of a series of environmental protection, consumer protection, housing, law enforcement, health, and welfare measures.

In November 1975, however, Mandel was indicted on federal corruption charges. He and five associates were charged with a "corrupt relationship" in which the governor's friends were said to have "bought" him with cash, travel, and jewelry. The indictment charged that Mandel had reciprocated by using his influence as chief executive to enhance the value of a Maryland racetrack that the five co-defendants had secretly bought, illegally concealing their ownership of it from state officials assigned to regulate the racing industry.

Mandel's first trial in 1976 ended in a mistrial because of jury tampering. In June 1977, prior to the start of his second trial, Mandel turned over his gubernatorial responsibilities to Lieutenant Governor Blair Lee, III, who became Acting Governor. Mandel's re-trial in 1977 resulted in his conviction on 15 separate counts of mail fraud and on another charge of racketeering. He thus became the first incumbent governor to be convicted of a federal crime in more than 50 years, and only the third chief executive in American history to be convicted while in office. He was sentenced to four years in prison on October 7, 1977. Although he refused to resign, upon his sentencing Mandel was automatically suspended from the powers of the gubernatorial office under state law. His sentence was delayed pending appeal, and during the intervening period Mandel served as a political consultant in Arnold, Maryland.

On January 11, 1979, a federal appeals court overturned Mandel's conviction and that of his five co-defendants. A three-judge panel of the United States Court of Appeals for the Fourth Circuit found that instructions to the jury in the previous trial might have been misleading. Nevertheless, the convictions were not reversed on any ground that could be regarded as repudiation of the original corruption charges. Indeed, the court said that the evidence in the case supported a third trial on the charges, although its ruling automatically empowered Mandel to reclaim the governorship for the final six days of his second term. Although he hesitated for several days before doing so, Mandel reclaimed the full powers of his office on January 15, 1979 for the final two days of his term. Citing "touching and sentimental reasons," he withdrew the terms of the June 1977 letter by which Lieutenant Governor Blair Lee, III had become acting governor. Mandel thus set into motion what historians called probably the first gubernatorial "triple play" in history. In three days, the Maryland government passed from Acting Governor Blair Lee, III to Mandel to Governor-elect Harry R. Hughes.

Mandel's conviction was reinstated on July 20, 1979 by a sharply divided United States Court of Appeals for the Fourth Circuit. In a ruling that nullified the January decision by a panel of the same court, the full court voted to uphold the convictions returned by a federal jury in August 1977. In November 1979 the Fourth Circuit Court of Appeals refused to rehear an appeal of the conviction, and in April 1980 the United States Supreme Court declined to hear Mandel's appeal.

Mandel began serving his prison term in May 1980. He served 19 months in all before President Ronald Reagan commuted his sentence on December 3, 1981. Mandel was freed on December 20, 1981, five months before he was due to be paroled. Offered a job as a budget analyst for the city of Baltimore, he eventually took a job with Charles J. Cirelli and Sons, a general contractor, with whom he was involved in real estate development and financing.

Bibliography: Frank F. White, Jr., *The Governors of Maryland, 1770-1970* (Annapolis, 1970); Congressional Quarterly, Inc., *Guide to U.S. Elections* (Washington, D.C., 1975); Roy Glashan, *American Governors and Gubernatorial Elections, 1775-1975* (Stillwater, Minn., 1975); Howard M. Epstein, ed., *Facts on File Yearbook, 1975* (New York, 1976); "Going After a Governor," *Time* (October 4, 1976); "Mandel's Mistrial," *Newsweek* (December 20, 1976); *New York Times*, April 6, June 2, June 26, August 24, August 28, October 8, and December 3, 1977, January 12-13, January 18, July 21, and November 7, 1979, April 15, 1980, December 3-4, December 6, and December 9, 1981; Michael Barone *et al.*, eds., *The Almanac of American Politics, 1978* (New York, 1977). MMM

Harry Roe Hughes (Credit: Office of the Governor, Maryland)

HUGHES, Harry Roe, 1979-

Born on November 13, 1926 in Easton, Maryland, the son of Jonathan Long-fellow and Helen (Roe) Hughes. An Episcopalian, Hughes married Patricia Ann Donoho on June 30, 1951, by whom he is the father of Ann Donoho and Elizabeth Roe.

Hughes grew up in Denton, Maryland, and was educated in Caroline County public schools. He served in the United States Navy Air Corps in 1944 and 1945, attended Mercersburg Academy in Mercersburg, Pennsylvania, and studied for a time at Mount Saint Mary's College in Emmitsburg, Maryland before receiving a B.S. from the University of Maryland in 1949. Hughes played briefly with the New York Yankees' Easton farm club. In 1952 he received an LL.B. degree from George Washington University School of Law. Admitted to the Maryland bar that year, he practiced law in Denton.

In 1954 Hughes was elected as a Democrat to represent Caroline County in the Maryland House of Delegates. He was elected to the Maryland Senate in 1958, where he served as Majority Floor Leader in 1965. Hughes chaired the Maryland Democratic Party in 1969 and 1970, and in the latter year served as Chairman of a commission to study the state's role in financing public education. That commission's report led to the assumption by Maryland's state government of most public school construction costs. In 1971 Hughes left both his law practice and the Maryland Senate when Governor Marvin Mandel named him to head the state's new Department of Transportation. While with the agency, he oversaw construction of the Baltimore, Maryland and Washington, D.C. subways, and the redevelopment of Baltimore's waterfront. Hughes resigned as Secretary in May 1977, over what he alleged was improper influence with state procedures in awarding contracts for the Baltimore subway. He then returned to the practice of law, this time with a firm in Baltimore, but afterwards entered the 1978 Democratic gubernatorial primary.

The incumbent governor that year was Blair Lee, a Democrat who had become chief executive when Marvin Mandel was convicted on numerous charges stem-ming from an alleged improper attempt to influence legislation concerning a racetrack in Upper Marlboro, Maryland. Although experts predicted that Lee would win the election, his connections with Mandel were damaging enough to cause voters to choose Hughes from among three candidates challenging the incumbent. Hughes was opposed in the general election by J. Glenn Beall, Jr., a former United States Senator and the offspring of an old and distinguished Maryland political family. Hughes received little support until the *Sun* news-papers of Baltimore decided to endorse his candidacy. He went on to defeat Beall by the largest popular vote margin in a century—718,328 votes to 293,635. In the election Beall took only rural Allegany and Garrett counties in the western part of Maryland.

On January 11, 1979, three judges of the United States Fourth Circuit Court of Appeals ordered a re-trial in the Mandel case, and the former governor was briefly reinstated as the lame-duck chief executive of the state. Hughes thus assumed office from Mandel, not Lee, when he was sworn in on January 17, 1979. The full Fourth Circuit Court confirmed Mandel's conviction about six months later. (At the same time Spiro Agnew, Mandel's immediate predecessor, was defending himself from civil charges stemming from his conviction on federal bribery charges.)

During his first year in office, Hughes approved a $144 million tax relief program. He sought reform of educational funding formulas in 1980, and entrusted the state's environmental regulations to the Department of Health and Mental Hygiene. Hughes also visited Mainland China. During his first term Maryland raised its legal drinking age and enacted a condominium conversion law.

In 1982 Hughes overcame light opposition in the primary from the veteran state legislator Harry McGuirk and faced Robert Pascal, also a state legislator, in the general election. Pascal charged the governor with being weak on crime, while others perceived Hughes as lacking in leadership. However, after Hughes called a special session of the Legislature to consider the state's response to federal cuts in unemployment benefits, this show of strength, coupled with Pascal's difficulty in raising campaign funds, enabled the incumbent to win easily. The final count was 705,910 votes for Hughes and 432,826 for his opponent, with Pascal showing real strength only in the Baltimore suburbs. Hughes' current term expires in 1987.

Bibliography: *Washington Post*, November 8, 1978, July 1, 1981, July 1 and November 3, 1982; *Maryland Manual, 1981-82* (Annapolis, Md., 1981). Mandel's appeal is reported as *United States v. Mandel*, 591 F.2d 1347 (4th Cir., 1979), *reversed en banc* 602 F. 2d 653 (4th Cir., 1979). JH

Michael S. Dukakis (Credit: Governor's Office, Massachusetts)

MASSACHUSETTS

DUKAKIS, Michael S., 1975-1979, 1983-

Born on November 3, 1933 in Brookline, Massachusetts, the son of Panos and Euterpe (Boukis) Dukakis, who were Greek immigrants. Dukakis is married to Katharine Dickson; he is the father of three children—John, Andrea, and Kara.

Dukakis attended Brookline High School, graduating in 1951. He received his B.A. degree in 1955 from Swarthmore College, where he earned highest honors in political science. He served in the United States Army from 1956 to 1958, including duty in Korea. Dukakis received an LL.B. from Harvard in 1960, graduating with honors. After being admitted to the Massachusetts bar, he practiced law. In 1962 Dukakis was elected to the Massachusetts House of Representatives, serving until 1970. There he sponsored legislation for housing, conservation, and consumer protection. He was the first legislator in America to introduce a no-fault automobile insurance bill, which was passed by the state in 1971. In 1970 Dukakis lost in an attempt to become Lieutenant Governor. He then returned to his private law practice, but remained active in public affairs. He served as moderator of ''The Advocates,'' a public television debate program, and helped to monitor state agencies to insure efficient government.

In 1974 Dukakis ran against incumbent Republican Governor Francis W. Sargent, after winning the Democratic gubernatorial nomination with 58 percent of the vote over Robert H. Quinn. Promising the most open campaign in Massachusetts history, he pledged to reduce the size of the governor's staff, balance the state budget, and reduce spending. Dukakis declared that the first thing he would do upon becoming governor was ''to begin to introduce the idea of productivity and efficiency goals and standards into state government.'' Helped by an anti-Republican year in an anti-Republican state, Dukakis took 56 percent of the vote.

As chief executive, Dukakis spent much of his time trying to correct the fiscal problems of Massachusetts. He reduced the number of public employees and made other cuts in state spending, which restored Massachusetts to fiscal responsibility. He worked to regulate state agencies, continued to support consumer protection, and was involved in efforts to alleviate the state's energy shortage.

Christened ''Jerry Brown East'' by the press, Dukakis impressed many voters by eliminating many of the trappings of the governor's office. He continued to live in his own modest home, grew vegetables in his garden, and got rid of his state limousine in favor of the Boston subway. Still, though citizens were impressed by his unquestioned honesty and competence, many were turned off by his lack of warmth. Dukakis was hurt most of all by the way he handled taxes. Elected as a liberal reformer intent on stopping the state's spiraling taxes and public spending, he did slash the budget and turn around the nearly bankrupt state. In the process, however, he was forced to approve the largest tax increase in Massachusetts history, after having given the voters a "lead pipe guarantee of no new taxes." In office Dukakis disappointed many of the liberals who had supported him by cutting state services and programs. He made enemies and antagonized allies in the Legislature, with whom he wrestled over the budget for almost his entire first year in office. He also earned the reputation of being a cold intellectual, who could not compromise with legislative interests. In retrospect, his governorship during his first term "cannot be said to have been a success," in the words of one political observer.

Nonetheless, Dukakis' defeat in the 1978 Democratic gubernatorial primary jolted liberals across the nation. His opponent was Edward J. King, the former director of the Massachusetts Port Authority and head of a business promotional group called the New England Council. King campaigned on a pledge to cut property taxes by $500 million, slash social spending, and create a pro-business atmosphere. Outspending Dukakis on advertising by a margin of two to one, he used sophisticated polling techniques to identify voter grievances against Dukakis. Dukakis, on the other hand, did little campaigning, relying on polls that showed him with a wide lead. In a stunning upset, he was defeated by King, 51 percent to 42 percent (with a third candidate garnering seven percent of the vote). King went on to defeat the Republican Francis Hatch, a moderate state representative, in the general election.

Dukakis' behavior after his defeat served to alienate him from an increasingly divided state Democratic Party. He was criticized especially for his failure to support King, a conservative, in the general election. Vulnerable because of his rigid stance against cronyism and his refusal to wheel and deal politically, Dukakis was even rebuffed by the Massachusetts Executive Council, which voted to ask President Jimmy Carter to keep him out of his Cabinet.

After leaving office, Dukakis assumed the position of lecturer and Director of Intergovernmental Studies at Harvard's John F. Kennedy School of Government, where he taught courses in management at the state and local level and joined a group of faculty members developing studies in the new field of public management.

By 1982, however, Dukakis was ready to make a surprising comeback and reclaim the governorship. In a rerun of their bitter 1978 contest, Dukakis challenged the incumbent King for the Democratic nomination in a primary billed as an early referendum on "Reaganomics." A conservative Democrat often referred to as "Ronald Reagan's favorite governor," King presented himself as an advocate of the common man, and took conservative positions on capital punishment, mandatory sentencing, and drunk driving. King's openly pro-business attitude, with its emphasis on tax-cutting, reduction in state regulation, and crackdown on welfare abuse, had pleased many businessmen, but voters were increasingly displeased with what they perceived as his inept handling of the budget and Legislature and his scandal-ridden administration. Not only did Dukakis attack King as a "cheerleader for Reaganomics," but he made effective use of the issue of corruption in state government. One of King's Cabinet secretaries was convicted and sent to prison for taking money; another old friend, a deputy commissioner in the Revenue Department, hanged himself after disclosure of a scandal over payoffs to revenue officials.

Dukakis hired professionals from Washington, D.C. to help project a campaign that highlighted integrity and competence. Running on the theme of "honest and effective leadership," he put together one of the largest field organizations ever assembled for a state-wide race. In expanding the organization of the liberal coalition that elected him in 1974, he raised $2 million from a broader base of small contributors than did King, and with it was able to overpower King's advantages of incumbency and his own substantial war chest. Dukakis was greatly aided by a resounding endorsement from the *Boston Globe*, which described the King administration as "one of the weakest in the modern history of the Commonwealth."

In May 1982 68 percent of the delegates to the state's first Democratic convention in eight years passed a non-binding resolution supporting Dukakis for the nomination. In the September 1982 primary, the most expensive in the state's history and one that received extensive national coverage, Dukakis defeated King, receiving 53 percent of the vote to the incumbent's 47 percent. The bitter grudge match drew the largest number of voters in the history of a Massachusetts primary. Dukakis' support had come from liberals, suburban residents, and the state's relatively large number of intellectuals, while King drew upon blue-collar workers in the old industrial cities and in Roman Catholic, Irish, and Italian communities.

In the general election, Dukakis faced Republican John Winthrop Sears, a well-to-do Boston city councilman. The race was billed as a classic contest between a liberal and a conservative, one that pitted an ethnic Democrat against a Brahmin Republican. Dukakis tried hard in his campaign to shed the reputation for humorlessness and arrogance which he had acquired as governor. He stressed his opposition to the death penalty, his support for gun control, and his concern about problems such as mass transit and human services. In a state where there are three Democrats for every Republican, Dukakis won handily, gaining 59 percent of the vote.

In his inaugural address, Dukakis pledged to "fight Reaganomics and its philosophy of indifference with all the energy I can summon." Serving with Lieutenant Governor John F. Kerry, he is once again facing difficult economic circumstances. Plans for his second term include the development of programs to aid the estimated hundreds of homeless Massachusetts citizens and to create jobs for the thousands of the state's unemployed.

Bibliography: Facts on File, 34-37 (New York, 1974-77); "Races to Watch," *Time* (October 21, 1974); "Routing the Republicans," *Time* (November 18,

1974); Congressional Quarterly, Inc., *Guide to U.S. Elections* (Washington, D.C., 1975); Roy Glashan, *American Governors and Gubernatorial Elections, 1775-1975* (Stillwater, Minn., 1975); *New York Times*, February 18 and November 1, 1978, January 5 and January 19, 1979, January 11, May 23, August 14, September 11, September 15-16, September 19, and October 25, 1982, January 7, 1983; "The Duke's Downfall," *Newsweek* (October 2, 1978); Michael Barone *et al.*, eds., *The Almanac of American Politics, 1978-80, 1984* (New York and Washington, D.C., 1977-79, 1983); "Getting a Second Chance," *Newsweek* (September 27, 1982); "Governors: Different Democratic Styles," *Time* (September 27, 1982); biographical information, Governor's Office, Commonwealth of Massachusetts. MMM

Edward Joseph King (Credit: King Committee)

KING, Edward Joseph, 1979-1983

Born on May 11, 1925 in Chelsea, Massachusetts, the son of Edward and Helen Veronica (Dawson) King. A Roman Catholic, King was graduated from Boston College in 1948 and did postgraduate work at the Bentley School of Accounting and Finance between 1951 and 1953. After leaving college he played guard for the Buffalo Bills in the National Football League in 1948 and 1949. In 1950 King played for the Baltimore Colts. On November 22, 1952, he married Josephine (''Jody'') Teresa Hurley. He has two sons—Brian Edward and Timothy D.

From 1953 to 1956 King was an accountant for a Boston firm. In 1956 he became associated with the Boston Museum of Science, and between 1959 and 1974 he held various offices at the Massachusetts Port Authority in Boston. King was President of the New England Council from 1975 to 1977. He was also active in charities such as the Little Sisters of the Poor and the Greater Boston Leukemia Society.

Outside the ranks of Democratic politicians in Massachusetts, King's background was that of a public administrator. Nevertheless, in the 1978 primary he defeated incumbent Governor Michael S. Dukakis by nearly 100,000 votes. In the general election he campaigned on a platform of cutting taxes and eliminating welfare abuse. He was supported by Howard Jarvis, the proponent of ''Proposition 13,'' a controversial measure in California which drastically cut state taxes and revenues. Edward F. King, the loser in the Republican primary, also supported King's candidacy.

On the other hand, Thomas P. O'Neill, III, the Democratic candidate for Lieutenant Governor and son of the Speaker of the United States House of Representatives, was so wary of King that he did not endorse the head of the Democratic ticket until the last days of the race. Still, King proceeded to win the general election, beating Francis Hatch, Jr., by 1,030,294 votes to 926,072. One deciding factor was a 30,000 vote advantage compiled by King in Boston.

Governor King soon called for a property tax freeze and signed a bill restoring capital punishment in the state in 1979. A dramatic tax cut was instituted in November 1980. In January 1981 King ordered home thermostats limited to 55 degrees during an acute natural gas shortage. He also supported Ronald Reagan's free-market economic policies; for example, Massachusetts deregulated hospital construction during King's tenure.

When President Reagan called King his ''favorite Democratic Governor,'' party regulars revolted. The 1982 Democratic State Convention refused to endorse King for renomination, and while United States Senator Edward M. Kennedy criticized Reagan strongly at that convention, his complaints were really aimed at King. Although the convention's action was only advisory, Democratic voters followed suit in September by choosing former Governor Dukakis over

King by a margin of 629,753 votes to 546,545. After leaving office, King joined the Boston office of Hill and Knowlton, a public relations firm.

Bibliography: Boston Globe, November 9, 1978, May 23 and June 9, 1982; Warren J. Mitofsky, ed., *Campaign '78* (New York, 1980); *Who's Who in America* (Chicago, 1982); *USA Today*, April 6, 1983. King's papers are at the Massachusetts State Archives in Boston. JH

William Milliken (Credit: Michigan Department of State Archives)

MICHIGAN

Born on March 26, 1922 in Traverse City, Michigan, the son of James Thatcher Milliken, the owner of the area's leading department store and an experienced politician who had served for ten years in the Michigan State Senate, and Hildegarde (Grawn) Milliken. An Episcopalian, Milliken is the brother of John and Ruth. He married Helen Wallbank in 1945, and is the father of William Jr. and Elaine.

Milliken attended Yale University, but his studies were interrupted when he was inducted into the armed forces in February 1943. He served with distinction as a non-commissioned officer in the Army Air Force, flying 50 combat missions as the waist gunner of a bomber. Milliken eventually returned to Yale, from which he was graduated in the spring of 1946. He then operated the family department store until his election in 1960 to the Michigan State Senate; he served as Republican Floor Leader of that body in 1963-64. In 1964 Milliken was elected Lieutenant Governor. Upon the resignation of Governor George Romney, he became Governor of Michigan on January 22, 1969.

Milliken continued the liberal policies which had made his predecessor so popular, and was elected Governor in his own right in 1970, defeating the Democrat Sander Levin by a vote of 1,338,711 to 1,294,600. Manifesting a special interest in the state's system of taxation, and in particular its method of funding public education, Milliken also sought to improve transportation and to relieve some of the problems confronting the state's urban areas. Although his policies often created dissension among more conservative Republicans, they made Milliken personally popular with the electorate. In 1974 he won re-election by again defeating Sander Levin, this time by a margin of 1,356,865 votes to 1,242,247.

In 1978 Milliken was unopposed in the Republican primary, and went on to score a convincing win over William Fitzgerald by a vote of 1,628,485 to 1,237,256. During the campaign, Fitzgerald accused Milliken of being slow to react in 1973, when livestock in Michigan were tainted accidentally with a chemical substance. The Milliken campaign responded by charging Fitzgerald with airing deceptive commercials concerning the incident, and the Columbia Broadcasting System finally postponed an episode from the "Lou Grant" television series, scheduled for election eve, which was a fictionalized account of the Michigan controversy.

Shortly after the fall election, Michigan's probate courts were overhauled in

December 1978. Milliken went on a trade trip to China in 1979, and announced a lottery program to aid the Chrysler Corporation, one of Michigan's largest employers, which was then on the brink of bankruptcy. In 1980 he strongly supported women's rights issues, backing the Equal Rights Amendment and freedom of choice on the abortion issue. That same year he was the center of a Republican National Convention *faux pas* of considerable dimensions, after telling news network reporters that Ronald Reagan had selected former President Gerald Ford as his running mate. (Reagan eventually named George Bush for the Vice-Presidential post.) Milliken concluded a long struggle with the Michigan Legislature in 1981 by approving a revision of the workmen's compensation laws.

In December of 1981 Milliken announced that he would not seek a fourth term in 1982. At the time, the state was experiencing high unemployment and a tough campaign loomed. A leader of Republican moderates in the United States, Milliken was a strong supporter of regulation and expansive social welfare programs, although he rolled back some of his own initiatives in those areas at the end of his administration. He was succeeded in office by a Democrat, the former Congressman James J. Blanchard.

Bibliography: D. Duane Angel, *William G. Milliken, A Touch of Steel* (Warren, Mich., 1970); *Detroit News*, October 21 and November 8, 1978, July 31, 1980, December 17, 23, 1981; Warren J. Mitofsky, ed., *Campaign '78* (New York, 1980). Milliken's papers are on deposit at the State Archives Unit, Michigan History Division, Michigan Department of State in Lansing. JH

Rudy Perpich (Credit: Governor's Office, Minnesota)

MINNESOTA

PERPICH, Rudy, 1976-1979, 1983-

Born in Carson Lake, Minnesota on June 27, 1928, the son of Anton and Mary (Vukelich) Perpich. A Roman Catholic, Perpich is the brother of Tony, Joseph, and George. He married Lola Simic of Keewatin, Minnesota on September 4, 1954, and is the father of Rudy Jr. and Mary Susan.

Perpich attended Hibbing High School and Hibbing Junior College in Minnesota, and received his A.A. degree in 1950; he was graduated from Marquette University with a D.D.S. in 1954. Perpich served in the United States Army as a Sergeant from 1946 to 1947. A member of Minnesota's Democratic-Farmer-Labor Party, he was on the Hibbing Board of Education from 1952 to 1962, served in the Minnesota Senate from 1963 to 1970, and was Lieutenant Governor of Minnesota from 1971 to 1976. On December 30, 1976, Governor Wendell Anderson resigned and Perpich was elevated to the office, as provided by Minnesota's constitution. Perpich then appointed former Governor Anderson to fill the seat of Walter Mondale, the Vice President-elect, in the United States Senate.

Perpich served as the 34th Governor of Minnesota from 1976 until January 1979. The son of immigrants from Eastern Europe, he became the state's first governor of that ethnic background, the first to come from the Iron Range region of Minnesota, and the first Roman Catholic. His success as a dentist and later as a politician was a classic American success story that endeared him to Minnesota's large Slavic population. Perpich's father Anton had moved to the state from Yugoslavia when he was 20 to work in the ore mines of the Iron Range, and Governor Perpich was later to claim that this background shaped him, leading him to champion the rights of the poor and minorities. His unorthodox personal style also proved to be exceptionally popular. A believer in the work ethic, he vowed to make government more productive, and to crack down on waste and inefficiency. Perpich ordered phones removed from state cars, cut down on travel and the use of state vehicles, and even banned coffee from his office in protest over its high price. Committed to providing citizens access to their chief executive, he maintained an open door policy and attracted attention by showing up unheralded and unexpectedly in public places. At one point, he even allowed reporters to rummage through his office drawers when they asked permission.

Nevertheless, the friendly and easygoing Perpich also had his critics. Some said he acted without thinking and often without heeding the advice of his staff; others claimed that he had no clear-cut program or vision for Minnesota. His biggest problem, however, was his link to the Democratic-Farmer-Labor Party that was drawing increasing criticism in the state. By early 1978 the Republicans had begun to make the point that all of Minnesota's top state-wide positions were filled by people who had not been elected to them—a view which the voters apparently shared, judging by the results of the 1978 elections. The DFL suffered some shattering defeats that year. Seeking election to his own term, Perpich was vulnerable on account of his role in the controversy which had ensued over Senator Anderson's appointment. He also faced a strong challenger in Republican Albert H. Quie, a 20-year veteran Congressman from Minnesota's First District.

Seizing on the popularity of "Proposition 13" sentiment in a high tax state, Quie advocated a 10 percent across-the-board tax cut and a constitutional amendment limiting state spending to growth in personal income. The voters responded positively, apparently reassured that Quie's reputation as a political moderate would keep him from slashing spending to ridiculous extremes. He defeated Perpich by a margin of 54 percent to 46 percent, in an election in which Perpich failed to carry some normally Democratic counties. Perpich attributed his upset defeat to poor campaign organization, and to a split between the conservative and liberal wings of his party. Quie's triumph was also widely interpreted as a victory for right-to-life groups in Minnesota. Although both men had taken anti-abortion stands, right-to-life groups felt that Quie had done more for them.

Perpich lived in Vienna after he left office in 1979. Working for Control Data Corporation overseas, he became Vice President and Executive Consultant to Control Data Worldtech, an international trade division of the Minneapolis-based computer concern. Perpich saw his new career as "an opportunity for me to promote Minnesota in international trade, breaking down barriers."

With Quie's retirement from office in 1983 after a single term and huge budget deficits, Perpich staged a comeback attempt in which he was widely perceived as the underdog. Still, he scored an upset victory in the Democratic primary that year, defeating popular State Attorney General Warren M. Spannaus and airline mechanic Ellsworth Peterson. Perpich earned 51 percent of the vote, winning huge majorities in his home base, the economically hard hit Iron Range.

Perpich was a strong favorite in the general election against Republican Wheelock Whitney, a wealthy businessman. The central focus of the 1982 campaign was on the financial health of Minnesota. Perpich, who contrasted the prosperous condition of the Treasury when he left office to its depleted state four years later, won an overwhelming victory, gaining 59 percent of the vote to Whitney's 40 percent.

With his victory, Perpich became the only person in Minnesota history to hold the gubernatorial post for two non-consecutive terms. He was sworn in as the state's 36th governor on January 3, 1983. Early in his second term, he named a 20-member task force to propose ways of attracting an NBA franchise to the state. Perpich's term expires in January 1987.

Bibliography: Congressional Quarterly, Inc., *Guide to U.S. Elections* (Washington, D.C., 1975); "From the 'Dumps' to Governor," *New York Times Biographical Service*, 7 (December 1976), 1775-76; *New York Times*, December

31, 1976, April 10, 1977, November 2, 1978, January 10, 1979, November 1, 1980, February 16, September 15, and November 1, 1982, January 5, 1984; Bob Hollingsworth, ed., *Facts on File Yearbook, 1976* (New York, 1977); "Minnesota: Rudy's Disappearing Act," *Newsweek* (April 11, 1977); Stephen Orlofsky, ed., *Facts on File Yearbook, 1977* (New York, 1978); Michael Barone *et al.*, eds., *The Almanac of American Politics, 1980, 1984* (Washington, D.C., 1979, 1983); biographical information, Office of the Governor, State of Minnesota. MMM

Albert H. Quie (Courtesy: Albert H. Quie)

QUIE, Albert H., 1979-1983

Born on September 18, 1923 on a farm in Wheeling Township, Rice County, near Dennison, Minnesota, the son of Albert K., a farmer, and Nettie (Jacobson) Quie. A Lutheran, Quie is the brother of Alice, Marjorie, and Paul. He attended elementary school in Nerstrand, high school in Northfield, and received a B.A. degree in political science from St. Olaf College in Northfield in 1950. In 1943 he joined the United States Navy, serving for two years as a naval pilot. On June 5, 1948, Quie married Gretchen Hansen of Minneapolis, Minnesota; they had five children—Frederick, Jennifer, Daniel, Joel, and Benjamin.

At the time of his marriage Quie briefly left college to operate his family's 240-acre dairy farm in southeastern Minnesota. He also engaged in the breeding and training of horses. In 1949 he returned to St. Olaf to complete work toward his degree. During the years 1949-52 he served as Clerk of District 43 School Board, and from 1950 to 1954 he was Supervisor of the Rice County Soil Conservation District. After a close but unsuccessful write-in campaign in the 1952 election, Quie's political career began in earnest when he was elected to a Senate seat in the Minnesota State Legislature in 1954, where he served from 1955 to 1958.

On February 18, 1958, Quie, then only 34, entered politics on the national level. Running as a Republican in a special election to succeed the deceased Congressman August H. Andresen of Minnesota's First District, he was elected by 603 votes out of more than 88,000 cast. In the general election in November he faced the same opponent and won by 18,000 votes. Over the next 20 years Quie never lost an election, winning 11 successive terms in the 85th through 95th Congresses. In all his campaigns he won handily, with margins ranging from over 10 percent in 1964 to better than 41 percent in the 1972 campaign.

In his Congressional career Quie built an impressive record of accomplishment. He served for a time on the House Agriculture Committee, was a member of the House Ethics Committee (which he helped to establish), and also served on the Republican Committee on Committees. By far his most important contributions resulted from his role as the senior Republican on the powerful House Education and Labor Committee, a post which allowed him to play a prominent part in the passage of important legislation. Quie became well known for designing policies to distribute federal funds to educational institutions, emphasizing greater state and local participation and less federal control. Congressional legislation in which he was involved included various federal programs for the elderly, which provided for extended and expanded federal grants authorized under the Older Americans Act of 1965. These enactments were signed into law in 1973.

Quie also played a major role in the passage of the Education for Handicapped Children Act of November 1975, which aimed at assuring free and adequate public school education for the nation's nearly eight million handicapped children. He was the major architect of the Vocational Education Acts of 1963-68 and 1976, which did much to modernize vocational training. Despite being a member of the minority party on the House Education and Labor Committee, Quie achieved success because he sought to cooperate with committee Democrats.

Quie's legislative contributions to education and labor resulted in numerous awards. During his career he received honorary LL.D. degrees from St. Olaf College, Gettysburg (Pennsylvania) College, Buena Vista (Iowa) College, Capital University in Ohio, and Gallaudet College in Washington, D.C. In addition, he was awarded honorary Public Service degrees from Greenville College in Illinois and Gordon College in Massachusetts.

In 1968 Quie was considered for Secretary of Agriculture in the Nixon Cabinet, but he was not interested in that position. Instead, he decided in 1977 to return home and campaign for Governor. Quie chose what turned out to be a good year to retire from Congress, since the Independent-Republicans in Minnesota were facing a divided Democratic-Farmer-Labor Party. In 1978 Quie won his party's nomination by an overwhelming margin of 174,999 votes to 34,406, and on November 7, running on a platform which included a strong anti-abortion plank and called for reduced income taxes through indexing, improved education, and return of the government to the people, he was elected Minnesota's 35th Governor. He defeated the DFL candidate, incumbent Governor Rudy Perpich, by a record vote of 830,019 to 718,244. Quie's campaign expenditures of more than $1 million set a new high for a gubernatorial race up to that time. Reflecting his moderate voting record during his 11 terms in the House, his victory was a boost for the moderate national wing of the GOP.

Nevertheless, almost from the beginning, Quie's administration was beset by problems. In June 1979 he declared a state of emergency and activated the National Guard during a nation-wide truckers' strike caused by rising diesel fuel prices, because blockades by truckers threatened to shut down the state's fuel distribution system. In July and August 1981 he had to cope with a 22-day strike over wages by 14,000 state employees. This strike was symptomatic of financial problems confronting Minnesota and other states as a result of the national recession. The state also faced a continuing series of budget shortfalls. In 1981 Minnesota had a deficit of over $600 million, due to incorrect projections of a slow but improving national and local economy in 1982.

Quie's task was not made easier by the fact that throughout his term he was forced to work with an opposition majority. The Senate during all four years remained in DFL hands and, after a 67-67 standoff in the House following the 1978 election, the DFL regained control there as well in 1980. Quie was forced to call eight special sessions of the Legislature, most of them to deal with the state's budget complications. He and the Legislature used a three-pronged approach to help solve these problems: tax increases, spending cuts, and bookkeeping shifts of state obligations into the next fiscal year. The last special session took place in December 1982, near the end of his term, when the state sales tax and the income surtax were raised as part of a $344.6 million budget-balancing bill.

Accomplishments during Quie's term of office included the indexing of state income taxes and the merit selection of state judges. He also successfully pushed for an improved energy conservation policy, which had positive results. Still, on January 25, 1982, in the face of persistent budget deficits, Quie announced his intention not to seek a second term. He retired into private life on January 3, 1983.

Bibliography: *Congress and the Nation*, vol. I, 1945-64; vol. II, 1965-68; vol. IV, 1973-76; vol. V, 1977-80 (Washington, D.C., 1965, 1969, 1977, 1981); *Biographical Directory of the American Congress, 1774-1971* (Washington, D.C., 1971); Congressional Quarterly, Inc., *Guide to U.S. Elections* (Washington, D.C., 1975); *1977 Congressional Directory*, 95th Congress, 1st Session (Washington, D.C., 1977); Wilfred Bockelman, *Politics With Integrity: Al Quie of Minnesota* (Minneapolis, 1978); "Governor of Minnesota," [undated] and Governor Al Quie, "Farewell Address, December 3, 1982," *Papers of Albert H. Quie*, Minnesota State Archives, St. Paul, Minnesota. Quie's papers are on deposit at the Minnesota State Archives in St. Paul. ECD

Charles Clifton Finch (Credit: Mississippi Department of Archives and History)

MISSISSIPPI

FINCH, Charles Clifton, 1976-1980

Born on April 4, 1927 near Pope, Mississippi, the son of Carl B. and Christine (McMinn) Finch. A Baptist, Finch married Zelma Lois Smith on November 20, 1952; he is the father of Janet, Anne, Charles Clifton II, and Stephen Nicholas.

Finch served in the United States Army from 1945 to 1947, and was graduated from the University of Mississippi with a degree in public administration in 1956; he received his LL.B. degree from the same institution in 1958, and began a law practice in Batesville, Mississippi. Finch was soon elected to the Mississippi House of Representatives, serving from 1958 to 1964; he also served from 1964 to 1972 as District Attorney of the 17th Circuit Court District. Later, as a candidate for Governor of Mississippi, he campaigned as the blue-collar candidate, working at a gasoline station and construction jobs one day a week. Finch won the Democratic Party primary runoff on August 26, 1975, defeating Lieutenant Governor William Winter by 442,864 votes to 308,298. He won the general election on November 4, 1975, accumulating 369,568 votes compared with 319,632 for Gil Carmichael, a Republican, and 17,713 for Henry J. Kirksey, an Independent. He was inaugurated on January 20, 1976.

During Finch's administration the State Legislature closed 34 private savings and loan associations to prevent a run on the deposits, as a result of mismanagement charges against the Bankers Trust Company of Jackson, Mississippi. Before reopening, savings and loan associations in the state were required to cover all deposits with the Federal Savings and Loan Insurance Corporation. Finch achieved a balanced budget without raising taxes; the State Department of Corrections was also established during his tenure. In 1978 he vetoed a bill calling for the "sunset" of certain state agencies, and failed in his attempt to win the Democratic nomination for the United States Senate. In September 1979 Finch sought and received federal disaster aid after Hurricane Frederic caused $200 million in damage to Biloxi and Pascagoula, Mississippi. Earlier that year he had sought a federal loan moratorium and convened a special legislative session to deal with problems caused by spring floods.

Unable to succeed himself as governor, Finch suddenly declared himself a candidate for the Democratic Presidential nomination on Christmas Eve of 1979, just before the deadline for entries in the New Hampshire primary. However, Finch lost the Mississippi caucus to Jimmy Carter, and his candidacy deteriorated further when he attracted only three percent of the vote in the Louisiana primary.

Bibliography: Congressional Quarterly, Inc., *Guide to U. S. Elections* (Washington, D.C., 1975); State of Mississippi, *Laws of Mississippi, 1976* (Jackson, 1976); *New York Times*, January 21, 1976; Bob Hollingsworth, ed., *Facts on File Yearbook, 1976* (New York, 1977); *New Orleans Times Picayune*, December 25, 1979. Governor Finch's papers are on file at the State Archives and Library in Jackson, Mississippi. JH

William Forrest Winter (Credit: Office of the Governor, Mississippi)

WINTER, William Forrest, 1980-1984

Born in Granada, Mississippi on February 21, 1923, the son of William Aylmer and Inez (Parker) Winter. A Presbyterian, Winter married Elise Varner on October 10, 1950; they are the parents of Anne, Elise, and Eleanor.

Winter received a B.A. from the University of Mississippi in 1943. Immediately after graduating, he entered the United States Army and served for three years. In 1946 he returned to the University of Mississippi, receiving an LL.B. in 1949. Winter was admitted to the Mississippi bar that year, and established a law practice in Granada. The previous year he had begun his political career, becoming a Democratic member of the Mississippi House of Representatives. Except for a brief stint in the United States Army in 1951, Winter served in the Mississippi Legislature until 1956, when he became State Tax Collector. In 1964 he became State Treasurer.

Winter was defeated in the Democratic gubernatorial primary in 1967 by John Bell Williams, who had split with the national party to support Barry Goldwater's 1964 Presidential campaign. Winter, characterized by Williams as "too liberal for Mississippi" during the campaign, eventually returned to private legal practice. He joined the firm of Ludlum, Winter, and Stennis (the last partner being the son of United States Senator John Stennis). In 1971 Winter was elected Lieutenant Governor, and the following year he received the Margaret Dixon Freedom of Information Award from the Associated Press. Winter's second try for the governorship failed in 1975, when he lost in the primary to Charles C. Finch. That year Winter was named the Outstanding Alumnus of the University of Mississippi. In 1979 Winter defeated Lieutenant Governor Evelyn Gandy in the Democratic primary runoff for Governor, and went on to win the general election over Republican Gil Carmichael, a Meridian, Mississippi businessman making his second attempt at the governorship, by a vote of 413,620 to 263,702. Winter took every county except Jackson, which he lost narrowly.

Soon after his election Winter tried to improve the state's cultural image by inviting such celebrities as Turner Catledge, Eudora Welty, Dean Rusk, Willie Morris, and William Styron for dinner and conversation at the governor's mansion. During his term a uniform state tax assessment was discussed by the Legislature, and a bill was introduced requiring that both the theory of evolution and Biblical explanations of the origin of man be taught in Mississippi schools. Winter sought to stimulate small business in the state, which had the lowest *per capita* income in the nation. He described Mississippi as being "picked on" when the federal government attempted, through the United States Supreme Court, to claim waters near a chain of islands located off the state's Gulf Coast. Winter also opposed the dumping of nuclear waste in salt domes situated along the coast.

Fearing the impoverishment of Mississippi counties in the face of lost federal payments, Winter worked to attract high-technology industries to the state, although he recognized that a school system with a 42 percent dropout rate could not easily sustain such industries. Consequently, he pushed for and obtained a compulsory school attendance law and mandatory kindergarten programs. (Previously, Mississippi had been the only state that did not require these educational standards.) Winter also obtained a one-half cent sales tax increase to fund educational programs. When President Reagan suggested that citizens who found their state's social services inadequate could "vote with their feet" by moving elsewhere, Winter responded that many native Mississippians might be forced to leave.

Since by Mississippi law he could not succeed himself, Winter relinquished his office early in 1984 to Bill Allain. Allain, a Democrat, had won the governorship in November 1983 by defeating the Republican Leon Bramlett by a vote of 406,703 to 286,431. Charles Evers, running as an Independent, polled 29,276 votes in that contest.

In the fall of 1984 Winter ran as the Democratic Party's candidate for a United States Senate seat from Mississippi, but lost to the Republican incumbent Thad Cochran by a vote of 584,112 to 371,693.

Bibliography: *Meridian Star*, August 8, August 29, and November 7, 1979; *New Orleans Times Picayune*, January 20 and October 26, 1980, May 16 and September 30, 1981, October 18 and December 22, 1982; Richard M. Scammon and Alice V. McGillivray, *America Votes*, 14 (Washington, D.C., 1981); *Who's Who in America* (Chicago, 1983); *Congressional Quarterly Weekly Report* (November 12, 1983); *New York Times*, November 8, 1984. JH

Christopher Samuel Bond (Courtesy: Christopher Samuel Bond)

MISSOURI

BOND, Christopher Samuel ("Kit"), 1973-1977, 1981-

Born in St. Louis, Missouri on March 6, 1939, the second son of Arthur Doerr and Elizabeth (Green) Bond. Bond is the grandson of A. P. Green, who founded the refractories company of that name in Mexico, Missouri. A sixth-generation Missourian, he attended school from grades one through four in Tucson, Arizona. He attended public school in Mexico, Missouri from the fifth through the tenth grades, and completed his secondary education at Deerfield Academy, Deerfield, Massachusetts, graduating in 1956. Bond received his college education at Princeton University, where he graduated *cum laude* from the Woodrow Wilson School of Public and International Affairs in 1960. He received his law degree in 1963 from the University of Virginia, graduating first in his class. On July 1, 1963, Bond accepted a clerkship with the United States Court of Appeals for the Fifth Circuit in Atlanta, Georgia, and served Chief Judge Elbert P. Tuttle. He held that position until June 30, 1964. In November 1964 he was employed by Covington and Burling, a law firm in Washington, D.C., where he remained until October 1967. Bond then returned to Mexico to practice law. He was married on May 13, 1967 to Carolyn Reid, in Lexington, Kentucky. They met in Atlanta, where she was employed as a speech therapist in the public schools. Mrs. Bond, who is from Owensboro, Kentucky, holds a master's degree in guidance and counseling from the University of Kentucky, where she was a member of Phi Beta Kappa. She also holds a bachelor's degree in speech and hearing therapy. The Bonds have one son, Samuel Reid Bond, born on January 26, 1981.

In 1968 Christopher Bond made an unsuccessful bid for the Ninth District seat in the United States House of Representatives. In January 1969 he became an Assistant Attorney General under Attorney General John C. Danforth, and served as Chief Counsel of the Consumer Protection Division; he resigned that position in June 1970, to run for State Auditor. Bond was elected State Auditor on November 4, 1970, and took office on January 12, 1971. The 28th State Auditor of Missouri, he was, at 31 years of age, the youngest person to hold the office up to that time. He won by over 200,000 votes, the largest margin by which a Republican ever had been elected to a state-wide office in the history of Missouri. He was State Auditor when he ran for chief executive in 1972 and defeated Democrat Edward L. Dowd by a vote of 1,029,451 to 832,751.

Bond was inaugurated as the 47th Governor of the state of Missouri on January 8, 1973, when he was 33 years of age. At the time he was the youngest governor in the nation and the youngest chief executive in the history of Missouri. Bond was the ninth Republican chosen governor, and his victory marked the first election of a Republican to that office in 32 years. During his first term Bond established a merit system of hiring, led a petition drive for a strict campaign contribution law, and secured passage of a strong open meetings law. Other accomplishments included the "circuit-breaker bill" (which provided property relief for low income senior citizens), increased funding for education, passage of a law requiring mandatory sentences for persons convicted of committing a crime with a gun, reinstatement of capital punishment for premeditated murder, establishment of the Department of Consumer Affairs, Regulation and Licensing to protect Missouri consumers, creation of the Office of Public Counsel to represent consumer interests before the Public Service Commission, and passage of a nationally recognized child abuse reporting law. Bond's economic development programs also brought many new jobs to the state. During his first term he served as Chairman of the Economic and Community Development Committee of the National Governors' Association, Chairman of the Midwest Governors' Association, and Chairman of the Republican Governors' Association. Bond was selected as one of the Jaycees' Ten Outstanding Young Men of America in 1974. He served as a Trustee of the School of the Ozarks, Point Lookout, Missouri, from 1970 to 1975. In 1973 he received an honorary Doctor of Laws degree from Westminster College, Fulton, Missouri, and William Jewell College, Liberty, Missouri.

In November 1976 Bond was narrowly defeated for re-election by Joseph P. Teasdale. From 1977 to 1979 he worked in Kansas City as President of the Great Plains Legal Foundation, a not-for-profit, public-interest law firm representing individual citizens and groups who could not otherwise afford an attorney in significant public policy battles before federal agencies and in the courts. The primary focus of the Great Plains Legal Foundation is to pursue cases where governmental regulatory barriers operate against the consumer. Bond resigned his position as President of the Foundation in the spring of 1980 to run again for the office of governor. During his campaign for a second term, he established as his priorities: bringing 200,000 jobs to Missourians, providing job training and preparation, providing better education for Missouri children, improving care for the elderly, meeting the needs of children, and improving crime prevention methods.

In November 1980 Bond was elected to a second term as Governor of Missouri, defeating Joseph Teasdale by a vote of 1,098,950 to 981,884. He took the oath of office on January 12, 1981. Immediately upon taking office, it was necessary to cut the operating budgets of state departments by $63 million to balance the budget. During 1981 and 1982 Bond's administration brought about a crackdown on welfare fraud, an aggressive plan to collect child support payments from absent parents, the establishment of the Governor's Commission on Crime, the establishment of the Silver Citizens Discount Card Program, increased efforts to collect delinquent state taxes, approval by the voters of a $600 million bond issue for capital improvements, and the signing of commercial agreements between both the Republic of China and Japan and the state of Missouri. Bond serves as Chairman of the National Governors' Association's Committee on Community and Economic Development.

Bond's current term ends in 1985, when he is scheduled to be succeeded by John Ashcroft. Ashcroft, Missouri's Republican Attorney General, won the state's gubernatorial contest that year over Democratic Lieutenant Governor Kenneth J. Rothman, by a vote of 1,189,442 to 901,584.

Bibliography: Roy Glashan, *American Governors and Gubernatorial Elections, 1775-1975* (Stillwater, Minn., 1975); Howard M. Epstein, ed., *Facts on File Yearbook, 1974* (New York, 1975); Howard M. Epstein, ed., *Facts on File Yearbook, 1975* (New York, 1976); *New York Times*, November 5, 1980, March 5, 1983, and November 8, 1984. AM

Joseph P. Teasdale (Courtesy: Joseph P. Teasdale)

TEASDALE, Joseph P., 1977-1981

Born in Kansas City, Missouri on March 29, 1936, the son of William B., a Kansas City attorney, and Adah (Downey) Teasdale. After attending St. Benedict's College in Atchison, Kansas from 1954 to 1955, Teasdale was awarded a B.S. degree in literature from Rockhurst College in Kansas City in 1957. Following in a family tradition, he then decided to study law. A member of the editorial staff of the *St. Louis Law Journal* from 1958 to 1960, Teasdale was admitted to the Missouri bar in 1960, the same year in which he received a law degree from St. Louis University. He was married to Theresa Ferkenhoff on October 13, 1973 at Conception Abbey, Conception, Missouri. Teasdale's wife attended Fontbonne College in St. Louis, and was employed by Braniff International Airlines prior to her marriage. They are the parents of one son, William Daniel, who was born on November 5, 1974.

A member of the United States Air Force Reserves from 1961 to 1967, Teasdale obtained an honorable discharge in 1967. Early in his legal career he served as a law clerk for Western District United States Court Judge Albert Ridge. Teasdale first held public office in 1962, when he was appointed Assistant United States Attorney General by Attorney General Robert F. Kennedy. In November 1966 he became the youngest Prosecuting Attorney in the history of Jackson County, Missouri. By 1968, he was being credited with having upgraded the professional staff operations in that office. Teasdale was re-elected prosecuting attorney for a second term in 1968. In 1969 he was honored as "Outstanding Man of the Year" by the Kansas City Junior Chamber of Commerce.

Although he ran unsuccessfully for the Democratic gubernatorial nomination in 1972, Teasdale earned the nickname "Walkin' Joe" after taking his campaign to the people by walking across the state. Four years later he used the media effectively to win the governor's office in a startling win over the incumbent Christopher Bond. Attacking Bond for his appointment of allegedly pro-utility members to Missouri's public service commission, the Democrat Teasdale defeated his Republican opponent by the narrow margin of 971,184 votes to 958,110. His four-year tenure was troubled, however, by a series of natural disasters and outbreaks of labor unrest.

In September of 1977, for example, at least 25 people were killed during flash floods which devastated the Kansas City, Missouri area, leading President Jimmy Carter to declare the state a major disaster area. Nature struck again in May 1980, when tornadoes damaged portions of Missouri, particularly the city of Sedalia. Early in 1979 a teachers' strike in St. Louis disrupted the Teasdale administration, and a year later Kansas City firemen struck for six days, in protest over the city's refusal to rehire union members dismissed because of an earlier work slowdown. The walkout of firemen was eventually resolved, but not before Teasdale had to dispatch members of the Highway Patrol and the National Guard to deal with the threat to public safety.

In the 1980 Missouri gubernatorial race, Teasdale again faced Christopher Bond, who sought to portray himself as an efficient and capable manager. Combined with his support for tax exemptions for the elderly, Bond's approach proved irresistible, and he won the election by a convincing margin of 1,098,950 votes to 981,884 (53 percent to 47 percent). Teasdale relinquished the governor's office to Bond on January 12, 1981.

Bibliography: *New York Times*, November 3, 1976, September 14-15, 20, 1977, January 17-18, 1979, March 18-24 and May 14, 1980; *St. Louis Globe-Democrat*, November 6-7, 1976; *St. Louis Post Dispatch*, March 20, 1977; Bob Hollingsworth, ed., *Facts on File Yearbook, 1976* (New York, 1977); Michael Barone *et al.*, eds., *The Almanac of American Politics, 1980-82* (New York and Washington, D.C., 1979-81); Richard M. Scammon and Alice V. McGillivray, *America Votes*, 14 (Washington, D.C., 1981). AM

Thomas L. Judge (Credit: Montana Historical Society, Helena)

MONTANA

JUDGE, Thomas L., 1973-1981

Born in Helena, Montana on October 12, 1934, the son of Thomas Patrick and Blanche (Guillot) Judge. A Catholic, Judge married the former Carol Ann Anderson of Helena in 1966. They have two children, Thomas Warren and Patrick Lane.

Judge received a B.A. in journalism from the University of Notre Dame in 1957, and did graduate work at the University of Louisville, from which he received a certificate in advertising in 1959. From 1958 to 1959 he served as an officer in the United States Army Adjutant General Corps at Fort Benjamin Harrison, Indiana. Following his active duty, he became an advertising executive with the *Louisville Courier Journal*, and served as Merchandising Director of the newspaper. In 1960 he started his own advertising and public relations agency in Helena.

Judge's political career began in 1961, when he became the state's youngest legislator by winning a seat in the Montana House of Representatives from Lewis and Clark County. Re-elected in 1963 and 1965, he served as Chairman of the House Business and Industry Committee. He was elected to the State Senate as a Democrat from Lewis and Clark County in 1967. Chairman of the Senate Natural Resources Committee, Judge served one term before being elected Lieutenant Governor of Montana in 1968. That year he defeated the Republican Tom Selstad by a vote of 146,527 to 124,322. As lieutenant governor, Judge was Chairman of the National Conference of Lieutenant Governors and was cited for his outstanding contributions to that organization.

Judge was elected Governor of Montana in 1972 after defeating the Republican Ed Smith; he attracted 54 percent of the vote to Smith's 46 percent. During his first term as chief executive, Judge reorganized the structure of state government and supervised the writing of a new state constitution. He also instituted a statewide referendum on property tax relief. In 1974 Judge organized a coalition of Rocky Mountain governors to pressure the federal government for increased state control over federal lands and resources located within their states, an issue that he continued to champion throughout his years in office. The highlight of Judge's early years as governor was his selection by *Time* magazine as one of America's top 200 young leaders. The one problem that surfaced during his first term was the increasingly vocal opposition of state environmentalists, who felt threatened by his vigorous efforts to promote tourism and to bring industry to the state.

Unopposed in the 1976 Democratic primary, Judge easily won his bid for a second term by soundly defeating Republican Attorney General Robert Woodahl with 63 percent of the vote to Woodahl's 37 percent. Political commentators, however, saw this as a rather unsatisfying victory, since charges of scandal had touched both men. Although Woodahl could not document his allegation that Judge was guilty of improprieties involving the state's workmen's compensation system, it was revealed that Judge had failed to disclose thousands of dollars in contributions to his 1972 campaign. Further into the campaign Woodahl himself was cited for contempt of court for his overzealous prosecution of the workmen's compensation controversy.

After his re-election, Judge continued his fight against federally imposed bureaucratic regulations that placed limitations on western states' use of land and resources. He attracted national press as part of a group of western governors concerned about the Carter administration's federal water policy. He also pushed hard for so-called "energy impact money," to be distributed among western states suffering unique problems because of the energy boom. Similar to the funds that the federal government provides when large installations, such as military bases, disrupt local economic conditions, these funds would help western states deal with the social problems of energy boom towns—increases in crime, social disintegration, and the cost of government services. In 1979 Judge drew the wrath of residents of eastern states because of his vociferous opposition to a planned consumer boycott of beef, called to protest high meat prices. Referring to the boycott as an attack on beef-producing Montanans, Judge attracted particular attention for his criticism of "arrogant Easterners." Because the boycott had first been suggested by New York City Consumer Affairs Commissioner Bruce Ratner, Judge warned New York's Mayor Ed Koch that he might retaliate by organizing a ten-state western tourists' boycott of New York City.

Although he was considered to have a rather liberal philosophy for the leader of a Rocky Mountain state, few political observers expected Judge to have serious trouble in winning re-election to a third term. Consequently, his defeat in the 1980 Democratic primary by Lieutenant Governor Ted Schwinden, 51 percent to 42 percent (with two others splitting the remaining seven percent of the vote), came as a surprise. Judge had never commanded real personal popularity in the state, whereas Schwinden, a folksy rancher, had made few enemies during his years in state government.

As chief executive, Judge served on the Executive Committee of the National Governors' Association and as Chairman of its task force on coal transportation and its subcommittee on agriculture. He was also Chairman of the Western Governors' Policy Office and state Co-Chairman of the Old West Regional Commission. A member of the Eagles, Elks, and Knights of Columbus, Judge has received various awards for his civic and political activities, including a citation from Notre Dame as its Man of the Year in 1966 and from the Montana Jaycees as their Outstanding Young Man of the Year in 1967.

Bibliography: "200 Faces for the Future," *Time* (July 15, 1974); Michael Barone *et al.*, *The Almanac of American Politics, 1978, 1982* (New York and

Washington, D.C., 1977, 1981); *New York Times*, January 14, 1978, April 12 and July 21, 1979; National Governors' Association, *Governors of the American States, Commonwealths, and Territories* (Washington, D.C., 1980); *Who's Who in American Politics, 1981-82* (New York, 1981); assorted political pamphlets and documents, Thomas Judge File, Montana Historical Society Library. MMM

Ted Schwinden (Credit: Office of the Governor, Montana)

SCHWINDEN, Ted, 1981-

Born on August 31, 1925 in Wolf Point, Montana, the son of Michael James and Mary (Preble) Schwinden. A Lutheran, Schwinden married the former Jean Christianson, a registered nurse, in 1946. They have three children—Mike, Chrys, and Dore—and two grandchildren—Jordan and Erin.

Ted Schwinden began his formal education in a rural one-room schoolhouse. After graduating from Wolf Point High School in 1943, he enlisted in the United States Army, serving in both Europe and Asia during World War II. He was honorably discharged as a Staff Sergeant in 1946. Schwinden then attended the Montana School of Mines in Butte for one year before transferring to the University of Montana in Missoula. There he received a B.A. in 1949 and an M.A. in 1950, both degrees in history and political science. From 1950 to 1954 he did postgraduate work at the University of Minnesota. Schwinden has owned and operated a grain farm in Roosevelt County, Montana since 1954.

A Democrat, Schwinden began his political career in 1958, when he was elected to the Montana House of Representatives from Roosevelt County. Named to the Legislative Council from 1959 to 1961, he served as House Minority Whip during the 1961 session. Over the course of the next decade, he held a variety of prestigious administrative positions and appointments. In 1965 he was elected President of the Montana Grain Growers Association, a position he held for two years. In 1968 he was selected by United States Secretary of Agriculture Orville Freeman to represent the United States on a wheat trade mission to Asia. Schwinden was named by Montana Governor Forrest Anderson to be Commissioner of State Lands in 1969. Reappointed by Governor Thomas Judge in 1973, he served until 1976. During this same period, from 1973 to 1976, he also served as Chairman of Montana's Bicentennial Advisory Committee.

In 1976 Schwinden was elected Lieutenant Governor of Montana, and he served from 1977 until 1981. In that capacity he was responsible for overseeing the state's role in natural resources, agriculture, and energy issues.

Characterized by political observers as a "folksy rancher with few enemies," Schwinden defeated incumbent Democratic Governor Thomas Judge to gain the Democratic gubernatorial nomination in 1980, gaining 51 percent of the vote to Judge's 42 percent. Two minor candidates shared the remaining seven percent. Although Judge, as the incumbent, had been expected to win re-election, or at the very least renomination, his liberal reputation may have worked against him. So too, some said, did his personal style and manner. After two four-year terms, his personality "did not wear well," wrote one political observer. In the general election Schwinden easily defeated Jack Ramirez, a Republican state legislator, by attracting 55 percent of the vote. Although Ramirez had won some popularity by pushing a tax cut through the Legislature, the fact that he was a corporate lawyer from Billings caused him to be viewed by some as a "city slicker and protector of monied interests." Schwinden carried all but a few scattered counties in the state, a testimony to the strength of the Democratic Party in Montana. It is still difficult for a Republican to win state-wide office, and the Democrats have now been in continuous control of the governorship since 1968.

Philosophically, Schwinden believes that Democrats have won governorships in the West by responding, in his words, to a popular desire for progress "coupled with protection." He feels that measured economic development and environmental protection can go hand in hand. Schwinden has achieved a certain amount of national publicity as part of a group of western governors anxious to ensure that the states, rather than Washington bureaucrats, have a greater voice in determining the nation's energy and water policies. "We know we have a responsibility to share our resources and be part of the energy solution," he told a reporter for *Newsweek* magazine. "What we don't want to do is turn over control to outsiders—and that means OPEC, Washington, and the East Coast." In 1982 Schwinden received extensive press coverage because of a dispute with Reagan administration Interior Secretary James Watt over mineral development and coal leases in the Powder River Basin of Montana and Wyoming. Schwinden also involved himself in a growing controversy among western states over interstate water sales and transfers. The lack of water is a crucial issue in the arid Rocky Mountain states, yet Schwinden gave his backing to a proposal that would clear the way for Montana to sell some of its own surface water to developers in other states. This, he said, would not only enable the state to earn money, but would also help to expand markets for Montana's huge coal reserves. (Presumably, the water would be used in coal slurry lines to move coal across the country.) Some members of Schwinden's own party attacked the plan, however, which they say could touch off a water war in the West.

During his first term in office, Schwinden also vetoed controversial legislation designed to eliminate the United States Supreme Court's exclusionary rule in Montana. Despite strong objections from the insurance industry, he signed a bill that made Montana the first state in the nation to prohibit discrimination based on sex or marital status in all types of insurance and pension plans.

Governor Schwinden won a second term as chief executive in November 1984 by easily defeating Republican State Senator Pat Goodover. Schwinden captured 70 percent of the vote in that election, compared with Goodover's 26 percent.

Bibliography: "The Angry West vs. the Rest," *Newsweek* (September 17, 1979); *New York Times*, November 5, 1980, April 23, 1981, April 26 and November 22, 1982, February 18 and April 23, 1983, November 8, 1984; Michael Barone and Grant Ujifusa, eds., *The Almanac of American Politics, 1982* (Washington, D.C., 1981); Alan Ehrenhalt, ed., *Politics in America, 1982* (Washington, D.C., 1981); *Who's Who in American Politics, 1981-82* (New York, 1981); "When Governors Sound Off on Reagan's New Policy," *U.S. News and World Report* (March 8, 1982); National Governors' Association, *Governors of the American States, Commonwealths, and Territories* (Washington, D.C., 1983); biographical information, Governor's Office, State of Montana. MMM

John James Exon

NEBRASKA

EXON, John James, 1971-1979

Born on August 9, 1921 in Geddes, South Dakota, the son of John J., a businessman, and Luella (Johns) Exon. An Episcopalian, Exon married the former Patricia Pros of Omaha. They have three children—Stephen, Pamela, and Candy—and four grandchildren.

Raised in the small rural community of Lake Andes, South Dakota, Exon moved to Nebraska to attend the University of Omaha from 1939 to 1941. With the outbreak of World War II, he entered the Army Signal Corps, serving in New Guinea, the Philippines, and Japan. Honorably discharged as a Master Sergeant in 1945, he continued in the Army Reserve until 1949. Exon was a businessman before entering politics, employed as Branch Manager of the Universal Finance Corporation between 1946 and 1954. He started his own office equipment business, Exon's Inc., in 1954.

His grandfather had served as County Judge in the South Dakota community where Exon was raised, and his parents held leadership positions in the South Dakota Democratic Party. Exon began his political involvement in the early 1950s, working for Frank B. Morrison during his 1952 Congressional race, and serving on various Nebraska state committees for Lieutenant Governor Philip Sorenson, United States Representative Clair Callan, and Governor Ralph Brooks. In 1959 he was Campaign Manager for the ''Morrison for Governor,'' state campaign, and in 1964 he became a member of the Executive Committee of the Nebraska Democratic Party and State Coordinator for the Johnson-Humphrey campaign. A Delegate to the Democratic National Convention in 1964 and an Alternate Delegate in 1972, he was Vice Chairman of the Nebraska Jefferson-Jackson Day Dinner in 1964, Vice Chairman of the Nebraska State Democratic Central Committee from 1964 to 1968, and Democratic National Committeeman from Nebraska between 1968 and 1970.

In 1970 Exon secured the Democratic gubernatorial nomination and went on to defeat incumbent Republican Norbert T. Tiemann by a vote of 248,552 to 201,994, a 55 percent victory. A conservative Democrat in a Republican state, Exon promised lower taxes and government spending. He thus sought to capitalize on the unpopularity of Tiemann, who had enacted state income and sales taxes. Political observers believed it was the tax issue that ''crippled'' Tiemann's bid for a second term. Indeed, public disenchantment with the incumbent governor was so great that he had nearly been defeated in his own party's primary. Exon had no problem winning re-election in 1974. His fiscal austerity programs produced a state government surplus that year, and he had achieved a broad base of support by keeping a tight hold on state spending and by speaking up for the state's farmers. After overwhelming Richard D. Schmitz in the Democratic primary, 88 percent to 12 percent, he defeated Republican Richard Marvel and Independent Ernest Chambers in the general election, gaining 59 percent of the vote to their 35 percent and five percent, respectively.

During his two terms in office, Exon, according to political commentators, "achieved a popularity that few Nebraska governors ever have attained." Major accomplishments of his administration included the control of state spending through a business-like approach to state government, the establishment of a Nebraska Department of Environmental Control, the creation of a Mexican-American Commission, and the organization of an obscenity law enforcement seminar (the first of its kind in the nation). Exon's administration was also marked by an emphasis on highway safety and safety legislation, an intensified interest in and promotion of agriculture, the initiation of programs for senior citizens (including property tax relief), the adoption of a state personnel pay plan, the adoption of penal reform and rehabilitation programs, and an emphasis on care of the mentally retarded through both institutional and community-based programs and model mental health programs.

During his tenure as governor, Exon served as a member of the Education Commission of the States, a member of the executive committees of the National Governors' Association and the Democratic Governors' Conference, Vice Chairman and Chairman of the Midwest Governors' Conference, Chairman of the Old West Regional Commission, and Chairman of the National Governors' Association Committee on Agriculture. He was honored by the *Omaha World Herald* with its Man of the Year Award. Exon also received the KMTV Man of the Year Award, the B'nai B'rith Citizenship Award, the Ak-Sar-Ben Agricultural Leadership Award, and the Highway Safety Leadership Award.

No one doubted that Exon could easily have won a third term in 1978 had he been constitutionally eligible to run. Instead, he ran for the United States Senate. Unopposed in his race for the Democratic nomination, his opponent in the general election was Republican Donald E. Shasteen, the former aide of retiring four-term Senator Carl T. Curtis. From the start, political observers predicted an easy win for Exon, despite Shasteen's last-minute attempt to impugn Exon's integrity with charges that he had used his years in office to benefit his office equipment firm. The charges were never documented, and Exon summarily and colorfully denounced the allegations as the "slime of Shasteen." Exon carried 92 of the state's 93 counties and polled 68 percent of the vote, becoming the first governor of Nebraska to be elected directly to the Senate. His election also gave Nebraska two Democratic senators for the first time in its history. Since Exon enjoys an apparently solid political home base, observers feels that he can probably remain in the Senate for some time. Indeed, despite President Ronald Reagan's landslide victory in November 1984, Exon won re-election to the Senate that year, defeating the Republican Nancy Hoch by a margin of 53 percent to 47 percent.

Exon serves on the Senate Armed Services Committee, the Committee on Commerce, Science, and Transportation, the Budget Committee, and six additional subcommittees. He is also a member of the Board of Visitors of the United States Military Academy at West Point. Especially vocal in espousing his philosophy of fiscal conservatism, he has consistently voted in favor of the Budget Committee's goal of a balanced federal budget as the number one means of easing inflation, and he has successfully co-sponsored legislation consistent with that goal. He is not as close to Democratic Party policy positions as most other midwestern Democrats, most of whom have less heavily Republican constituencies. Exon takes a rather hard line on defense issues, is solicitous of the grain industry (important to Nebraska's interests), and is best known for co-sponsoring an amendment to the 1980 rail deregulation bill that protected farmers from shipping rates which would have risen and fallen according to demand. He was a member of the Democratic National Committee in 1981.

Exon continues to be active in civic and professional organizations, including the VFW, American Legion, Masons, Shriners, Elks, and Eagles. He is a Past President of the Lincoln Optimists Club, and a former Lieutenant Governor of District 10, Optimists International.

Bibliography: Michael Barone *et al.*, eds., *The Almanac of American Politics, 1978-82* (New York and Washington, D.C., 1977-81); *New York Times*, May 9, 11, July 1, and September 10, 1978, March 14 and July 28, 1981, November 8, 1984; Alan Ehrenhalt, ed., *Politics in America, 1982* (Washington, D.C., 1981); *Who's Who in American Politics, 1981-82* (New York, 1981); biographical information, United States Senate Offices, Washington, D.C. MMM

Charles Thone

THONE, Charles, 1979-1983

Born on January 4, 1924 on a farm near Hartington, Nebraska. A Presbyterian, Thone is married to the former Ruth Raymond of Scottsbluff, Nebraska; he has three daughters—Ann, Mary, and Amy.

Thone served in the United States Army Infantry in World War II and in the Army Field Artillery and Army Air Corps. He was graduated from the University of Nebraska College of Law in 1950, and was the managing law partner in the firm of Davis, Thone, Bailey, Polsky, and Hansen between 1959 and 1971.

Since 1950, Thone has held a continuous string of political and public service appointments and positions. He has been Deputy Secretary of State for Nebraska (1950-51), Assistant Nebraska Attorney General for Clarence Beck (1951-52), Assistant United States Attorney in charge of the Lincoln, Nebraska office (1952-54), and Administrative Assistant to United States Senator Roman L. Hruska (1954-59). Active in state Republican politics, he was Chairman of the Lancaster County Young Republicans in 1951, State Chairman of the Nebraska Young Republicans in 1952, National Committeeman for the Nebraska Young Republicans in 1953, and State Chairman of the Nebraska Republican Party and a member of the Republican National Committee from 1959 to 1962. Thone was also Delegate-at-Large to the Republican National Convention in 1952 and 1960, and a Republican Presidential Elector for Nebraska in 1952, 1956, 1960, and 1968. The one disappointment in his early political career was an unsuccessful race for Lieutenant Governor in 1964.

Thone was first elected to Congress in 1970, representing Nebraska's First District, and was subsequently re-elected in 1972, 1974, and 1976. A member of the House Agriculture Committee, he assisted in drafting the complete revision of the Packers and Stockyards Act and the initial Commodities Futures Trading Act, as well as the overall Agricultural acts of 1973 and 1977. Thone was a member of the House Government Operations Committee and of its Select Committee on the Kennedy-King Assassinations. The senior Republican on the Oversight and Research Subcommittee and Government Activities and Transportation Subcommittee, he served as Assistant Minority Whip, and was a member of the Executive Committee of the Republican Congressional Campaign Committee between 1971 and 1979. Thone was also a Delegate to the Mexican-American Interparliamentary Congress.

In 1978 Thone decided to seek to succeed the extremely popular two-term Democrat J. James Exon, who was constitutionally ineligible to run for another term. Although many Republican insiders had urged him to challenge Exon's bid for the Senate, since Thone was considered to be the strongest possible Republican candidate for that position, he declined. Claiming to be wary of Washington, D.C., Thone explained that being Governor of Nebraska was a boyhood dream.

To gain the Republican nomination, he faced four other candidates in the primary: Stanley Juelfs, a millionaire oilman from Kimball in the Nebraska panhandle; Robert A. Phares, former Mayor of North Platte; Vance D. Rogers of Lincoln, former President of Nebraska Wesleyan University; and Richard M. Hedrick of Waverly, a locomotive engineer. The principal issues in the primary were the cost of Juelfs' campaign (he spent more than $300,000, most of it his own money), and Thone's refusal to debate the others. Thone received 45 percent of the vote in the five-man primary, and went on to face Lieutenant Governor Gerald T. Whelan in the general election, who had defeated Grand Island businessman Robert V. Hansen to gain the Democratic nomination. Although both men campaigned as fiscal conservatives, Thone capitalized on his ability to work well with the Legislature, whereas Whelan promised to keep the Legislature in line. The key to Thone's victory was his popularity in his own First District, which includes Lincoln and the agricultural counties to the north and south. By carrying Lincoln solidly and by winning 62 percent of the vote in his home district, Thone defeated Whelan with 56 percent of the vote overall, compared to the Democrat's 44 percent. With his victory, Thone restored to Nebraska Republicans the Statehouse, which had been held by Democrats for all but four of the preceding 20 years.

As chief executive, Thone was Chairman of the National Governors' Association Committee on Agriculture and Chairman of its Agriculture Export Committee, Chairman of the Old West Economic Development Commission, Vice President of the Council of State Governments, Chairman of the Midwestern Governors' Association, Vice Chairman of the Great Plains Water Study Commission, and a member of the Executive Committee of the Interstate Oil Compact Commission.

During his administration a new abortion statute was passed, requiring women to wait 48 hours after asking for an abortion and girls under 18 to consult with their parents or guardians. In the first few years of his term, Thone managed to avoid major controversies at a time when Nebraska was doing better economically than more industrial midwestern states. Faced with a prospective surplus in the State Treasury, he lowered tax rates on both personal and corporate income, saving taxpayers more than $100 million. By the last year of his administration, however, Nebraska's agricultural economy had suffered a downturn. While Thone himself was not responsible for falling farm prices, voters blamed him for a Nebraska farm economy described by some as the bleakest since the 1930s. In common with many governors, he had to seek tax increases since the recession had forced the state budget into deficit.

Nonetheless, Thone was viewed as a competent incumbent, and political observers felt that he would have no trouble winning a second term in 1982. The result, however, was a surprise. Thone's contest with restaurant owner Robert Kerrey was referred to by the *New York Times* as "one of the more interesting battlegrounds in the 1983 election." A young and colorful Kennedyesque Democrat who had won a Medal of Honor for Vietnam combat action in which his foot was blown off, Kerrey was an unusual political commodity in a conservative state that had given Ronald Reagan his third largest majority (72 percent) in 1980. An editorial in the *North Platte Telegraph* entitled "Strangely, a Nebraskan," described Kerrey as political kin to Jerry Brown of California, and the conservative Thone organization attempted to portray him as an ultra-liberal who had participated in anti-war activities and who, as a member of Lincoln's Human Rights Commission, had led an unsuccessful effort to enforce an equal rights ordinance for homosexuals. Although they viewed Kerrey, who had never before held an elective office, as a novice in agricultural matters, voters continued to hold Thone responsible for sagging farm prices and high interest rates. Kerrey promised to attract jobs with more aggressive economic development, and took advantage of the fact that Thone had made enemies, notably the state's education lobby, through his support of unaccredited fundamentalist schools. Most important was the difference in style between the two men. Thone liked to tell audiences that he was "what Nebraska is all about," an honest, hard-working fellow who came off the farm and thinks of himself as more of a "workhorse than a showhorse"—all in contrast to the polished and city-bred Kerrey. Nevertheless, voters were swayed by what the Nebraska Democratic chairman called Kerrey's "extraordinary political organization and his charismatic ability to move people." Kerrey is considered to have run one of the most effective campaigns in Nebraska's history. Even a visit from President Reagan couldn't save Thone. He lost the election narrowly, gaining 49 percent of the vote to Kerrey's 51 percent.

Throughout his long political career, Thone has been involved in various civic and community activities. He was Commander of Lincoln American Legion Post No. 3 in 1952-53, honored as Lincoln's outstanding young man in 1953, President of the Nebraska Jaycees in 1953-54, and named by the national Jaycees as that organization's Outstanding State President. Thone was also Judge Advocate of the Nebraska Department of the American Legion in 1954-55, National President of the University of Nebraska Alumni Association in 1961-62, a member of the Executive Board of the Boy Scouts of America (Cornhusker Council) and Chairman of the Scouts' Special Gifts Committee from 1963 to 1968. He has served as President of the Holmes School (Lincoln) PTA from 1966 to 1967, Chairman and charter member of the Lincoln Human Rights Commission from 1967 to 1969, a member of the Nebraska Supreme Court Judicial Nominating Commission from 1969 to 1971, and a member of the Board of Governors of the John G. Neihardt Foundation from 1968 to date. Thone holds life memberships in the Nebraska PTA, the Nebraska Broadcasters Association, the Nebraska State Historical Society, the Nebraska Jaycees, the Nebraska B.P.O. Elks, the Lincoln American Legion, the Hartington VFW, and the Washington, D.C. Capitol Hill Club. Presently a lawyer in private practice in Lincoln, he is a member of President Reagan's Export Council and Chairman of its Committee on Agricultural Exports.

Bibliography: New York Times, May 9-10, 1978, March 20 and November 18, 1979, November 7, 1980, January 21, September 23, October 22, and

November 4, 1982; Michael Barone *et al.*, eds., *The Almanac of American Politics, 1980-82* (New York and Washington, D.C., 1979-81); National Governors' Association, *Governors of the American States, Commonwealths, and Territories* (Washington, D.C., 1980); "Fresh Faces in the Mansions," *Time* (November 15, 1982); biographical information furnished by Charles Thone. MMM

Donal Neil O'Callaghan (Credit: Nevada Historical Society)

NEVADA

A big, baldish man who lost a leg in the Korean War, "Mike" O'Callaghan was one of the most popular governors Nevada ever had. Born on September 10, 1929 in La Crosse, Wisconsin, the son of a power shovel operator, he joined the United States Marine Corps after high school and served with the Pacific Fleet as an anti-aircraft gunner during World War II. After his discharge, he was employed as an ironworker in Washington State before earning an associate of arts degree at Boise (Idaho) Junior College in 1950. When the Korean War began that summer, O'Callaghan joined the Air Force and was assigned as an intelligence operator in Alaska and the Aleutians. Qualified to attend Army Officer Candidate school at Fort Ord, California, he was assigned to the Army and sent to Korea, where he received both the Bronze and Silver stars. It was while trying to rescue some wounded companions that he was hit in the left leg by an 82mm mortar round, and lost the leg below the knee. O'Callaghan also received the Purple Heart during his military career.

Following his return to Idaho, O'Callaghan attended the University of Idaho at Moscow, where he received both bachelor of science and master of education degrees in 1956, and was honored as one of the top ten students of the year. He taught government and history at Henderson, Nevada High School for the next five years, and also worked closely with young athletes, especially in boxing. In 1959 O'Callaghan was elected President of the Southern Nevada Amateur Athletic Union (AAU). During the summer of that year, he worked for Nevada Senator Howard Cannon while studying at Georgetown's School of Foreign Service. O'Callaghan grew increasingly active in southern Nevada politics after that experience. Appointed Chief Probation Officer and Director of Court Services in Clark County in 1961, he also served as that county's Democratic Chairman in 1962 and 1963. When the Nevada Legislature created the Department of Health and Welfare in 1963, O'Callaghan was named its first Director; he served in that capacity until 1964. The post was the first of several appointive positions he held before choosing to run for Governor in 1970. When the Job Corps was created, O'Callaghan was named Project Management Director for the Job Corps Conservation Centers in Washington (1964-66). He later served as a United States Commerce Department representative, working from 1966 to 1967 mainly to help Indian reservations qualify for federal funds to establish industries. Finally, he was appointed Director of the western region of the Office of Emergency Planning in Santa Rosa, California (1967-69), where one of his biggest challenges was leading the clean-up of California beaches after the Santa Barbara oil spill incident and the California floods. In 1969 O'Callaghan left the federal government to open a research, planning, and development corporation in Carson City, Nevada.

When Republican Governor Paul Laxalt did not stand for re-election in 1970, O'Callaghan entered the race, his second try at state-wide office. In 1966, when he sought the Democratic nomination for lieutenant governor, he had run third in a field of seven candidates. This time, however, he was a surprise winner, defeating Republican Ed Fike by 6,000 votes. Although Fike had hoped to profit from Laxalt's popularity, stressing the economic growth in Nevada under the Republican administration and the accumulation of the largest surplus in the state's history, O'Callaghan avoided direct criticism of the previous administration. Instead, he maintained that the surplus should be used to raise teacher salaries and to improve schools and prisons, rather than to repeal the state sales tax on groceries, as his opponent had suggested. O'Callaghan, a Roman Catholic himself, also made a muted appeal to the Catholic vote. When asked if gamblers had contributed to his campaign, he bluntly and frankly answered, "You bet. Any politician in Nevada who tells you he got no money from gamblers isn't telling the truth. But I took none from anybody who had something he wanted from me. I turned down some. And a lot of casinos didn't even offer me any campaign help....I don't owe any of them anything."

Integrity and competence were the hallmarks of O'Callaghan's administration, which was generally considered to be honest and economy-minded. During the first term he enacted a fair housing law, strong anti-pollution measures, and a bill to reapportion the Legislature. He also pushed for stronger laws to control Nevada gambling interests. Although his 1970 victory had been by a small margin, in his 1974 campaign for re-election he was considered "unbeatable." He defeated two candidates, Republican Shirley Crumpler and Independent James Ray Houston, by gaining 67 percent of the vote to their 17 and 16 percent, respectively.

After serving as chief executive for eight years, O'Callaghan chose to retire in 1978. State political observers believed that he could easily have won a third term, but he honored the probable intent of a rather ambiguous clause in the Nevada Constitution and decided not to seek re-election. Instead, he joined the staff of the *Las Vegas Sun*, a paper with a lively interest in politics. A member of the Knights of Columbus, Lions International, and the Veterans of Foreign Wars, O'Callaghan has always had a great interest in education. Besides his B.S. and M.Ed. degrees, he earned an LL.D. at the University of Nevada, Las Vegas in 1972, and did postgraduate work at the University of Nevada, Colorado State University, Georgetown University, and the Claremont Graduate School. In 1971 he was installed in the University of Idaho's Hall of Fame. O'Callaghan and his wife Carolyn have five children—Michael, Mary, Teresa, Brian, and Timothy.

Bibliography: New York Times, November 4 and November 27, 1970; Michael

Barone *et al.*, *The Almanac of American Politics, 1978* (New York, 1977); *Who's Who in America, 1978-79*; official biography of Governor O'Callaghan, published by the Nevada State Library. MMM

Robert Frank List (Credit: Nevada Historical Society)

LIST, Robert Frank, 1979-1983

Born in Visalia, California on September 1, 1936, the son of Franklin Way and Alice A. (Dove) List. A Presbyterian, List and his wife, Kathryn Sue Geary, have three children—Suzanne, Franklin, and Michelle.

List received his B.S. from Utah State University in 1959, and his law degree from the University of California Hastings College of Law in San Francisco in 1962. A practicing attorney in Carson City from 1962 to 1966, he was also active in a variety of Republican organizations. List was Chairman of the Young Republican Club in Carson City from 1963 to 1964, a Delegate to the Young Republican National Convention in 1963, 1965, 1967, and 1969 (and Chairman of its Platform Committee in 1969), and Chairman of the Young Nevadans for Laxalt in the popular Republican's 1964 senatorial and 1966 gubernatorial campaigns. List was Ormsby County District Attorney between 1967 and 1970. He was elected as Nevada's Attorney General in 1970, a position he held until his election as Governor in 1978.

List's involvement in national Republican politics included service as a Delegate to the Republican National Convention in 1968 and 1976; he also served as Chairman of the Nevada delegation in 1972. In 1968 List was a Young Republican Delegate to a NATO conference in Brussels, and in 1972 President Richard Nixon appointed him to a Commission for the Review of National Policy Toward Gambling.

In 1978 List defeated three other candidates in the Republican gubernatorial primary, receiving an astounding 89 percent of the vote to gain his party's nomination. In the general election he faced Lieutenant Governor Robert Rose, a Democrat from Las Vegas. There were great similarities between the two men: both were about 40, both were born outside the state, and both favored the Equal Rights Amendment in a state which to that point had refused to ratify it. Although Rose tried to identify himself with Las Vegas, the home town factor seemed to matter little in a state made up of only two large urban centers. List also benefited from the endorsement of the popular outgoing Governor "Mike" O'Callaghan, who had chosen not to seek re-election and who had crossed party lines to support List. Another factor in List's victory was Rose's stand on the state's foreign gaming law. His criticism of this law, which prevents Nevada casino owners from setting up branches in other states which legalize gambling unless they meet Nevada standards, may have made him seem overly sympathetic to casino owners in a state where voters have routinely been wary of them. List won a decisive victory, gaining 56 percent of the vote.

As chief executive, List was a member of the President's State Planning Council on Radioactive Waste Management, and served as Chairman of the National Governors' Association Committee on Criminal Justice and Public Protection from 1980 to 1981. He also chaired the Western Governors' Conference in 1981. At home, however, List faced two special problems that severely affected Nevada's number one industry—New Jersey's entry into competition for legalized gambling dollars, and the increase in air fares due to higher jet fuel prices. Even Republicans were doubtful about his chances for a second term because, in the words of one observer, "controversial local issues had made him a host of enemies and gained him few friends." In fact, List did lose his bid for re-election in 1982 to Democratic Attorney General Richard H. Bryan, who received 54 percent of the vote to List's 43 percent.

Bibliography: Michael Barone and Grant Ujifusa, eds., *The Almanac of American Politics, 1982* (Washington, D.C., 1981); "Where the GOP Will Hold Its Own," *U.S. News and World Report* (October 4, 1982); *Who's Who in America, 1982-83*. MMM

Meldrim Thomson, Jr. (Credit: Equity Publishing Company, N.H.)

NEW HAMPSHIRE

THOMSON, Meldrim, Jr., 1973-1979

Born on March 8, 1912 in Pittsburgh, Pennsylvania, the son of Meldrim Thomson, a testing engineer, and Beulah (Booth) Thomson. Thomson was married to Anne Gale Kelley on October 29, 1938; he is the father of Peter, David, Thomas, Marion Gale, Janet, and Robb.

After graduating from Miami (Florida) High School in 1930, Thomson studied at the University of Miami for two years; he later attended Mercer University Law School in Macon, Georgia, and Washington and Jefferson College in Washington, Pennsylvania. Thomson was graduated with an LL.B. degree from the University of Georgia Law School. He joined the Florida National Guard in 1931, and was honorably released in 1933. Following a brief period as an Instructor of Political Science at the University of Georgia, Thomson was accepted by the Florida bar in March 1936, but almost immediately joined the publishing company of Edward Thompson in Brooklyn, New York. He remained with that firm from 1936 until 1951, when he formed the Equity Press, a legal publishing company that prints official codes.

In 1954 Thomson moved the company and his family home to Orford, New Hampshire, where he has lived since. A lifelong Republican, he is a member of the Baptist Church. Thomson had earlier served for six years as a member and Chairman of the school board in Stony Brook, New York, and he was elected to the Orford School Board from 1959 to 1962. There he first achieved prominence by opposing federal aid for remedial reading. Worried about the increasingly liberal drift of American politics in the 1960s, Thomson entered state politics as an unsuccessful candidate for the House of Representatives in 1964; that same year, however, he won election to New Hampshire's Constitutional Convention.

Thomson sought the governorship in 1968 and 1970, but lost both times in the primary election. (In 1970 he ran as the American Independent Party's candidate.) In the 1972 Republican gubernatorial primary Thomson received 43,611 votes, defeating Walter Peterson (41, 252) and James Koromilas (3,975); in the general election that year he polled 133,702 votes to beat Democrat Roger J. Crowley (126,107) and Malcolm McLane, running as an Independent (63,199). Thomson repeated his victory in 1974 by defeating David L. Nixon and Ralph W. Brewster in the primary, and then beating Democrat Richard W. Leonard in the general election by a vote of 115,933 to 110,591. In the September 1976 primary, Thomson won over Gerard Zeiller and Ralph Brewster; he earned a third term in the November general election by defeating Democrat Harry Spanos, 197,589 votes to 145,015. With this last victory, Thomson became the only Republican ever to serve three consecutive gubernatorial terms in New Hampshire.

Governor Thomson soon earned a reputation as "one of the most vocal conservatives in Republican ranks." Adamantly opposed to the imposition of any broad base taxes (New Hampshire remains the only state in the Union with no general sales or personal income tax), he ran for office on the basis of slogans such as "Ax the Tax," "Protect Your Pocketbook," and "Vote for Mel Thomson for What You Moved to New Hampshire For." A controversial figure, he drew national media attention for his outspoken views and unconventional actions; attacking the Reverend Dr. Martin Luther King and former United Nations Ambassador Andrew Young; praising the government of South Africa; ordering a state university instructor discharged for publishing unflattering remarks about him; proposing to arm the New Hampshire National Guard with atomic weapons; inviting Nantucket to leave Massachusetts and join New Hampshire; and lowering flags to protest Jimmy Carter's pardon of Vietnam-era draft resisters. Soon after he took office, Thomson sent one of his top aides to examine the confidential state tax records of his political opponents, a move declared unconstitutional by the New Hampshire Supreme Court. In 1978 his attempt to have all state flags lowered in commemoration of Good Friday was challenged as unconstitutional by the New Hampshire Civil Liberties Union. Thomson took his losing crusade all the way to the United States Supreme Court.

Although he was often embroiled in conflicts with the moderate wing of the Republican Party in New Hampshire, who claimed he was trying to push the party to the "far right," Thomson enjoyed the support of the staunchly conservative Manchester *Union Leader*, the state's largest newspaper. He built his reputation on a tight-fisted fiscal policy, and during his administration New Hampshire prospered as did no other state in the East. Population increased by one-fourth in the 1970s, businesses moved into the state or started up there, wages and salaries increased, and even old factory towns like Manchester and Nashua showed signs of growth. When the budget deficit started to mount in 1977 because of the exhaustion of federal revenue sharing funds, Thomson's administration endorsed a plan to legalize casino gambling, but it was defeated by the Legislature. A strong supporter of nuclear power, Thomson drew criticism for his ardent championing of the Seabrook nuclear generating plant. At one point he sought to bar any state employee from criticizing that nuclear installation.

The Seabrook facility proved to be Thomson's undoing when he made a bid for an unprecedented fourth term as chief executive in 1978. Easily defeating former Governor Wesley Powell in the Republican primary, he lost to former State Representative Hugh Gallen in the general election, an upset termed one of the most prominent gains scored by Democrats that year. The key issue in the race was Thomson's support for a 17 percent surcharge that the local utility was charging customers to build the plant. Convinced the utility would halt construction without the surcharge, Thomson encountered considerable opposition from the public when he vetoed a bill that would have repealed it. Gallen's victory, just over 49 percent of the vote, was also attributed to his extensive use of TV advertising, rarely employed in New Hampshire political campaigns until then. Thomson garnered 45 percent of the vote, while former Governor Wesley Powell, running as an Independent, drew five percent.

Gallen beat Thomson again in 1980, increasing his winning percentage to 59 percent. Although Thomson tried to depict the Gallen administration as paving the way for a state-wide sales or income tax by its excessive spending, Gallen continued to insist on his opposition to any new tax or tax increase. By 1980, the main issue in the election had come to be Thomson himself, with many Democrats and even some Republicans contending that he was an embarrassment to the state because of his right-wing activities and often abrasive behavior. An ultra-conservative, Thomson was both a member and officer of the John Birch Society at the time of the election. In the 1982 campaign, Thomson threatened to run as an Independent if the eventual Republican gubernatorial nominee refused to promise to veto a sales or income tax. Although he did file as an Independent, he later agreed to support John H. Sununu, winner of the Republican primary after a close three-way race. In the November election Thomson, whose name remained on the ballot, drew two percent of the vote to Sununu's 51 percent and Gallen's 47 percent.

At various points in his career, Thomson attempted to bring his conservative crusade to the national political stage. In 1974 he emerged as perhaps the most staunchly pro-Nixon of all the nation's governors. He has served as Chairman of the National Conservative Caucus. In 1976 Thomson threatened to run against President Gerald Ford in the Republican Presidential primaries if Ronald Reagan failed to do so. In 1979 he abandoned the Republican Party as not conservative enough, and announced that he was forming a new "Constitution Party" to make the run for President. Urging voters to "support a candidacy that is trying to save America," he vowed "to fight in the cause of freedom without compromise or accommodation until the struggle for survival prevails." Thomson dropped out of the Presidential race in April 1980, citing a lack of support and mounting campaign debts. He also decided against making a run for the United States Senate in 1980.

After his gubernatorial defeats in 1978 and 1980, Thomson returned to his publishing business and his farm in Orford.

Bibliography: *The Brown Book of the New Hampshire Legislature* (1973); State of New Hampshire, *Manual for the General Court* (1973, 1975); Howard Gaines, "Meldrim Thomson, Jr.: An American Success Story," *New Hampshire Times* [Concord] (October 20-26, 1976); *New York Times*, May 11, August 28, and November 24, 1977, February 18, March 22, March 30, April 26, September 14, and November 8-9, 1978, November 1 and November 20, 1979, April 15, May 14, August 24, October 26, and November 5, 1980, September 15 and October 30, 1982; Michael Barone *et al.*, eds., *The Almanac of American Politics, 1978-84* (New York and Washington, D.C., 1977-83). MMM

Hugh J. Gallen (Credit: Michael Cornelius, State Comptroller)

GALLEN, Hugh J., 1979-1982

Born in Portland, Oregon on July 24, 1924, the son of Hugh J. and Mary (O'Kane) Gallen. A Roman Catholic, Gallen moved to Medford, Massachusetts at the age of six and was graduated from high school there. During the Depression he joined the Civilian Conservation Corps, moving to New Hampshire to work on the roads and campsites at Mount Kearsage. Gallen's short stint as a minor league pitcher ended after an arm injury. On October 16, 1948, he married Irene Carbonneau; they had three children—Kathleen A., Michael J., and Sheila M., all of whom were grown by the time Gallen was elected Governor.

At about the same time as his marriage, Gallen began a career as an automobile salesman in Littleton, New Hampshire, and in 1964 he became a full owner of Hugh Gallen, Inc., an automobile dealership. Between 1962 and 1965 he served on the Littleton Planning Board; in 1967 he served on the National Advisory Council of the Small Business Administration. In 1969 Gallen became President and Chairman of the Board of a Littleton bank, an enterprise that he had helped to establish. The same year he became Director and Chairman of the New Hampshire-Vermont Development Council, which had been founded to encourage business growth. Gallen also served at about the same time as Director of White Mountain Community Services, a mental health facility. In 1971 and 1972 he served as Democratic State Chairman, and he acted as a Delegate to the 1972 Democratic National Convention. Gallen served in the New Hampshire House of Representatives in 1973, becoming the first Democrat elected to that body from Littleton.

In 1978 Gallen won the Democratic nomination for Governor by defeating Delbert Downing in the primary by a margin of almost three to one. In the general election he defeated incumbent Governor Meldrim Thomson, who ran as a Republican, and former Governor Wesley Powell, who campaigned as an Independent after losing the Republican primary. Gallen received 133,133 votes to Thomson's 122,464 and Powell's 12,349, as the rift in the Republican Party contributed to his election.

Gallen called out the National Guard in 1979 to protect the Seabrook nuclear power plant from demonstrators protesting the use of nuclear generating stations in the United States. In 1980 he beat Thomas Wingate handily in the Democratic primary and won re-election in the general election when he again defeated Thomson, this time by a count of 226,436 to 156,178 with only a small Independent vote. Gallen again summoned the National Guard in June 1981 to staff mental hospitals and juvenile facilities after most of the state's 9,200 workers staged a "sick out" to draw attention to their demands for higher pay. The governor promptly agreed to a nine percent increase, but the Republican-dominated Legislature agreed to only a six percent raise. Gallen then vetoed the budget, the first to be rejected by a New Hampshire chief executive in many years. Despite these actions, he insisted that he was opposed to either a state income or a state sales tax.

In 1982 Gallen ran unopposed in the Democratic primary, while John H. Sununu defeated a large field to capture the Republican race. During Gallen's second term William Loeb, the editor of the Manchester *Union Leader*, died. Loeb had long been the most powerful man in New Hampshire politics, and his paper continued to exercise a major influence even after his death. The paper's editorials vigorously opposed Gallen, who had refused to pledge that he would not support a state sales or income tax if re-elected. On election day of 1982 Gallen was narrowly beaten, becoming the only incumbent Democratic governor in the United States to lose that year. The final vote was 132,287 for Gallen, 145,389 for Sununu (who had taken a "no taxes" pledge), and 4,785 for Thomson (whose name was on the ballot as an Independent, although he did not actively campaign).

Shortly after the election Gallen contracted a blood infection and was hospitalized. He died on December 29, 1982, eight days before his term as chief executive would have ended. Between Gallen's death and Sununu's inauguration on January 6, 1983, Vesta Roy, President of the New Hampshire Senate, carried out the state's gubernatorial duties.

Bibliography: Richard M. Scammon and Alice V. McGillivray, *America Votes*, 13-14 (Washington, D.C., 1979-81); *Manual for the General Court* (Concord, 1981); *New York Times*, October 30 and December 30, 1982. Gallen's papers are on deposit at the New Hampshire Department of Administration and Control, Division of Records Management and Archives, Concord. JH

Vesta M. Roy (Credit: Office of Vesta Roy, New Hampshire Senate)

ROY, Vesta M., 1982-1983

Born on March 26, 1925 in Detroit, Michigan. A Roman Catholic, Roy is married to Dr. Albert Roy, an optometrist. She is the mother of five children, and the grandmother of eight. Roy graduated from Wayne State University. A World War II veteran of the Royal Canadian Air Force, she was named Leading Air Woman (1943-45).

Roy was Special Agent for Prudential Insurance, and served as the first woman Commissioner for Rockingham County. A Republican, she is currently serving her third term in the New Hampshire Senate. She has also been a New Hampshire State Representative (1973-74); a Salem Checklist Supervisor (1971-73) and Selectman; a Delegate to the New Hampshire Constitutional Convention; Co-Chairman of the Republican State Committee; an unsuccessful District 3 Executive Council candidate in 1976 (losing to Dudley Dudley, a Democrat from Durham); a Gerald Ford Delegate to the 1976 Republican National Convention; and a member of state and town Republican committees.

During her legislative career, Roy has served as Assistant Senate Whip, Assistant Senate Majority Leader, and Chairman of the Public Institutions/Health and Welfare Committee of the New Hampshire Senate. She has been a member of the Finance, Ways and Means, Public Affairs, Insurance, Interstate Cooperation, and Internal Affairs committees. Roy's legislative priorities have included: reorganization of executive departments; resolution of the state's fiscal crisis by setting priorities and by keeping expenditures within projected revenues; and examination of proposals to combine the Laconia State School and New Hampshire Hospital. She has been an opponent of off-track betting in the state and of the nuclear weapons freeze.

Roy has been on the Board of Directors of Castle Business College; an advisor for New Hampshire elderly affairs and the New Hampshire Seacoast Council on Aging; counselor to the New Hampshire Manpower Service; a Trustee of the New England College of Optometry; Fundraising Committee Chairman of the Salemhaven Nursing Home; a former President of the New Hampshire Optometric Association; and a Director of the New Hampshire Easter Seal Society. She has been a member of American Legion Post 63, the National Counties Health and Education Steering Committee, the New Hampshire State Manpower Services Council, and the Salem Association for Retarded Citizens. In 1980 the Salem Business and Professional Women's Club honored Roy with its annual Woman of Achievement Award. She was chosen New Hampshire Woman of the Year in 1983.

Vesta Roy became Acting Governor of New Hampshire under circumstances that tested the state's constitutional provisions for the orderly continuation of public leadership in times of crisis. In the November 1982 gubernatorial election, incumbent Hugh J. Gallen was defeated by Republican John H. Sununu. Shortly after the election and more than a month before Sununu's scheduled inauguration on January 6, 1983, Gallen was hospitalized for a blood infection. Under terms of the New Hampshire constitution, the president of the Senate serves as acting chief executive in the event of the governor's incapacity or absence from the state. On December 1, 1982, Vesta Roy was elected Senate President in an organizational meeting of the newly-elected Legislature. She defeated Senator Norman Champagne, a Democrat from Manchester, by a 13 to 11 vote on the second round of a highly unusual secret ballot for the post. Roy then became acting governor of the state following Gallen's hospitalization. Her election as Senate President makes her the first woman in state history to hold that post; she is also the first woman to serve as acting governor of New Hampshire.

When Governor Gallen died of kidney and liver failure on December 29, 1982, Vesta Roy chose to continue as acting governor and not exercise her prerogative as Senate president to take the oath as governor. With Governor-elect Sununu to be sworn in exactly one week later, and with no votes scheduled in the Senate, Roy maintained that she envisioned no problems as to the leadership of the state in the brief interim. Had she chosen to become governor, she would have been required to resign from the Senate: one provision of New Hampshire's constitution precludes a governor from also holding a Senate seat, while another requires selection of a new Senate president within 30 days.

Meanwhile, since assuming the governorship from Roy, Sununu has gained re-election in November 1984 over Chris Spirou, the minority leader in the New Hampshire House. Sununu won by a margin of 244,144 votes to 122,915, in a contest that centered on the issue of New Hampshire's controversial Seabrook nuclear power plant.

Bibliography: *Women in Public Office* (New York, 1976); Manchester [New Hampshire] *Union Leader*, November 23, December 1-2, and December 30, 1982; *New York Times*, December 20, 1982, January 4, 1983, and November 8, 1984; *New Hampshire Elected Officials, 1983-84*. MMM

Brendan Thomas Byrne (Courtesy: Brendan Byrne)

NEW JERSEY

BYRNE, Brendan Thomas, 1974-1982

Born on April 1, 1924 in West Orange, New Jersey, the son of Francis A., President of the Essex County (New Jersey) Tax Board, and Genevieve Thecia (Brennan) Byrne. A Roman Catholic, Byrne married Jean Featherly on June 27, 1953; he is the father of Brendan Thomas, Susan, Nancy, Timothy, Mary Anne, Barbara, and William Byrne.

Byrne served in the United States Army Air Force from 1943 to 1945, receiving the Distinguished Flying Cross and the Air Medal with three oak leaf clusters. He was awarded an A.B. from Princeton in 1949 and an LL.B. from Harvard Law School in 1951. Admitted to the New Jersey bar in 1951, Byrne practiced law in Newark, New Jersey from 1951 to 1955. He was appointed Assistant Counsel to Governor Robert B. Meyner in 1955 and Executive Secretary in 1956, serving in the latter capacity until 1958. Named Deputy Attorney in charge of the Essex County Prosecutor's Office in 1959, Byrne held that position until 1968. He served as President of the New Jersey Public Utilities Commission from 1968 to 1970, Judge of the Superior Court of New Jersey from 1970 to 1972, and Assignment Judge of Morris, Essex and Warren counties from 1972 to 1974.

The Democratic Party's gubernatorial candidate, Byrne was elected Governor of New Jersey on November 6, 1973, defeating the Republican candidate, Charles W. Sandman, Jr., by a vote of 1,397,613 to 676,235; he was inaugurated on January 15, 1974. A major concern of his first term was the personal income tax issue. In a 1973 decision of the New Jersey Supreme Court, that state was ordered to devise a new way to finance public education, which in the past had been based on 70 percent of local property taxes. Several attempts at passing a personal income tax failed, but when the New Jersey Supreme Court ordered the public schools closed on July 1, 1976 because the Legislature had not provided an alternative to the local property tax system, Byrne signed New Jersey's first law providing for a state-wide income tax on July 8, 1976. Other legislation approved during Byrne's first term included required public financing of gubernatorial election campaigns (with private contributions limited to $600 per person), legalization of casino gambling in Atlantic City, and an increase in the state sales tax.

In the 1977 gubernatorial election Byrne was re-elected, defeating the Republican Raymond Bateman by a vote of 1,184,564 to 888,880. The following year the New Jersey Supreme Court upheld the governor's right to require disclosure of personal finances by high officials in the state administration. Byrne's second term in office was also marked by the threat of the New York Stock Exchange to move to New Jersey to avoid a New York city tax, a brief job action by state employees, passage of a bill permitting the state to take over commuter rail and bus lines, and a controversy involving the state's Attorney General (a Byrne appointee), who ran afoul of licensing agencies in an attempt to exert greater control over professional licensing standards. The state also went through considerable turmoil associated with the effort to establish legalized gambling in New Jersey. Byrne sought revisions in the law governing the Casino Control Commission in 1981, and the subtle aspects of the gambling statutes consumed the attention of the New Jersey courts.

During Byrne's administration New Jersey decided to construct a sports complex in the "Meadowlands," the flat area on the west side of the tunnels leading to New York City. The New York Giants decided to occupy the football stadium, while a nearby arena was eventually filled by a professional basketball and professional hockey team. New Jersey residents were critical of Byrne, however, when Meadowlands officials named the new arena in his honor.

Byrne's term ended in 1982, and he has returned to private legal practice.

Bibliography: *New York Times*, November 7, 1973 and May 19, 1981; Congressional Quarterly, Inc., *Guide to U.S. Elections* (Washington, D.C., 1975); Roy Glashan, *American Governors and Gubernatorial Elections, 1775-1975* (Stillwater, Minn., 1975); Bob Hollingsworth, ed., *Facts on File Yearbook, 1976* (New York, 1977). Byrne's papers are at the Archives Division of the New Jersey State Library in Trenton. JH

Thomas H. Kean (Credit: Office of the Governor, New Jersey)

KEAN, Thomas H., 1982-

Born in New York, New York on April 21, 1935, the son of Robert Winthrop and Elizabeth (Stuyvesant) Kean. Kean is married to Deborah Bye of Wilmington, Delaware; he is the father of Reed, Thomas, and Alexandra.

Kean's father served in the United States House of Representatives from 1939 to 1959. His ancestors include William Livingston, who was Governor of New Jersey from 1776 to 1790. Kean attended St. Marks School, and was graduated from Princeton University. He earned an M.A. at Columbia University, but abandoned plans to go on for a Ph.D. after joining William Scranton's unsuccessful bid for the Republican Presidential nomination in 1964. Kean taught American history and English in high schools for three years, directed a camp for disadvantaged children, and took part in the White House Conference on Youth in 1970 and 1971. He taught political science at Rutgers, New Jersey's state university, and worked as a commentator on the New Jersey Educational Network's evening news program. Kean also was President and Chairman of the Realty Transfer Company of Elizabeth, New Jersey.

A member of the New Jersey General Assembly from 1967 to 1977, Kean was named Speaker of that body in 1972, despite the fact that Republicans did not hold a majority of the seats. David Freidland, the Democratic Minority Leader of the previous Assembly, had been passed over for the nomination as speaker in favor of a black pastor from Trenton. Freidland and two others retaliated by defecting to Kean, the Republican Minority candidate. One disgruntled Democrat noted that ''Jesus Christ has his Judas, the Democrats now have David Friedland.''

Kean managed President Gerald Ford's successful New Jersey campaign in 1976, and in the following year lost the gubernatorial primary to State Senator Raymond H. Bateman. Four years later, however, Kean defeated seven other candidates to win the nomination. (Kean's principal opponent in that primary was Lawrence Kramer, the Mayor of Paterson, New Jersey.) Kean then met James Florio, a Democratic Congressman from South Jersey, in the general election. Both men were rather moderate liberals—for instance, Kean had introduced New Jersey's first rent control bill—but Kean nevertheless spent much of his time disassociating himself from President Ronald Reagan. The final count was extremely close: 1,145,999 votes for Kean and 1,444,202 for Florio, with about 25,000 votes divided among 11 independent candidates. Although there were allegations that the national Republican Party had tried to scare Democratic voters away from the polls by using a ''ballot security'' force, in the end Florio conceded the election without a court fight. In a referendum held the same day as the election, New Jersey abolished the pocket veto.

Two months after Kean took office, Harrison A. Williams of New Jersey resigned from the United States Senate following his indictment as a result of the so-called ''Abscam'' investigation (which also implicated a Democratic Congressman from the state). Kean appointed Nicholas F. Brady to the Senate for a few months until the next general election. For the first time ever, the New Jersey Supreme Court in 1982 issued a writ of election after State Senator William V. Musto refused to resign after being indicted for receiving kickbacks. In 1983 the Legislature considered repeal of the state's no-fault automobile law when New Jerseyans found themselves paying the nation's highest insurance rates. Kean's current term expires in 1986.

Bibliography: *New York Times*, October 26, 1981; *Newark Star Ledger*, November 4, 1981; *Manual of the Legislature of New Jersey* (Trenton, N.J., 1982).
JH

Jerry Apodaca

NEW MEXICO

APODACA, Jerry, 1975-1979

A former football star at the University of New Mexico, the boyishly handsome Apodaca was the first Spanish-surnamed governor of New Mexico since 1918 and the first state chief executive to have a Spanish surname since 1921. Born to bilingual parents Raymond and Elisa Apocada in Las Cruces, New Mexico on October 3, 1934, Apodaca was held back in the first grade in order to improve his English—an experience friends believe may have fueled his furious drive to succeed. (Significantly, during his tenure as governor, he made kindergartens mandatory throughout the state so that Chicano children might become bilingual earlier.) Following an all-star football career in high school, he won a scholarship to the University of New Mexico, where he majored in education. Apodaca taught history and coached football at an Albuquerque high school after graduating from college, and then opened a successful storefront insurance agency that blossomed into a real estate business and some retail shoe outlets.

Apodaca assisted in a friend's unsuccessful mayoral campaign in 1964. He soon decided to try politics for himself, losing his first bid for state senator because—he believed—of his nervousness as a public speaker. In 1966, after taking speech lessons, he won the race, marking the start of an eight-year career in the New Mexico Senate. There Apodaca acquired the reputation of a maverick. In 1973, for example, he risked the anger of a Democratic governor by blocking a bill that would have let him run for another term. Chairman of the Legislative School Study Committee from 1969 to 1970, Apodaca was also a Delegate to the 1968 Democratic National Convention, State Chairman of the Democratic Party from 1969 to 1970, and a member of the National Democratic Policy Council.

When he entered the Democratic gubernatorial primary in 1974, Apodaca was, at 39, the youngest candidate in a six-man field, but his youth, energy, and Hispanic background helped him to win the nomination. In the primary he defeated his closest challenger, Albuquerque lawyer Bobby Mayfield, by more than 10,000 votes. In the general election against conservative Republican Joseph Skeen, Apodaca made his anonymity a virtue. Posing for a series of billboards emblazoned with the slogan, "The Man Nobody Owns," he won by only 3,700 votes. He did, however, attract 62 percent of the vote in the state's Hispanic areas, the best showing any Democrat had made among that constituency in years.

As chief executive, Apodaca created the first Cabinet in the history of New

Mexico, and charged it with special goals to improve the governor's ability to manage state agencies, improve decision making, and make state operation more cost effective, accountable, and responsive to the needs of New Mexico's citizens. He streamlined the state's bureaucracy, which he had once called a "700 pound marshmallow," and fired many state employees, as well as issuing orders cutting back on long lunches and forbidding government employees from drinking during the work day. Apodaca was also the first New Mexico governor to adopt the cautious approach to development that has been rather popular in the Rocky Mountain states in recent years.

Apodaca eventually acquired a national reputation. Indeed, it was while helping Apodaca that Jimmy Carter met Tim Kraft and Chris Brown, who became key staff aides in his 1976 primary victories. Co-Chairman of the Democratic National Convention in 1976, Apodaca was rumored to have been in line for a Cabinet post in the Carter White House. During his tenure as chief executive, he also served as Chairman of the Western Governors' Association Regional Energy Policy Office.

Because New Mexico law prevented him from succeeding himself, Apodaca retired from office in 1979. In June 1982 he was defeated in his bid to gain the Democratic nomination for the United States Senate, when New Mexico Democrats chose Attorney General Jeff Bingamon to oppose Senator Harrison Schmitt in the fall general election. A Roman Catholic, Apodaca and his wife Clara Melendres have five children—Cindy, Carolyn, Jerry, Jeff, and Judy.

Bibliography: *New York Times*, November 7, 1974; *New Mexico Blue Book, 1977-78*; Michael Barone *et al.*, eds., *The Almanac of American Politics, 1978* (New York, 1977); Kent Demaret, "New Mexico Governor Jerry Apodaca Survives the Agony of the Boston Marathon—But Barely," *People* (May 1, 1978). MMM

Bruce King

KING, Bruce, 1971-1975, 1979-1983

Because New Mexico's constitution prohibits incumbent governors from serving a second consecutive term, Bruce King's eight-year tenure in the Statehouse has been an interrupted one. Born in Stanley, New Mexico on April 6, 1924, the son of Molly Schooler and rancher William King, he attended the University of New Mexico between 1943 and 1944 and then served in the Field Artillery of the United States Army from 1944 to 1946. A rancher and livestock feeder by trade, and co-owner of King's Butane Company, he entered state politics as Sante Fe County Commissioner in 1954. King held that post for the next four years, and eventually served as Chairman of the Board of Commissioners from 1957 to 1958. He was a member of the New Mexico House of Representatives for the next decade, from 1959 to 1969, and served as Speaker of the House from 1963 to 1969. Positions as State Democratic Chairman (1968-69) and President of the New Mexico State Constitutional Convention in 1969 preceded King's first race for the governorship in 1970. With the strong support of organized labor, he defeated the Republican Pete Domenici, a former Chairman of the Albuquerque City Commission. King was the first chief executive of New Mexico elected to a four-year term, under the provisions of a constitutional amendment adopted in 1970.

King's first administration saw New Mexico pass the Equal Rights Amendment to the United States Constitution, organize a Department of Corrections, establish a State Capitol Improvement Fund, and create a Children's Court Division of the District Courts. King also served as Vice Chairman of the Western Governors' Conference from 1973 to 1974.

Retiring to his ranching and cattle investments in 1975, he was succeeded in the governorship by Jerry Apodaca, who had previously been a member of the New Mexico Legislature. Although Apodaca is a Democrat, the two men are not political allies, and have been very different governors. King's interest in politics continued during his retirement, and he served as a Delegate to the Democratic National Convention in 1976.

Two years later he returned to politics, seeking his party's gubernatorial nomination in the 1978 primary. Although King soundly defeated his opponent Robert Ferguson, gaining 61 percent of the vote, he had a more difficult time in the general election against Joseph Skeen, a very conservative Republican who attacked King on the right-to-work issue. New Mexico Republicans had been gaining strength in state-wide contests, and King, a moderate Democrat, just managed to defeat Skeen by a 51-49 percent margin, gaining only about one percent more of the total vote than had Apodaca in 1974. Yet, like Apodaca, he did well in Hispanic areas, and he ran stronger than Apodaca in so-called "Little Texas," the southeast corner of the state.

A Delegate to the 1980 Democratic National Convention, King was ineligible to seek re-election as governor in 1982. His successor this time was former

Democratic Attorney General Toney Anaya, who had served as King's administrative assistant during his first term as chief executive. A Baptist, King and his wife Alice Martin have two sons, Bill and Gary.

Bibliography: Michael Barone *et al.*, eds., *The Almanac of American Politics, 1978-80* (New York, 1977-79); *New Mexico Blue Book, 1979-80.* MMM

Hugh L. Carey (Credit: Library of Congress, Congressional Collection)

NEW YORK

CAREY, Hugh L., 1975-1983

Born on April 11, 1919 in Brooklyn, New York, the son of Dennis J. and Margaret (Collins) Carey. A Roman Catholic, Carey married Helen Owen on February 27, 1947, who died in March 1974; he is the father by his first marriage of Alexandria, Christopher, Susan, Peter, Hugh L., Michael, Donald, Marianne, Nancy, Helen, Bryan, Paul, Kevin, and Thomas. Carey married Evangeline Gouletas, a divorcee and part-owner of a condominium-conversion company, on April 11, 1981.

During World War II Carey served in the United States Army, rising to the rank of Major and Lieutenant Colonel of the New York National Guard. He received both the Bronze Star and France's Croix de Guerre with Silver Star. Admitted to the New York bar in 1951 after graduating from St. John's University Law School that year, Carey began his private law practice in Brooklyn. He is the former Director of several industrial firms.

Carey was a member of the United States House of Representatives from 1960 to 1975, representing a district in Brooklyn. While serving in that capacity, he authored the first federal aid to education act for all school children. He has also been a member of the Board of Governors for the National Democratic Club, a member of the Board of Visitors of the United States Merchant Marine Academy, and a Delegate to the Interparliamentary Union Conference in Brussels in 1961. Carey has been awarded numerous honorary degrees during his political career. Other professional associations include the Veterans of Foreign Wars, the American Legion, the Catholic War Veterans, the Emerald Association (which he served as Director), and the Boy Scout Finance Committee. Carey was named a Knight of the Holy Sepulchre of Jerusalem by Pope Pius XII.

The candidate of both the Democratic and Liberal parties, Carey was elected Governor of New York on November 5, 1974, receiving 3,028,503 votes compared to 2,219,667 cast for Malcolm Wilson, the Republican incumbent and Conservative Party nominee. Carey was sworn into office on January 1, 1975. During his first term New York's food stamp plan was invalidated, offshore oil leasing by the United States was upheld, and the oil tariff was declared illegal. In 1976 the Democratic National Convention met in New York City; it would do so again in 1980. That city faced a severe financial crisis during Carey's administration, a crisis which resulted in the creation of the Municipal Assistance Corporation.

In 1978 supposed voter dissatisfaction with the Carey administration led both

Lieutenant Governor Mary Ann Krupsak and Jeremiah R. Bloom to challenge him in the Democratic primary. After scoring an impressive win in that contest, he faced veteran state legislator Perry B. Duryea in the general election. While he was backed by a united Republican Party, Duryea ran a lackluster campaign and lost ground as questions emerged concerning his finances. In the election Carey amassed a 500,000 vote lead in New York City, and won the state by a popular vote margin of 2,429,272 to 2,156,404, with 130,000 votes going to Mary Jane Tobin, the Right to Life candidate.

During 1979 a proposal to fund medicaid payments for abortions provoked considerable controversy, although it was eventually approved. Rejected, however, was a Carey proposal to establish an ombudsman's office headed by the new lieutenant governor, Mario Cuomo. In 1980 the Winter Olympic Games were held at Lake Placid, New York, with the Games' most emotional feature being a surprise gold medal for the United States hockey team. Late in Carey's second term the New York Court of Appeals ruled that the chief executive could not spend money received from the federal government without the consent of the Legislature.

On January 15, 1982, Carey announced that he would not seek a third term, since he had decided to concentrate his energy on completing his legislative initiatives rather than campaign for re-election. Some observers questioned whether Mrs. Carey's financial interests might have produced conflict of interest issues had the governor continued in office. Unfortunately for Carey, the Legislature became preoccupied with the issue of reapportionment, and little was done to enact his program. Carey, who was succeeded as governor by Mario Cuomo, entered the same law firm as former New York City Mayor Robert F. Wagner after leaving office.

Bibliography: *Congressional Directory, 1972* (Washington, D.C., 1972); Congressional Quarterly, Inc., *Guide to U.S. Elections* (Washington, D.C., 1975); Roy Glashan, *American Governors and Gubernational Elections, 1775-1975* (Stillwater, Minn., 1975); Howard M. Epstein, ed., *Facts on File Yearbook, 1975* (New York, 1976); Bob Hollingsworth, ed., *Facts on File Yearbook, 1976* (New York, 1977); *New York Times*, November 8, 1978, April 12, 1981, and January 16-17, 1982; Warren J. Mitofsky, *Campaign '78* (New York, 1980). Carey's papers are in Albany, New York at the University of the State of New York, Department of Education, State Archives. JH

James Baxter Hunt (Credit: Office of the Governor, North Carolina)

NORTH CAROLINA

HUNT, James Baxter, 1977-

Born on May 16, 1937 in Greensboro, North Carolina, the son of James B. Hunt, a farmer and soil conservationist, and Elsie (Brame) Hunt, a teacher. A Presbyterian, Governor Hunt is the brother of Robert Brame Hunt. He married Carolyn Joyce Leonard on August 20, 1958, by whom he is the father of Rebecca, Baxter, Rachel, and Elizabeth.

Hunt was graduated from Rock Ridge High School and attended North Carolina State University, receiving a B.S. degree in agricultural education in 1959 and an M.S. in agricultural economics in 1962. He received a J.D. from the University of North Carolina Law School in 1964, eventually establishing a law practice in Wilson. Hunt served as Chairman of "Young Voters for Terry Sanford" in 1960, and as National College Director for the Democratic National Committee in 1962-63. In 1964 he went to Nepal for two years under the sponsorship of the Ford Foundation, where he became an economic advisor to the government. Elected President of the State Young Democratic National Convention, Hunt was appointed Assistant State Party Chairman in 1969.

In the Democratic primary for Lieutenant Governor on May 6, 1972, Hunt defeated Roy Sowers, Margaret Harper, Allen Barbee, and Reginald Grazier. Reversing a Republican trend in the state, he was elected Lieutenant Governor in the November election, defeating John Walker, the Republican candidate, by over 200,000 votes. Four years later Hunt sought the Democratic nomination for Governor, and in the August 1976 primary he received 52.3 percent of the vote, defeating Edward M. O'Herron, Jr., George M. Wood, Thomas E. Strickland, and Jetter Braker. In the general election he attracted 1,081,293 votes, compared to 564,102 for the Republican candidate, David T. Flaherty. Hunt was inaugurated on January 6, 1977.

In his inaugural address, Hunt called for a "new beginning" which would "eliminate the last vestiges of discrimination." He advocated a renewed emphasis on the teaching of reading in the public schools, and supported a new utilities regulation structure that would reflect consumer interests. Hunt named a black and a woman to high level posts, and actively promoted the appointment of blacks to judicial positions. In 1978 he was urged by a number of organizations, including Amnesty International, to free the "Wilmington 10"—a group of nine black men and one white woman accused of firebombing a Wilmington, North Carolina grocery store. The Soviet Union contended that the imprisonment of this group was a human rights violation, and critics of the trials maintained that the defendants had been convicted in a politically-charged atmosphere which included tampering with evidence by state officials. Hunt declared that there had indeed been a fair trial, although he decided that the sentences were too long and reduced the terms for the prisoners. All ten were on parole within a year.

In 1980 Hunt, who could succeed himself after the passage of a 1977 constitutional amendment, engaged in a primary struggle with former Governor Robert Scott. Scott asserted that Hunt had failed to deal adequately with mill workers' claims that they had contracted brown lung disease while on the job, but Hunt still managed to win the primary. Later in 1980 Hunt was the focus of a brief assassination scare while attending the Democratic National Convention. In November of that year he easily defeated Beverly Lake, the Republican candidate, by 1,847,432 votes to 691,449. Those counties which Hunt lost in the election were located predominantly in the mountainous western region of the state. In 1981 Hunt had a difficult time meeting the state's need for government services in the face of federal budget cuts. His term is scheduled to end in 1985, when he will be succeeded by James G. Martin, a North Carolina Congressman who becomes only the second Republican governor of the state in this century. Martin defeated State Attorney General Rufus Edmisten by a margin of 1,183,331 votes to 998,979.

Meanwhile, following a particularly acrimonious campaign against Jesse Helms, the conservative Republican incumbent, Hunt lost his bid for a United States Senate seat in 1984. Helms won that contest by polling 1,137,885 votes compared to 1,055,592 votes for Hunt.

Bibliography: Daily News [Greensboro], November 19, 1972; *News and Observer* [Raleigh], January 9, 1977; *Washington Post*, January 25, 1978 and May 6, 1980; *New York Times*, December 15, 1979, December 8, 1981, and November 8, 1984; Richard M. Scammon and Alice V. McGillivray, *America Votes*, 14 (Washington, D.C., 1981). The State Archives in Raleigh is the repository for gubernatorial papers, and those of Governor Hunt will eventually be deposited there. The North Carolina Collection in Chapel Hill also contains documents, including a clipping file. JH

Arthur A. Link

NORTH DAKOTA

LINK, Arthur A., 1973-1981

Born on May 24, 1914 in Alexander, North Dakota, the son of homesteader parents. A Lutheran, Link married the former Grace Johnson; he is the father of five sons and one daughter.

Link attended North Dakota Agricultural College (now North Dakota State University), where he majored in agriculture and applied science. His career in public service has been a long and distinguished one. Link served as a member of the Randolph Township Board for 28 years, and of the McKenzie County Welfare Board for 21 years. He served on his local school board for 18 years and is a past county and state Farm Security Committee member. A Democrat, he served in the North Dakota House of Representatives from 1947 to 1971. Speaker of the House in 1965, he completed seven terms as Minority Floor Leader. Link worked on various House committees, such as Education, Finance, and Industrial and Labor relations; he also chaired an interim committee on legislative procedure and arrangements for the Subcommittee on Education. Link was Chairman of the State Advisory Council for Vocational Education from 1969 to 1971. He served one term in the United States House of Representatives, winning election in an upset victory in 1970. However, Link's Congressional career came to an abrupt halt in 1972. After the size of North Dakota's Congressional delegation was reduced to one at-large seat following the 1970 census, he decided to run for Governor rather than challenge the state's other Congressman, the popular Republican Mark Andrews.

Link won North Dakota's 1972 gubernatorial contest when he defeated the Republican Richard Larsen, compiling 51 percent of the vote to Larsen's 49 percent. Although North Dakota is historically a Republican state, political observers believe the Democrats were able to retain the governorship because of the popularity of outgoing Governor William Guy, who had held the office since 1961. Link won re-election in 1976. Unopposed in his party's primary, he took the general election by defeating Republican Richard Elkin, whom political pundits considered to be a formidable opponent. Link received about 52 percent of the vote compared to Elkin's 47 percent.

During Link's administration the state's agricultural economy prospered, with farmers planting more and receiving higher prices for their products. The North Dakota Legislature also passed laws which reformed income and property taxes, and reapportionment became a major topic of debate and argument. Above all, the energy crisis came to assume important dimensions, with those anxious to exploit the state's mineral wealth lining up against those more concerned with environmental protection. Strip mining was an important question during these years, and Link was more willing to regulate the industry than his predecessor had been. (The strip mining issue was particularly significant in the western part of the state, where great veins of lignite coal lie directly beneath wheat fields and grazing land.) Political observers consider Link's position on energy and the environment to be the most important part of his record. Especially during the second term, he came to national attention because of the energy issue. Meeting with Carter administration energy advisors, he suggested that North Dakota would be more cheerful about sacrificing for the energy program if it could be assured of getting its fair share of water, a precious commodity in this part of the country.

Political observers feel that Link's position on energy-related issues may have played a role in his unsuccessful bid for a third term in 1980. His opponent, Republican State Attorney General Allen I. Olson, charged that Link favored too high a severance tax on mineral exploitation. Instead, Olson promised to encourage more development, a position in line with the Reagan administration's policy of exploiting American mineral and energy resources more extensively. His position obviously appealed to North Dakota voters, who gave him 54 percent of the vote to Link's 46 percent.

During his gubernatorial tenure Link was Chairman of the Resolutions Committee of the Farmers Union Grain Terminal Association, a post he held for three years. He also chaired the National Governors' Association Committee on Agriculture in 1979, and served on the NGA's Executive Committee from 1977 to 1978. A Delegate to the Democratic National Convention in 1976, Link was Chairman of the Midwestern Governors' Conference in 1978. He is a former state Co-Chairman of the Old West Regional Commission.

Link has been a board member of the Williston University Center Foundation since its inception, and is a past board member of the McKenzie County Historical Society and the Lewis and Clark Trail Museum. A charter member of the National Cowboy Hall of Fame, he has also been active in the Lions Club.

Bibliography: Michael Barone *et al.*, eds., *The Almanac of American Politics, 1978-82* (New York and Washington, D.C., 1977-81); *New York Times*, July 21, 1979 and September 3-4, 1980; National Governors' Association, *Governors of the American States, Commonwealths, and Territories* (Washington, D.C., 1980); Alan Ehrenhalt, ed., *Politics in America, 1982* (Washington, D.C., 1981); *Who's Who in American Politics, 1981-82* (New York, 1981). MMM

Allen Ingvar Olson

OLSON, Allen Ingvar, 1981-

Born on November 5, 1938 in Rolla, North Dakota, the son of Elmer and Olga (Sundin) Olson. A Presbyterian, Olson is married to the former Barbara Benner of Grand Forks. They have three children—Kristin, Robin, and Craig.

Olson grew up on a farm near Sarles in northeastern North Dakota, a few miles from the Canadian border. He earned his B.A. in 1960 and his LL.B. in 1963, both from the University of North Dakota, where he was a member of Lambda Chi Alpha. He entered the United States Army in September 1963 as a lawyer in the Judge Advocate General Corps. Stationed at the Pentagon in Washington, D.C. and later in West Germany, Olson handled cases at both the trial and appellate levels. His last assignment was as Chief of Military Justice for a major overseas command, and he received an army commendation medal for his services.

Returning to North Dakota in 1967, Olson became Assistant Director of the Legislative Council at the State Capitol in Bismarck, where he directed research on the state's first comprehensive study of strip mining, soil banks, and land reclamation. He was also involved in legislative studies on vocational education. From 1969 to 1972 Olson was in private practice with the Bismarck law firm of Conmy, Rosenberg, Lucas, and Olson. He first entered political life in 1972 when, running as a Republican, he was elected to the post of North Dakota Attorney General; he was re-elected to a second four-year term in 1976. That same year, he was a Delegate to the Republican National Convention.

In 1980 Olson won 76 percent of the vote to defeat Labor Commissioner Orville W. Hagen and gain the Republican gubernatorial nomination. Although North Dakota is historically a Republican state, the Democrats had been in control of the Statehouse for 20 years. By 1980, however, incumbent Democrat Arthur A. Link, seeking his third term as chief executive, was politically vulnerable. Olson charged that Link favored too high a severance tax on mineral exploitation, an issue of great importance in a state with rich deposits of lignite coal. By contrast, Olson ran on a platform that called for more development. His position, which was closer to the Reagan administration's policy of exploiting America's mineral and energy resources more extensively, enabled Olson to win the general election with 54 percent of the vote to Link's 46 percent. On January 6, 1981, he was sworn in as the 28th chief executive of North Dakota.

Governor Olson has received national publicity as one of the governors from five western coal-producing states who have pushed the Reagan administration for a stronger state role in determining the pace of coal development. Weakening oil prices and subsequently reduced state royalties, coupled with low farm prices, also forced Olson to devote attention to the problem of falling state revenues. Faced with the necessity of budget cuts midway through his first term, Olson chose to cut building funds, state raises, and grants to localities.

Olson is a member of North Dakota's Emergency Commission, Industrial

Commission, Board of University and School Lands, Water Commission, Indian Affairs Commission, and Board of Pardons. By statute, he also serves on a number of other boards and commissions, but he has delegated much of this authority to Lieutenant Governor Ernest M. Sands, who is the first occupant of that office to serve as a direct member of a North Dakota governor's administration.

Despite Ronald Reagan's landslide Presidential victory in November 1984, Olson was unexpectedly defeated in North Dakota's gubernatorial race that year. He lost the contest, by a convincing margin of 55 percent to 45 percent, to George Sinner, a Democratic State Representative. Olson's term is scheduled to end in January 1985.

Governor Olson is Chairman of the Western Governors' Policy Office. A member of the Executive Committee of the National Governors' Association, he is a member of the NGA's Agriculture Committee and Committee on Community and Economic Development. In addition, he chairs the NGA's Soil Conservation Task Force and its Legal Affairs Committee, as well as the Legal Committee of the Interstate Oil Compact Commission. Olson continues to be active in a number of national, state, and community organizations, including the Elks, American Legion, YMCA, Sons of Norway, and the Masonic Lodge. He has also been a member of the National Association of Attorneys General and of the American and North Dakota Bar associations.

Bibliography: *New York Times*, September 3-4, 1980, November 22-23, 1982, March 5, 1983, and November 8, 1984; Michael Barone and Grant Ujifusa, eds., *The Almanac of American Politics, 1982* (Washington, D.C., 1981); *Who's Who in American Politics, 1981-82* (New York, 1981); National Governors' Association, *Governors of the American States, Commonwealths, and Territories* (Washington, D.C., 1983); biographical information, Office of the Governor, State of North Dakota. MMM

James A. Rhodes (Credit: Ohio Historical Society)

OHIO

RHODES, James A., 1963-1971, 1975-1983

Born in Coalton, Jackson County, Ohio on September 13, 1909, the son of James Allen Rhodes, a coal miner who died in 1917, and Susan (Howe) Rhodes. A Methodist, Rhodes is the brother of two sisters. He married Helen Rawlins, and is the father of Suzanne, Saundra, and Sharon.

Rhodes attended South High School in Springfield and Ohio State University, but he was forced to leave before graduating from college in order to support his mother and sisters, by operating a restaurant near the Ohio State campus. He began his political career as a member of the Columbus Board of Education between 1937 and 1939. Rhodes was elected Auditor of the city of Columbus in 1939, and served in that capacity until 1944. He became Mayor of Columbus in 1948, the same year in which he was selected to represent the United States at the Olympic Games in London. Rhodes was elected Auditor of the state of Ohio in 1953, and during his ten years in office he gained a reputation for efficiency and economy in handling the state's finances. In May of 1950 he lost the Republican gubernatorial primary; he won the primary four years later, but lost the general election to Frank Lausche by a vote of 1,405,262 to 1,192,528.

In 1962 Rhodes was again the Republican nominee for governor. Running on a platform that called for economy in government, he defeated the Democratic incumbent, Michael DiSalle, by a vote of 1,836,190 to 1,280,521. He was easily re-elected in 1966, defeating Frazier Reams by a count of 1,795,277 to 1,092,054. Following his second term Rhodes retired from public life for four years, but in 1974 he returned to defeat John Gilligan in an extremely close contest. Polling 1,493,679 votes to Gilligan's 1,482,191, Rhodes withstood a delay of several days before he was declared the winner. Finally, in 1978 he was challenged in the Republican gubernatorial primary by Charles F. Kurfess, the party's leader in the Ohio House of Representatives. Although he conducted a vigorous campaign, Kurfess lost by a margin of about two to one. In the general election Rhodes faced Richard F. Celeste, Ohio's Lieutenant Governor. Celeste sought to break the connection between the Ohio property tax and public education; he also attacked recent utility rate increases. Nevertheless, Rhodes won the contest by a vote of 1,402,167 to 1,354,631, losing the Cleveland and Dayton areas by considerable margins but scoring well in other parts of the state. About 95,000 votes in the election were scattered among three independent candidates. The 1978 Ohio gubernatorial race is likely to be the last contest between an incumbent governor and an incumbent lieutenant governor, since it represented the first year in which both positions were chosen in the same election. Henceforth, both offices will be held by the same political party.

Early in his career as governor, Rhodes instituted an austerity program in an effort to wipe out a deficit of $83 million. He reduced DiSalle's proposed budget and required state departments to trim expenditures, a strategy that resulted in the unemployment of 4,000 state employees. These and other measures, however, enabled Rhodes to balance the budget and turn Ohio's deficit into a surplus. Rhodes also established an Ohio Youth Commission to deal with juvenile crime, originated Ohio's "Teenage Hall of Fame," and wrote a book on that program.

In his final term Rhodes unleashed a bitter attack on environmental regulations, blaming them for the energy crisis and the difficulties faced by American steel manufacturers. On the other hand, he supported continued federal control of the trucking industry. In 1980 Rhodes backed a proposal for a temporary sales tax increase; he later supported a permanent increase in the levy. Rhodes also signed a bill permitting counties to increase sales taxes. In 1981 he approved legislation allowing a 25 percent interest charge on certain loans and credit cards. Rhodes headed a particularly effective political organization in Ohio, and was frequently credited with bringing victory to Republican Presidential candidates in the state.

Since he could not run again for governor in 1982, Rhodes considered opposing United States Senator Howard Metzenbaum, but ultimately he decided not to seek a Senate seat. Rhodes is the author of *Johnny Shiloh, The Trial of Mary Todd Lincoln*, and *The Court Martial of Commodore Perry*. His continuing interest in sports is demonstrated by his membership in the Professional Golfers Association (he is also a founder of the National Caddie Association) and his service on the United States Olympic Committee. Rhodes has promoted a series of events and organizations for youth and has worked to increase state aid to education, including state teachers' salaries. He was succeeded in office by Richard Celeste in 1983.

Bibliography: Edward J. Mowery, "James Allen Rhodes: Taxpayer's Governor," *Bookmailer* (1963); Office of the Secretary of State, *Ohio Blue Book* (Columbus, 1964-77); S. Winford Smith, "James A. Rhodes," *Governors of Ohio* (Columbus, 1969); "No Place for Fortas," *Time* (May 19, 1969); D. Hess, "Rhodes: Ninth Inning Optimist," *Biographical News* (January 1975); *Cleveland Plain Dealer*, November 8, 1978; Richard M. Scammon and Alice V. McGillivray, *America Votes*, 14 (Washington, D.C., 1981). Rhodes' papers are at the Ohio Historical Society, Archives-Manuscript Division in Columbus. JH

David Lyle Boren (Credit: Senator Boren's Offices, Washington, D.C.)

OKLAHOMA

BOREN, David Lyle, 1975-1979

Born in Washington, D.C. on April 21, 1941, the son of Christine (McKown) Boren and former United States Representative Lyle H. Boren. A Methodist, Boren has two children, Carrie and David. Following his divorce from Janna Lou Little in 1976, he married Molly W. Shi in 1977.

A *summa cum laude* and Phi Beta Kappa graduate of Yale University, Boren received a Rhodes scholarship to attend the University of Oxford, from which he received an M.A. in government in 1965; he later went on to obtain his law degree in 1968 from the University of Oklahoma School of Law, where he was named the outstanding graduate in his class by the law school faculty. Although an attorney by profession, Boren also served as Chairman of the Division of Social Sciences and Professor of Political Science at Oklahoma Baptist University between 1969 and 1974, before embarking on a political career.

After serving four consecutive terms in the Oklahoma House of Representatives from 1966 to 1974, Boren decided to run for Governor in 1974 on a platform emphasizing welfare and campaign spending reform, the elimination of waste and mismanagement from government and, most important, political integrity. Although few pundits took him seriously, his reputation as a political outsider and reformer helped him attract voters infused with a post-Watergate consciousness and disgusted with scandals in their own state, where Governor David Hall was under investigation on corruption charges that were later to send him to prison. Using a broom as his campaign symbol, and promising to clean up state government, Boren easily defeated Republican Jim Inhofe by capturing 64 percent of the vote, a bigger margin than that won by all but two chief executives in the state's history.

Boren ran a clean and fiscally austere administration, fulfilling his campaign promise to reorganize state government. He also won national attention as a spokesman for his state's oil producers, and sought to keep his distance from the Carter administration when its policies on the deregulation of gas and oil prices proved not to his liking. "To me," Boren has said, "being pro-oil means being pro-Oklahoma." His gubernatorial record brought him far more business support than most Democrats can expect in Oklahoma, and he could almost certainly have become the first Oklahoma governor to win consecutive terms in office had he decided to run again in 1978. Instead, however, he took the riskier path and decided to seek the Senate seat being vacated by Dewey F. Bartlett, who was retiring because of ill health.

Boren, as an oil industry loyalist, was a clear favorite until a minor candidate charged that he was a homosexual. Finally swearing on a Bible that the innuendo was untrue, Boren nevertheless had to face a runoff election against former Congressman and two-time Senatorial candidate Ed Edmondson in order to win his own party's nomination. He captured the general election handily, defeating Republican Robert Kamm with 65 percent of the vote.

In Washington, Boren is generally regarded as one of the brighter Senate newcomers in recent years. He was one of the few Democrats to endorse the Kemp-Roth tax cut plan, and usually supports the conservative fiscal policies of the Reagan administration: cutting federal spending, lowering taxes, decreasing federal regulation, and removing energy price controls. Two of his pet ideas were incorporated in the June 1981 tax cut bill—an exemption from the oil windfall profits tax for royalty holders, and an end to the federal inheritance tax between spouses.

Boren easily retained his Senate seat in November 1984, defeating Republican Bill Crozier by a margin of 76 percent to 23 percent.

Bibliography: Michael Barone *et al.*, eds., *The Almanac of American Politics, 1978-82* (New York and Washington, D.C., 1977-81); Oklahoma Department of Libraries, *Governors of Oklahoma: 1890-1979* (Oklahoma City, 1979); *New York Times*, November 8, 1984. MMM

George Patterson Nigh (Credit: Photography Center, Inc.)

NIGH, George Patterson, 1963, 1979-

First elected to the governorship in 1978 and re-elected in 1982, Democrat George Nigh will go down in Oklahoma history as the first chief executive to serve consecutive terms in office. Born in McAlester, Oklahoma on June 9, 1927, he is the son of Wilbur R. and Irene (Crockett) Nigh, who were grocery store owners. A Baptist, he and his wife Donna Skinner Mashburn have two children, Michael and Georgeann.

Nigh served a tour of duty aboard an aircraft carrier with the United States Navy from 1945 to 1946, after graduating from McAlester High School in 1945. He returned to Oklahoma to complete his education, received an associate degree from Eastern Oklahoma Agricultural and Mechanical College at Wilburton, and was graduated from East Central State Teachers College, Ada, with a B.A. degree in 1950. Before entering political life, Nigh taught history and government in McAlester High School, was a partner in a McAlester grocery, and owned and managed a public relations firm in Oklahoma City.

In 1950, at the age of 23, Nigh was elected to the Oklahoma House of Representatives, the youngest member ever to have been chosen to serve in that body at the time. Representing Pittsburg County, he remained in the House for four terms before winning the post of lieutenant governor in 1958. At 31, he was the youngest person ever elected to that office in the history of Oklahoma. Nigh served four terms as lieutenant governor—1959-63, 1967-71, 1971-75, and 1975-79. In 1962 he waged an unsuccessful campaign for the Democratic gubernatorial nomination. Yet he did serve as chief executive for nine days in 1963 when, as lieutenant governor, he succeeded to the unexpired term of Governor J. Howard Edmondson, who had resigned. Nigh quickly appointed his predecessor to fill the United States Senate seat left vacant by the death of Robert S. Kerr on January 1, 1963.

In 1978, after Democratic Governor David L. Boren chose not to seek re-election but to run for the United States Senate instead, Lieutenant Governor Nigh faced a stern challenge to gain his party's nomination. The leading vote-getter in a three-man field, he was forced into a runoff against Attorney General Larry Derryberry, whom he eventually defeated with 58 percent of the vote. In the general election he travelled around the state in a "white hat brigade," an apparent attempt to imitate the housecleaning campaign that Boren had waged so successfully four years earlier, when he toured the state with a broom as his symbol. In the 1978 race Nigh narrowly defeated Republican candidate Ron Shotts, a 32-year-old former University of Oklahoma football star, who polled 47 percent of the vote to Nigh's 52 percent. After Governor Boren, also successful in his 1978 campaign, resigned to take his Senate seat, lieutenant governor Nigh became governor on January 3, 1979. The term to which he had been officially elected began five days later, with his inauguration on January 8, 1979. Nigh was the first lieutenant governor to be elected governor, and the only person to serve four times as the state's chief executive. In his 1982 campaign for re-election, he handily defeated Tom Daxon, Oklahoma's State Auditor.

Governor Nigh is a former Chairman of the National Conference of Lieutenant Governors. He is Chairman of the Southern Growth Policies Board, and serves as Vice President of the Council of State Governments. Active in many civic affairs, Nigh is a member of the American Legion and various Masonic organizations. He has also served in several executive capacities with the Oklahoma Jaycees.

Bibliography: Wilbur Johnson, ed., *Directory of Oklahoma* (Oklahoma City, 1975); Oklahoma Department of Libraries, *Governors of Oklahoma: 1890-1979* (Oklahoma City, 1979); Michael Barone and Grant Ujifusa, eds., *The Almanac of American Politics, 1982* (Washington, D.C., 1981); *New York Times*, November 4, 1982; National Governors' Association, *Governors of the American States, Commonwealths, and Territories* (Washington, D.C., 1983). MMM

Robert William Straub (Credit: Oregon Historical Society)

OREGON

STRAUB, Robert William, 1975-1979

An Oregon builder, land developer, farmer, and rancher, Bob Straub held a variety of positions in state government before his election to the governorship in 1974. He was born in San Francisco, California on May 6, 1920, the son of Thomas J. and Mary (Tulley) Straub. Straub earned both his B.A. (1943) and M.B.A. (1947) at Dartmouth College. A Protestant, he and his wife Pat have two sons and three daughters.

Straub, who was an Army enlisted man and Corporal during World War II, first moved to Oregon in 1946, where he worked as an executive with the Weyerhauser Timber Corporation and as a building contractor before entering politics in 1955. A Democrat, he served as Commissioner of Lane County, Oregon from 1955 to 1959, Oregon State Senator from 1959 to 1963, and State Treasurer from 1964 to 1972. Straub was also a Delegate to the Democratic National Convention in 1968. He made two unsuccessful runs for the governorship, one in 1966 and the next in 1970.

According to some political observers, Straub's 1974 gubernatorial victory, after these two defeats, was a result not only of his own efforts, but of a conservative swing among Oregon's declining number of registered Republicans. In a massive upset in the Republican primary, voters rejected the candidacy of liberal Secretary of State Clay Myers, giving the nomination instead to conservative State Senator Victor Atiyeh, who had waged an aggressive campaign. While in the primary Atiyeh had managed to capitalize on certain irregularities in the Secretary of State's office, in the general election he proved not to have the strong appeal of outgoing Governor Tom McCall. Oregon voters were looking for someone likely to continue the policies of the popular incumbent, who had chosen not to run again, and they gave the victory to Straub by the convincing margin of 58 percent to 42 percent.

Major accomplishments during Straub's term as chief executive include the reduction of the unemployment rate from 12 to five percent (the first time in ten years Oregon's unemployment rate was below the national figure), increased direct property tax relief, utility rate relief for senior citizens and an attempt to establish a fair regional power plan through the United States Congress, and important changes in Oregon's land use planning laws. Another significant development during his term was his appointment of more women, handicapped, and minorities to head state agencies and divisions than had any previous Oregon governor. Under Straub basic school support for local grade and high schools increased, educational programs for the handicapped were expanded, duplicative state agencies were consolidated for better services and tax savings, and more than 50 clean, labor intensive firms were attracted to Oregon.

In his 1978 bid for re-election, however, Straub fell victim to an increasing conservative mood of voters, especially in the West. It was the year of "Proposition 13," which cut property taxes in California, and the Oregon election turned on Straub's opposition to, and Republican challenger Victor Atiyeh's support for, an almost identical version of the California referendum proposal. In this replay of their 1974 contest, Straub lost to Atiyeh, winning only 45 percent of the vote to the conservative Republican's 55 percent.

Bibliography: Michael Barone *et al.*, eds., *The Almanac of American Politics, 1978* (New York, 1977); *Oregon Blue Book, 1977-78; New York Times*, November 6, 1978; Official 1978 Oregon General Voters' Pamphlet. MMM

Victor G. Atiyeh (Credit: Photo Art Commercial Studios, Inc.)

ATIYEH, Victor G., 1979-

First elected governor in 1978 following an unsuccessful campaign four years earlier, Republican Vic Atiyeh has had a long history of involvement in Oregon's political and civic affairs. Born in Portland, Oregon on February 20, 1923, he and his wife Dolores have two children. Atiyeh is an Episcopalian.

After attending the University of Oregon in Eugene for two years, Atiyeh joined Atiyeh Brothers, the Portland rug and carpet firm his father had established at the turn of the century. Widely known for his work with the Boy Scouts, where he holds the highest council and regional adult leadership awards, he served in the Oregon Legislature as a member of the Oregon House of Representatives from 1959 to 1964 and as a State Senator from 1965 to 1978. Atiyeh was also Senate Republican leader for three legislative sessions, and served as a Delegate to the Republican National Convention in 1968, 1972, and 1976. As a legislator with a conservative reputation, he won the 1974 Republican gubernatorial primary in an upset, but lost to Robert Straub in the general election.

Atiyeh again won the Republican nomination for governor in 1978, only this time he was able to capitalize on Governor Straub's failure to provide strong leadership in the tradition of his predecessor Tom McCall, who had gained widespread publicity with his amusing suggestion that people visit Oregon for the scenery but then go back home rather than become a permanent drain on the state's resources. Projecting a forceful image, Atiyeh won a decisive victory against Straub, attracting 55 percent of the vote. As a conservative, he benefited from the post-"Proposition 13" climate, and his proposals to cut both taxation and government spending proved highly popular with Oregon's voters. Yet Atiyeh was also careful to campaign as a supporter of environmental measures in a state whose residents remained keenly aware of the importance of natural resources. His campaign literature heralded the fact that he had introduced major air and water quality bills into the Oregon Legislature more than a decade earlier, and he continued to insist that both conservation and the development of alternative energy sources were critical for the state's future.

Among the accomplishments of Atiyeh's first term were improvements in state management and productivity, reform in workers' compensation and welfare, and major new programs in energy and economic development. He also cut his own salary three times to help balance the budget. Although national news magazines reported that he was "running scared" in his 1982 campaign for re-election because of a depressed economy, especially in the critical lumber industry, Atiyeh continued to command widespread respect. He defeated his opponent, Democratic State Senator Ted Kulongowski, by winning 61.6 percent of the vote, Oregon's largest gubernatorial margin in 32 years. Atiyeh's record as a good administrator and his promise to broaden the state's economic base by bringing in new industries had particular appeal to Oregon voters in this election.

After his inauguration Governor Atiyeh announced that his priorities for his second term would include property tax limitation, land use planning reform, renewed aid and commitment to higher education, continued emphasis on economic development, and establishment of special programs for public safety and Oregon's fishing and lumber industries.

Currently, Atiyeh is Chairman of the Western Governors' Conference and Vice Chairman of the Republican Governors' Association.

Bibliography: Official 1978 Oregon General Voters' Pamphlet; *Oregon Blue Book, 1979-80, 1981-82, 1983-84*; Official 1982 Oregon General Voters' Pamphlet; "Where the GOP Will Hold Its Own," *U.S. News and World Report* (October 4, 1982); National Governors' Association, *Governors of the American States, Commonwealths, and Territories* (Washington, D.C., 1983). MMM

Milton Jerrold Shapp (Credit: Commonwealth Media Services)

PENNSYLVANIA

SHAPP, Milton Jerrold, 1971-1979

Born Milton Jerrold Shapiro on June 25, 1912 in Cleveland, Ohio, the son of Aaron, a hardware wholesaler, and Eva (Smelsey) Shapiro. A Jew, Shapp married Muriel Matzkin on May 20, 1947; he is the father of Richard, Joanne, and Dolores.

Shapp attended public schools in Cleveland, Ohio; he later studied at Case Institute of Technology, receiving his B.S. in electrical engineering in 1933. He worked as a truck driver and as a salesman in Philadelphia, and had his name legally changed to Shapp. After serving in the United States Army Corps during World War II, he was discharged in 1946 as a Captain. In 1948 Shapp founded the Jerrold Electronics Corporation, which pioneered in the development of the cable television industry; that venture made him a millionaire. A Democrat, he served as consultant to the Peace Corps, the Department of Commerce, and the National Public Advisory Committee on Area Redevelopment during President John F. Kennedy's administration.

In 1966 Shapp ran unsuccessfully for Governor of Pennsylvania, after winning the Democratic nomination over a candidate endorsed by the state's big political machines. Despite huge sums spent on a media campaign, he was defeated by Raymond P. Shafer, the Republican standard bearer, by a vote of 2,110,349 to 1,868,719. In 1970, however, Shapp was victorious, defeating Republican Raymond J. Broderick with over 55 percent of the vote. Under a new law which permitted Pennsylvania governors to succeed themselves, Shapp ran again in 1974. He defeated two candidates, Martin P. Mullen and Harvey Johnston, to win the Democratic gubernatorial nomination with 70 percent of the vote, and went on to defeat Republican Andrew L. Lewis in the general election. The first chief executive of Pennsylvania since the 1870s to win two consecutive terms, he won re-election in 1974 by a 300,000 vote margin, garnering 54 percent of all votes cast.

Governor Shapp promised that he would be ''the people's advocate.'' He stood up for what he believed was right even when it was politically unpopular— for example, by ordering an end to discrimination against homosexuals in state employment. Shapp won national attention for his consumer advocate policies, innovative programs for the elderly and handicapped, and sweeping welfare reforms. Among the programs he pioneered were: full financial disclosure for state officials, the most comprehensive ''sunshine law'' in the nation, a strict code of ethics for all state employees, and a rigorous code of campaign conduct;

property tax relief and free public transit for senior citizens; a toll-free hotline to the Governor's Office for citizen problems; close supervision of the insurance industry, enactment of no-fault auto insurance, and sweeping reforms to control rising health costs; strict control over the state budget and payroll, leading to an across-the-board tax cut in 1974; programs of strip mine control and land reclamation; and use of the Pennsylvania Industrial Development Authority to stimulate business development. Shapp instituted a state-wide lottery designed to yield a yearly $60 million, 30 percent of which was to be used to reduce the property taxes of poor elderly citizens. He appointed a number of consumer activists to state offices and agencies, among them the popular Insurance Commissioner Dr. Herbert S. Denenberg, who sought to lower the cost and improve the quality of service in hospitalization and in life and auto insurance. In February 1974, when independent truckers went on strike, Shapp brought together all sides and helped negotiate an end to the national strike. One month later he helped avert a shutdown of the nation's gas service stations, and he defused a second truckers' strike in May 1974. Shapp was also credited with whittling down the number of patronage jobs in state government, and with attracting a Volkswagen plant to western Pennsylvania.

Despite such achievements, Shapp was a controversial chief executive. Never a strongly partisan Democrat, he had problems getting on well with the Legislature, even when it was controlled by his own party. He even feuded with some of his most popular appointees, including Denenberg. Unfortunately, some of Shapp's political appointments proved unwise, and scandal tainted the final years of his administration. In his eight years in office, about 60 public officials were indicted, resulting in a number of convictions. Two of his campaign workers were fined for falsifying campaign contributions to his ill-fated 1976 Presidential campaign.

Barred by state law from seeking a third term, Shapp nevertheless became the chief target of all candidates looking to succeed him. Disenchantment with malfeasance in his administration ran so high that 11 candidates sought the gubernatorial nomination of their respective parties in 1978, four of them former prosecutors. Even the eventual Democratic nominee, former Pittsburgh Mayor Peter F. Flaherty, sought to disassociate himself from Shapp's administration. Issuing a stinging rebuff to any offer of support from Shapp, he promised throughout his campaign that the first thing he would do as governor would be "to fire Shapp's pals and cronies."

Interested in ridding their state of what they obviously perceived to be corruption and political cronyism in Shapp's administration, Pennsylvania voters in 1978 gave their support to Republican Richard Thornburgh, a Deputy Attorney General in Washington, D.C. who had a reputation for impeccable honesty.

Bibliography: Roy Glashan, *American Governors and Gubernatorial Elections, 1775-1975* (Stillwater, Minn., 1975); Congressional Quarterly, Inc., *Guide to U.S. Elections* (Washington, D.C., 1975); *New York Times*, November 13, 1977, April 18, April 23, September 27, and November 8, 1978, February 3,

1979; Michael Barone *et al.*, eds., *The Almanac of American Politics, 1978-80* (New York, 1977-79); biographical information, Governor's Office, Commonwealth of Pennsylvania. MMM

Richard Lewis Thornburgh (Credit: Office of the Governor, Pennsylvania)

THORNBURGH, Richard Lewis, 1979-

Born in Pittsburgh, Pennsylvania on July 16, 1932, the son of Charles Garland and Alice (Sanborn) Thornburgh. An Episcopalian, Thornburgh married Virginia Hooton, a childhood sweetheart, who was later killed in a 1960 automobile accident. He is the father of John, David, and Peter by his first wife. On October 12, 1963, Thornburgh married Virginia Judson, a former New York school-teacher, by whom he is the father of a son named William.

Thornburgh received a bachelor of engineering degree from Yale University in 1954, and an LL.B. with high honors from the University of Pittsburgh in 1957. He has received honorary degrees from Washington and Jefferson College, Bucknell University, LaSalle College, Temple University, Lincoln University, Villanova University, St. Francis College, College Misericordia, Lehigh University, and Wheaton College in Massachusetts. Admitted to the Pennsylvania bar in 1958, Thornburgh was employed by the Aluminum Company of America for two years. He then joined the Pittsburgh law firm of Kirkpatrick, Lockhart, Johnson, and Hutchinson, where he worked until 1969. In that year the Nixon administration named him United States Attorney for the Western District of Pennsylvania. Thornburgh impanelled the first grand jury in the United States to investigate racketeering under the Organized Crime Control Act of 1970. He has personally never lost a legal case. In 1975 Thornburgh became Deputy Attorney General in charge of the Criminal Law Division of the Department of Justice, where he served until President Jimmy Carter took office. He then returned to his old Pittsburgh firm.

Running as an Republican, Thornburgh defeated Philadelphian Arlen Specter and five other candidates in the 1978 gubernatorial primary. He opposed Pete Flaherty, the former Mayor of Pittsburgh, in the general election. Flaherty was expected to win easily, but instead he lost most of eastern Pennsylvania except Philadelphia, a development which cost him the election. The final vote was 1,966,042 for Thornburgh and 1,737,888 for Flaherty. During the campaign Thornburgh attacked Flaherty's record as Pittsburgh's mayor, but he was careful to avoid raising that issue while in the Pittsburgh area. Traditional Democratic groups like the teachers' union were annoyed by Flaherty's fiscal conservatism and backed Thornburgh, who also did well with black voters.

Soon after being sworn in, Thornburgh faced the grave responsibility created by the Three Mile Island nuclear power plant accident. While there was no danger of a nuclear explosion, some radiation did escape as a result of the accident and a leakage of disastrous proportions was feared by responsible persons at the scene. Thornburgh's office was effective in avoiding panic and acting as a clearinghouse of reliable information, and the governor himself made a number of key decisions involving the public's safety. In the most crucial of these, Thornburgh proposed the evacuation of pre-school youngsters and pregnant women who were within five miles of the plant.

Pennsylvania's economy was severely disturbed during Thornburgh's first term, partly as a result of major cutbacks in federal aid to the state. In 1981 the economic situation was further complicated when a drought emergency was declared in the Delaware River basin.

Thornburgh received the 1982 Republican gubernatorial nomination without opposition. In the general election he defeated Allen Ertel, a Congressman from the Harrisburg-Williamsport, Pennsylvania area. Ertel had tried to link the incumbent to the Reagan administration's economic policies, while Thornburgh emphasized property tax reform and his plan to end the policy of state-owned liquor stores. Ertel lost considerable ground when he failed to disclose his tax returns, after attempting to portray himself as the "poor man's candidate." The final vote was 1,872,784 for Thornburgh and 1,772,353 for Ertel, who won the Philadelphia vote handily but did not do well outside of the eastern part of the state.

As Thornburgh began his second term in 1983, his administration was seeking to resolve some persistent problems. In 1978 the state signed a consent order with the Environmental Protection Agency and a citizens' group, requiring mandatory vehicle emission tests in certain areas of the state. The Pennsylvania Legislature, however, overrode Thornburgh's veto and refused to appropriate funds to begin the tests. The United States Court of Appeals for the Third Circuit then blocked the use of $91 million in highway funds by the state. Eventually, the Legislature backed down and vehicle tests began. Yet another contentious issue concerned the reorganization of rail commuter lines in the Philadelphia area, as the Southeastern Pennsylvania Transit Authority took over commuter rail service from Conrail. Labor difficulties stemming from this change caused a brief shutdown of service, and a state judicial inquiry and review board later charged that Pennsylvania Supreme Court Justice Rolf Larsen had tried to organize opposition to the re-election of one of his fellow members of the Court. Those charges were still pending in 1983.

Bibliography: Philadelphia Inquirer, November 8, 1978 and November 3, 1982; *New York Times*, April 6, 1979, December 14, 1980, and September 10, 1982; Michael Barone *et al.*, eds., *The Almanac of American Politics, 1980* (New York, 1979); *The 1978-1979 Pennsylvania Manual* (Harrisburg, Pa., 1979); Richard M. Scammon and Alice V. McGillivray, *America Votes*, 13 (Washington, D.C., 1979); Mark Stephens, *Three Mile Island* (New York, 1980); *National Law Journal* (June 27, 1983). JH

John Joseph Garrahy (Credit: Office of the Governor, Rhode Island)

RHODE ISLAND

GARRAHY, John Joseph, 1977-

Born on November 26, 1930 in Providence, Rhode Island, the son of John and Margaret (Neylon) Garrahy. A Roman Catholic, Garrahy married Margherite De Pietro in 1956; he is the father of Colleen, John, Maribeth, Sheila, and Seanna.

Garrahy attended the University of Buffalo in 1952 and the University of Rhode Island in 1953. A member of the United States Air Force from 1953 to 1955, he was elected to the Rhode Island Senate in 1962, where he served until 1968. He also acted as Deputy Majority Leader of the Rhode Island Senate from 1963 to 1968. Garrahy has served on the Board of Directors of the National Council on Vocational Rehabilitation and the Governors' Council on Youth Opportunities. Running as a Democrat, he was elected Lieutenant Governor of Rhode Island in 1968. In 1976 Garrahy defeated Giovanni Falcarelli in the Democratic gubernatorial primary; he then defeated James L. Taft in the general election by a vote of 218,561 to 178,254. Garrahy took the oath of office on January 4, 1977.

In 1978 Rhode Island endorsed the building of Interstate Highway 84. The state also agreed to return 1,800 acres which allegedly had been taken illegally from the Narragansett Indians. Unopposed in the 1978 Democratic primary, Garrahy defeated the Republican Lincoln C. Almond and Joseph A. Doorley, an Independent candidate, in a three-man race. Garrahy did little campaigning during the contest, but still managed to accumulate 197,386 votes compared to Almond's 96,596 and Doorley's 20,381.

Garrahy travelled to the Soviet Union in 1979 along with other governors to discuss strategic arms limitation with the Soviet Union's Vasily V. Kuznetsov. In 1980 he was unopposed in the Democratic gubernatorial primary and again was elected by defeating Vincent A. Cianci, the Republican Mayor of Providence, by 299,174 votes to 106,729 in the general election. During his third term Garrahy tried to combat the state's image as "Poor Little Rhode Island;" he also allowed a ban on the sale of spray paint to minors to become law without his signature. In 1982 Garrahy again had no primary opposition. He proceeded to win a landslide victory over Vincent Marzullo by a vote of 246,566 to 79,602. Garrahy's present term expires in 1985, when he is scheduled to be succeeded by Edward D. DiPriete, the Republican Mayor of Cranston, Rhode Island. DiPriete defeated Democratic State Treasurer Anthony J. Solomon in Rhode Island's 1984 gubernatorial race, by a margin of 237,160 votes to 157,814.

Governor Garrahy is the author of *Rhode Island in the Year 1975, Campaign Spending and Practices—A Direction to Pursue*, and *Financial Aid Information—A Guide for Rhode Island High School Students.*

Bibliography: Congressional Quarterly, Inc., *Guide to U.S. Elections* (Washington, D.C., 1977); Bob Hollingsworth, ed., *Facts on File Yearbook, 1976* (New York, 1977); *New York Times*, January 5 and November 3, 1977, November 8, 1984; *Providence Journal*, November 8-9, 1978 and November 3, 1982; *Rhode Island Manual* (Providence, 1981). JH

James Burrows Edwards (Courtesy: James Burrows Edwards)

SOUTH CAROLINA

EDWARDS, James Burrows, 1975-1979

Born on June 24, 1927 in Hawthorne, Florida, the son of O. Morton and Bertie (Hieronymus) Edwards. Edwards married Ann Norris Darlington on September 1, 1951; he is the father of James B. and Catherine Darlington.

After receiving a B.S. degree from the College of Charleston, South Carolina in 1950, Edwards earned a D.M.D. from Kentucky's University of Louisville in 1955. He did postgraduate study at the University of Pennsylvania from 1957 to 1958, and was a resident at Henry Ford Hospital in Detroit, Michigan from 1958 to 1960. Edwards served in the United States Maritime Service from 1944 to 1947, and with the United States Naval Reserve from 1955 to 1957. He began his dentistry practice, specializing in oral surgery, in Charleston in 1960. Edwards became a consultant for the United States Public Health Service in Charleston in 1964. He was Vice President of the East Cooper Private School Corporation in Mount Pleasant, South Carolina in 1966, and a Clinical Associate in oral surgery at the Medical University of South Carolina at Charleston in 1968.

Edwards served as Chairman of the Charleston County, South Carolina Republican Committee from 1964 to 1969, a Delegate to the Republican National Convention in 1968, a member of the Steering Committee of the South Carolina Republican Committee from 1969 to 1970, and a member of the Steering Committee of the Charleston County Republican Committee from 1969 to 1972. He was also an unsuccessful Republican candidate for the United States House of Representatives in 1971. Edwards did, however, become a member of the South Carolina Senate in 1972. A Trustee of the Charles County, South Carolina Hospital from 1966 to 1970, he has held memberships in the East Cooper Chapter of Sertoma International, the American Board of Oral Surgery, the American College of Dentists (of which he is a Fellow), the International College of Dentists, the American Dental Association, the British Society of Oral Surgeons, and the Federation Dentaire International.

Unopposed in the 1974 Republican gubernatorial primary, Edwards was elected Governor of South Carolina on November 5, 1974. His victory came as something of a surprise to political pundits, and was attributed by many to the fierce infighting among the state's Democrats that year. Defeating Democrat William Jennings Bryan Dorn with about 51 percent of the vote, Edwards was sworn into office on January 21, 1975. He was the first Republican chosen as chief executive of South Carolina in nearly a century, becoming in the process a symbol of the Republican renascence across the South.

During Edwards' term of office, the South Carolina Legislature enacted malpractice insurance for doctors, several offshore drilling sites were discovered, and the United States Marine facility at Parris Island, South Carolina was investigated. An advocate of nuclear power, he concluded early in his administration that the economic development of the state was at risk because of a lack of energy resources, and he created the South Carolina Energy Research Institute to study alternative energy possibilities. Edwards also supported the reopening of a nuclear reprocessing plant in Barnwell, South Carolina that President Jimmy Carter had ordered closed as part of his nuclear nonproliferation policy. A staunch conservative and a passionate believer in private enterprise, Edwards opposed unionization of public employees, "overregulation" of the private sector, and efforts such as the antipoverty program, which he said benefited "only an elite few." He irritated many blacks by fighting a running battle with the state's Welfare Department over allegedly wasteful practices, but won plaudits even from his opponents for pressing an investigation in which five state policemen were sent to prison on racketeering convictions.

Edwards remained a popular governor who was considered open and accessible to both constituents and lawmakers. Political analysts concluded that he had "turned in a more creditable performance than most observers had expected." Barred by law from seeking a second consecutive term, Edwards retired to his Charleston dental practice, amid speculation that he would run for the United States Senate or at the very least make a second bid for the governorship.

A long-standing backer of Ronald Reagan (in 1976, as governor, he was the major force in delivering most of the South Carolina delegation to Reagan in his drive for the Republican nomination), Edwards was rewarded with a Cabinet post in the Reagan administration. While serving as Secretary of the Department of Energy from 1981 to 1982, he espoused a pro-nuclear, free enterprise approach to the energy shortage. Believing that the government itself was responsible for the nation's energy problems, he spoke of "streamlining" the department whose very creation he had once opposed. Edwards also favored abolition of price controls on crude oil and gasoline.

Edwards left office in November 1982 to become President of the Medical University of South Carolina. Looking back at his period in Washington, D.C., he has said that he felt he contributed to an historic reversal of increasing and debilitating federal intervention.

Bibliography: Congressional Quarterly, Inc., *Guide to U.S. Elections* (Washington, D.C., 1975); Roy Glashan, *American Governors and Gubernatorial Elections, 1775-1975* (Stillwater, Minn., 1975); Howard M. Epstein, ed., *Facts on File Yearbook, 1975* (New York, 1976); Bob Hollingsworth, ed., *Facts on File Yearbook, 1976* (New York, 1977); *New York Times*, April 13 and July 25, 1977, December 28, 1979, January 13, 1981, June 19 and November 1, 1982; Michael Barone *et al.*, eds., *The Almanac of American Politics, 1978-82* (New York and Washington, D.C., 1977-81); "James Burrows Edwards," *New York Times Biographical Service*, 11 (December 1980), 1720; "A Dentist for

Energy,'' *Newsweek* (January 5, 1981); ''Rating Reagan's Cabinet,'' *U.S. News and World Report* (July 27, 1981). MMM

Richard Wilson Riley (Credit: Office of the Governor, South Carolina)

RILEY, Richard Wilson, 1979-

Born on January 2, 1933 at Greenville, South Carolina, the son of Edward Patterson and Martha (Dixon) Riley. A Methodist, Riley was graduated in 1954 from Furman University, receiving an A.B. with honors. He was operations officer on a minesweep control ship in the United States Navy from 1954 to 1956. On August 23, 1957, he married Ann Osteen Yarborough; they have four children—Richard W. Jr., Anne Y., Hubert D., and Theodore D. In 1959 Riley received an LL.B. from the law school of the University of South Carolina. That same year he became legal counsel for the Judiciary Subcommittee of the United States Senate.

Riley became a Democratic member of the South Carolina House of Representatives in 1963, and in 1967 he was elected to the South Carolina Senate. In the Legislature he advocated judicial reform and local autonomy. In 1970 Riley pleaded for harmony in the face of an order requiring rapid school desegregation. He left his own children in the public schools during this period. He resigned from the Legislature in 1975 to become Jimmy Carter's state campaign manager. In 1978 Riley placed second in the initial primary for Governor, but he defeated Lieutenant Governor W. Brantley Harvey in the runoff primary. In the general election he defeated Edward Young, a former United States Congressman, by 385,016 votes to 236,946, taking every county in the state but Lexington.

As chief executive, Riley has been prominent particularly as an environmentalist. He refused to permit the dumping of nuclear waste from the Three Mile Island nuclear generator in his state after the accident at that plant. Riley urged a federal solution to the difficulty. In 1980 President Carter named him to the Nuclear Waste Disposal Council. Riley and his wife received an award from conservationists in 1982, when they designed the grounds of the governor's mansion to be hospitable to wildlife.

Midway in Riley's term the state constitution was amended to permit a chief executive to succeed himself. Riley thus ran again in 1982; no one challenged him in the primary. Former Governor and then United States Secretary of Energy James Edwards initially considered opposing Riley in the general election, but Edwards decided that Riley was too popular to defeat. Ultimately, Riley ran against William Workman, a retired newspaper editor, whom he beat easily by 468,819 votes to 202,806. Governor Riley reportedly passed up an opportunity to run for the United States Senate in 1984.

Bibliography: South Carolina Legislative Manual (1975); *Washington Post*, April 23 and November 24, 1979, May 7, 1981; Warren J. Mitofsky, ed., *Campaign '78* (New York, 1980). JH

Richard Francis Kneip (Credit: South Dakota State Historical Society)

SOUTH DAKOTA

Born in Tyler, Minnesota on January 7, 1933, the fifth of eight children born to Frank J. and Bernice D. (Peterson) Kneip. A Roman Catholic, Kneip married Nancy Lou Pankey of Rardin, Illinois on April 19, 1957. He is the father of Kevin, Keith, Paul, Kent, Kurt, Phillip, Patrick, and Michael.

A 1950 graduate of Arlington High School in Arlington, South Dakota, Kneip entered the United States Air Force in 1951 and served with the German occupational forces in Europe until 1955. He received the German Occupational Medal for his services. After attending South Dakota State University at Brookings and St. John's University in Collegeville, Minnesota, he started a dairy business in Salem, South Dakota that grew to become a state-wide wholesale milk equipment dealership. Kneip entered South Dakota politics as a Democrat in 1964, and represented McCook, Hanson, and Sanborn counties in the State Senate. A member of the Senate from 1964 to 1971, he served as Minority Leader between 1967 and 1971. As a state legislator, Kneip was also a member of the Executive Board of the Legislative Research Council and a member of South Dakota's Constitutional Revision Commission.

Labelled a "folksy, breezy politician" by political analysts, Kneip was first elected Governor in 1970, defeating Republican incumbent Frank L. Farrar by a margin of 55 percent to 45 percent. That election marked the beginning of a startling shift in state voting patterns as South Dakota, which had been solidly Republican in the past, elected a Democrat to the governorship and to both of its Congressional seats. In 1972 South Dakota Democrats enjoyed an even better year. Kneip easily won re-election to a second term, defeating Republican Carveth Thompson with 60 percent of the vote to his opponent's 40 percent. The Democrats also took majorities in both houses of the State Legislature and won five out of seven of the most important state-wide offices.

During his first four years in office, Kneip consolidated into 16 what had been 160 agencies, boards, and departments of South Dakota's government. He also established a state personnel system based on civil service, and formalized plans for the first degree-granting medical school in the state. Because South Dakota had become the scene of nationally publicized disturbances among its large Indian population, the most famous being the episode at Wounded Knee in 1973, Kneip worked with a task force to solve disputes between tribal governments and the state government. For all these efforts during his first years in office, Kneip was honored by *Time* magazine in 1974 as one of America's "200 Leaders for the Future."

However, Kneip's star dimmed somewhat as he campaigned for re-election to a third term in 1974. A primary contest with Lieutenant Governor Bill Dougherty, an old friend of South Dakota's Senator George McGovern, exposed the discord between South Dakota Democrats. As a conservative, Kneip was a different kind of Democrat than the liberal McGovern and his supporters. Although Kneip won the primary with 66 percent of the vote to Dougherty's 34 percent, his margin was sharply reduced in the general election. The Democrats were suffering from widespread dissatisfaction with their performance and, as the party in power, they could no longer campaign as outsiders. Indian disturbances at Wounded Knee also harmed the Democrats. Perceived as being more sympathetic to the Indian cause, they fell victim to a white backlash against the Indians. Still, despite a poor showing in the western part of the state, Kneip defeated Republican John E. Olson, gaining 54 percent of the vote to Olson's 46 percent. Due to a change in state law, Kneip was elected to South Dakota's first four-year gubernatorial term.

Kneip's biggest problem during his third term in office was taxes. Convinced that the rising level of state expenditures warranted a tax increase, he attempted unsuccessfully to push such a measure through the Legislature. By the 1976 legislative elections, Republicans controlled both houses of the State Legislature by wide margins. Because of such startling shifts in state-wide voting patterns, political observers began to predict that Kneip's chances for re-election would be "risky." His appointment by President Jimmy Carter as United States Ambassador to Singapore in the summer of 1978 kept him from a potentially tough gubernatorial race. Upon his resignation, Kneip was succeeded in office by his Lieutenant Governor, Harvey Wollman.

During his years as chief executive, Kneip served as a member of the five-state Old West Regional Commission, as a member of the Executive Committee of the National Governors' Conference, and as a Presidential appointee on the Advisory Committee on Intergovernmental Relations. He was also Chairman of the Democratic Governors' Conference from 1977 to 1978.

In the *Foreign Service Journal*, a former aide wrote a rather unflattering description of Kneip's work as ambassador to Singapore, a description that reflected unfavorably on his knowledge of the host country. Though Kneip was not named in the article, his identity was quickly confirmed by the Associated Press, and the story received publicity in the national press. Kneip left the post in the fall of 1980, replaced by Harry E.T. Thayer, a career diplomat.

Bibliography: "200 Faces for the Future," *Time* (July 15, 1974); *South Dakota Legislative Manual, 1977*; Michael Barone *et al*., eds., *The Almanac of American Politics, 1978* (New York, 1977); *New York Times*, February 4 and December 7, 1980; *Who's Who in American Politics, 1981-82* (New York, 1981). MMM

Harvey Wollman (Credit: South Dakota Department of Education and Cultural Affairs)

WOLLMAN, Harvey, 1978-1979

Born on May 14, 1935 in Frankfort, South Dakota, the son of Edwin and Katherine Wollman. A member of the Ebenezer Mennonite Brethren Church, he married the former Anne Geigel of Manitowoc, Wisconsin on December 30, 1958. They have two sons, Michael and Daniel, and one daughter, Kristine.

Wollman was graduated from Doland High School in 1953, and attended Bethel College in St. Paul, Minnesota before graduating with a B.A. from Huron College in Huron, South Dakota in 1961. He served for two years in the United States Army, and was stationed in Europe from 1958 to 1960. Before entering politics he taught government and history at Doland High School between 1961 and 1965, did graduate work in history at the University of South Dakota, and engaged full-time in a farming operation along the banks of the James River in the Hitchcock, South Dakota area.

A Democrat, Wollman was first elected to the South Dakota Senate in 1968, and re-elected in 1970 and 1972. Chosen Senate Minority Leader in 1970 and Majority Leader in 1972, he was named Chairman of the Midwest Conference of the Council of State Governments in 1972, and elected to the National Executive Board of the Council of State Governments in 1973. Wollman was appointed by Lieutenant Governor Bill Dougherty to the state's Constitutional Revision Commission in 1972; he was also Chairman of the Legislative Research Council Executive Board from 1973 to 1974. As a state legislator, Wollman wrote the bill that created the South Dakota State Investment Council. The chief sponsor of bills authorizing multi-district vocational education centers and establishing the Developmental Disabilities Act, he was a key figure in the effort to create the South Dakota Housing Development Authority. Wollman was also Chairman of the Medical Education Subcommittee whose work led to the creation of a degree-granting medical school in the state.

As the running mate of Governor Richard F. Kneip, Wollman became Lieutenant Governor in 1974. He took over the lieutenant governor's spot from Bill Dougherty, who had lost the race for the Democratic gubernatorial nomination to Kneip by a two to one margin. Wollman had had his own plans to seek the governorship in 1974, but quickly abandoned them when the incumbent Kneip decided to try for an unprecedented third term in office.

Wollman was lieutenant governor until the post of governor was vacated by the increasingly unpopular Kneip, who resigned after being appointed United States Ambassador to Singapore by President Jimmy Carter. Wollman officially took over the responsibilities of chief executive on July 24, 1978. He was Governor of South Dakota for less than six months, however, having narrowly lost the Democratic gubernatorial nomination in the June 1978 primary to State Senator Roger D. McKellips. State law prevented him from seeking the governorship as an Independent.

"I realize my input will be very, very limited," Wollman said on taking office, but he explained that his goal would be to establish some direction for solving problems left unfinished by Kneip. In his inaugural address he promised to concentrate on protecting and increasing the state's water resources, one of South Dakota's most serious issues. He sought to streamline the water bureaucracy, to create a water rights defense fund to defend the state against any challenge to its water use rights, and to lay the foundation for mutual cooperation on water issues with South Dakota's Indian tribes. Other programs he hoped to initiate included the institution of program budgeting in the field of higher education, the repeal of the state's personal property tax, the encouragement of alternative energy sources, and the establishment of plans to improve the efficiency of the state's owned and operated cement plant in the face of national and regional shortages of cement.

Wollman left office on January 6, 1979, succeeded by Republican William Janklow, who had defeated McKellips in the general election. Wollman retired to his farm in Hitchcock, South Dakota. He is a member of major farm organizations and of several fraternal organizations.

Bibliography: *Rapid City* [South Dakota] *Journal*, March 23, 1977; *New York Times*, June 2 and July 25, 1978; Governor Harvey Wollman, "The Inaugural Message," July 24, 1978; *South Dakota Legislative Manual, 1979*; biographical information, South Dakota Department of Education and Cultural Affairs; official biography, Governor's Office, Pierre, South Dakota. MMM

William John Janklow (Credit: South Dakota Department of Education and Cultural Affairs)

JANKLOW, William John, 1979-

Born on September 13, 1939 in Chicago, Illinois. A Lutheran, Janklow is married to the former Mary Dean Thom, a native of Flandreau, South Dakota. They have three children—Russell, Pamela, and Shonna.

In 1956 Janklow enlisted in the United States Marine Corps, serving in Southeast Asia from 1956 to 1959. Following his discharge he enrolled at the University of South Dakota, graduating with honors with a B.S. in business administration in 1964. He earned his J.D. from the University of South Dakota School of Law in 1966.

As a Legal Services attorney, Janklow was chief officer at the Rosebud Indian Reservation from 1966 to 1973. There he developed a reputation both as a trial lawyer and administrator, as he and his staff handled over 43,000 requests for assistance in seven years. He personally defended Indians accused of murder or manslaughter in 30 cases, winning all 30, and filed a major civil rights case leading to reform of the jury selection process. During his years with the reservation, Janklow won an anti-discrimination case against Winner, South Dakota.

In 1973 Janklow was appointed Chief Prosecutor of South Dakota. As the chief trial attorney in the Attorney General's Office, he quickly earned a reputation as a top trial lawyer in one of the most difficult periods of the state's history. South Dakota has one of the largest Indian populations in the nation, and when Indian militants erupted into violence at Wounded Knee in 1973, Janklow's vigorous law and order stance drew widespread attention. Prosecuting 22 persons, most of whom were associated with the American Indian movement, on charges of rioting and arson, the conservative Janklow drew the wrath of many Indian leaders and pro-Indian liberals. He became known for his opposition to the land claims of the American Indian movement, and was christened by political analysts as the "premier anti-Indian politician in the state." This reputation endeared him to many South Dakota voters, however, who were disenchanted with Indian demands and methods.

In 1974 the Republican State Convention nominated Janklow for Attorney General. Campaigning on the theme, "a trial lawyer, not a politician," he pledged to clean up the "mess" in the Attorney General's Office and to reverse the state's rising crime rate. While Democrats captured most state offices that year, Janklow upset his former boss, Democratic Attorney General Kermit Sande, in a landslide that repudiated what he called Sande's "mudslinging, vicious campaign tactics." Sande, who was seeking a second term in office, had charged that Janklow had a criminal record, but he was unable to substantiate the accusation. Despite other inflammatory allegations by his opponent, Janklow won 67 percent of the vote and carried every county in the state.

As attorney general, Janklow continued to be active in the courtroom. He personally argued and won two cases before the United States Supreme Court, a first for a South Dakota attorney general. He also continued to attract publicity as Indian violence persisted in the state throughout the early 1970s. As the state's top law enforcement officer, Janklow even ordered that anyone found with dynamite should be detonated with it. Fortunately, the order never had to be carried out. When someone threw a firebomb into his home, Janklow let it be known that he was sleeping with an M-16 by his side, and that he would shoot to kill anyone trespassing on his lawn at night. The most famous of such colorful incidents came on July 4, 1976. Hearing that a man had taken hostages at the State Capitol, Janklow, working at home, grabbed his gun and went off to the rescue.

Justifiably labelled "flamboyant" by political observers on account of such episodes, Janklow was elected Governor in 1978. After defeating State Senator Leroy Hoffman, a millionaire farmer, rancher, and former concert singer, and rancher Clint Roberts to gain the Republican gubernatorial nomination (the vote totals were 51 percent, 33 percent, and 16 percent, respectively), he then benefited from the discord plaguing South Dakota's Democrats. Three-term incumbent Richard Kneip had resigned to become United States Ambassador to Singapore, and his successor, Lieutenant Governor Harvey Wollman, was narrowly defeated by State Senator Roger D. McKellips in the Democratic primary. McKellips himself got into trouble because of his party's position on the Oahe Irrigation Project, a once-popular program endorsed by many Democrats but increasingly opposed by South Dakota voters. Janklow won the election with a solid 57 percent of the vote to McKellips' 43 percent.

Political commentators see Janklow as highly intelligent, intense, and articulate, a man of high energy and with strong populist tendencies. A conservative, he balanced the state's books and avoided tax increases for several years through job attrition and a series of bookkeeping maneuvers. Janklow is a strong supporter of a constitutional amendment requiring the federal budget to be balanced. Indeed, he has stated publicly in the national press that the time has come "to protect the future economy of the nation with a measure of this kind." Unopposed in the 1982 Republican primary, he won re-election to a second term overwhelmingly, defeating the Democratic nominee, State Senator Mike O'Connor, with 71 percent of the vote to O'Connor's 29 percent, the largest margin of victory for a governor in South Dakota history.

During his years as chief executive, Janklow's style has continued to gain him a measure of notoriety. His decision to allow a San Francisco-based energy concern to siphon water from Lake Oahe and pipe it 260 miles west to the coal fields of the Powder River Basin near Gillette, Wyoming provoked outrage and court challenges from conservationists, the Sioux Indians, and several states downstream. Although Janklow defended his decision by arguing that it would bring the state hundreds of millions of dollars that could pay for badly-needed projects to get more water into arid western South Dakota, the other states of the Missouri River basin feared that the deal presaged the extensive commercial exploitation of their primary water source. Under Janklow's direction South Dakota, which has no corporate or personal income tax and lower wages than surrounding states, also began an aggressive bid to attract businesses to the state. When almost 60 companies relocated to South Dakota from adjacent Minnesota, a high tax state, Janklow became the target of invective from neighboring governors. His public dispute with Minnesota Governor Rudy Perpich, which saw both men feuding over which state offered the better business climate, drew considerable attention. Both men appeared together on public television's "McNeil-Lehrer Report" and, in the words of a *New York Times* reporter, "verbally assaulted each other with considerable zeal." At times, Janklow's past has returned to haunt him. In 1983 he sought to remove all copies of a book entitled *In the Spirit of Crazy Horse* from the shelves of South Dakota bookstores, because he believed the book libeled him. A biography of Leonard Peltier, a leader of the American Indian movement, the book contained passages critical of Janklow when he was an attorney on the Rosebud Indian Reservation.

Governor Janklow is a member of the Executive Committee of the National Governors' Association, and serves as Chairman of its Task Force on Agriculture Transportation. He has received numerous awards and honors during his career in public service, including the South Dakota Academy of Family Physicians Distinguished Public Service Award, the South Dakota Association of the Deaf Leadership Award, the Toastmasters International Award for Outstanding Communications and Leadership, and the Associated School Boards of South Dakota Strong Support for Public Education Award. Janklow has also won the South Dakota Library Association Friend of the Library Award, the Reverence for Law Award, the Liberty Bell Award, the South Dakota Army National Guard Meritorious Service Award, and the Appreciation Award from the South Dakota Peace Officers Association. He has received a National Award for Legal Excellence and Skill, and an Honorary Doctor of Humane Letters degree from Huron College.

Janklow is a member of the American and South Dakota Bar associations, the American and South Dakota Trial Lawyers associations, and the American Judicature Society. He has also served on the Board of Directors of the Sky Ranch for Boys.

Bibliography: *Rapid City* [South Dakota] *Journal*, November 6, 1974; Michael Barone *et al.*, eds., *The Almanac of American Politics, 1978-82* (New York and Washington, D.C., 1977-81); *New York Times*, June 2, 1978, June 1, June 4 and August 11, 1982, March 5, April 7, and May 1, 1983; *South Dakota Legislative Manual, 1979*; Molly Ivins, "It's Rarely Politics as Usual to South Dakota Governor," *New York Times Biographical Service*, 11 (August 1980), 1123; *Who's Who in American Politics, 1981-82* (New York 1981); National Governors' Association, *Governors of the American States, Commonwealths, and Territories* (Washington, D.C., 1983); biographical information, Governor's Office, State of South Dakota. MMM

Ray Blanton (Credit: Secretary of State, State of Tennessee)

TENNESSEE

BLANTON, Ray, 1975-1979

Born on April 30, 1930 in Hardin County, Tennessee, the son of Leonard, a farmer and public official, and Ovie (DeLaney) Blanton. Blanton is the brother of Gene Allen and Sarah (Blanton) Gray. He is married to Betty Littlefield, and is the father of Debbie Blanton Flack, David, and Paul.

Educated in Hardin County public schools, Blanton earned a B.S. in agriculture from the University of Tennessee in 1951. After graduation, he taught agriculture in an Indiana high school for one year, and then returned to his home town of Adamsville to organize the B&B Construction Company, a general contracting firm.

Blanton made his political debut in 1964, when he was elected to the Tennessee House of Representatives from Chester and McNairy counties. Two years later, with the backing of Governor Frank Clement, he challenged 12-year incumbent Tom Murray for the Democratic nomination for Congress. Blanton won both the nomination and the general election, and returned to the House in 1968 and 1970. As a member of Congress, he served on the Interstate and Foreign Commerce Committee, the House District of Columbia Committee, and the House Subcommittee on Commerce and Finance. In 1971 Blanton became a member of the Special Subcommittee on Investigations. The next year he decided to compete for the United States Senate seat of Howard Baker but, in the Republican landslide of that year, he suffered his only political defeat. Baker polled 62 percent of the vote, compared with Blanton's 38 percent.

In 1974 Blanton entered the Democratic primary and won the gubernatorial nomination over 11 other candidates, receiving 23 percent of the vote. In the general election of that Watergate year, he faced Republican Lamar Alexander. Alexander's previous position as a Nixon White House aide may have worked against him. He was also hurt by general dissatisfaction with the Republican administration of outgoing Governor Winfield Dunn. Stressing his experience in contrast to that of the 34-year-old Alexander, Blanton waged a populist campaign in which he forged a black-labor coalition. He won with 56 percent of the vote.

The ''outsider mentality'' of the former West Tennessee farm boy was considered to be one key to his election. Once in office, he turned away from old-line Democrats and looked to remote counties for advisors and appointees. Blanton emphasized fiscal responsibility, government efficiency, and economic development. He held the line on state spending, worked to expand the state's tourist industry, reorganized the state government, lobbied for public service jobs for the unemployed, increased highway construction, supported better educational opportunities for Tennesseans, and took the lead in developing international trade. In March 1976 he invited all of the permanent representatives of the United Nations to visit Tennessee. The visit by U.N. Secretary General Kurt Waldheim and 101 other diplomats marked an unprecedented excursion outside New York. Blanton also led a trade delegation of Tennessee businessmen on an extended tour of Europe, Africa, and the Middle East.

On March 7, 1978, state voters approved a constitutional amendment allowing governors to stand for re-election. Although Blanton interpreted the referendum results as an endorsement, and confidently predicted that he could win another term, he declined to seek re-election. His surprise announcement came in the midst of a heightening investigation into charges of corruption in his administration. Blanton's tenure had been a controversial one. He was frequently in the news because of his running battles with the press, his patronage committees, the trial and acquittal of a state transportation commissioner in connection with illegal sales of surplus cars, and a federal investigation of state pardons and paroles. He had also been criticized for expensive travels in the state executive jet.

As his term drew to a close, Blanton came under increasing fire for his generous pardoning policies. In late December of 1978 three of his key aides were arrested on charges of selling pardons and commutations of sentences, and Blanton himself became the object of a federal grand jury probe. As the investigation widened in the last days of his term, and amid calls for his resignation, Blanton granted clemency to 52 convicts, including the son of a close political ally. He justified the commutations by citing the fact that the State Correction Department was under a court order to reduce the prison population and to eliminate overcrowding. Nevertheless, his actions drew such a storm of bipartisan protest that Governor-elect Lamar Alexander hurriedly took the oath of office in an emergency ceremony on January 17, 1979, three days ahead of schedule, because a federal prosecutor had warned state officials that Blanton would free subjects in the pardon-selling investigation unless removed from office. Even after Blanton learned that he had been summarily removed from office, he and his legal counsel were still trying to commute the sentences of an additional 30 convicts when law enforcement agents and aides of Alexander moved into the Capitol to take control of the state government.

The controversy drew national attention, and Nashville country musicians even put out a record called "Pardon Me, Ray," based on the governor's conduct. Democratic party leaders were said to be "embarrassed and humiliated" by the affair, with one calling Blanton's actions "the grossest breach of a chief executive's discretionary power in the history of the state."

The clemency scandal in Blanton's administration was the subject of a book, *Marie: A True Story*, by best-selling writer Peter Maas, author of *Serpico*. The book detailed the story of Marie Ragghianti, the woman who went to the FBI to tell about irregularities involving the Tennessee Board of Pardons and Paroles, to which Blanton had appointed her chairman.

After Blanton hurriedly left office in January 1979, a widening federal probe revealed his to have been one of the most corrupt administrations in state history. In March 1979 the federal grand jury investigating allegations of parole selling indicted four Blanton aides, a Nashville lawyer, and a Democratic Party committeeman, but declined to accuse Blanton himself of any wrongdoing. In October 1980, however, he and two of his former aides were named in a federal indictment which accused them of conspiring to sell state liquor store licenses for 20 percent of the profits while Blanton was in office. On June 9, 1981, a federal jury in Nashville convicted Blanton of 11 counts of mail fraud, extortion, and conspiracy in the issuance of 12 Nashville liquor licenses to friends and political supporters. He was sentenced to three years in prison and fined $11,000. The conviction was upheld by the United States Court of Appeals for the Sixth Circuit on September 29, 1983. Reversing a decision by a three-judge appellate panel that overturned the conviction because of possible juror bias resulting from pre-trial publicity, the court ruled by a margin of six to four that Blanton and his aides had received a fair trial when they were convicted by a federal jury in Nashville in June 1981.

Blanton entered Maxwell Air Force Base Federal Prison Camp in July 1984.

Bibliography: *Tennessee Blue Book* (1967-68, 1975-76, 1977-78); "Races to Watch," *Time* (October 21, 1974); "Routing the Republicans," *Time* (November 18, 1974); Michael Barone *et al*., eds., *The Almanac of American Politics, 1978-80* (New York, 1977-79); *New York Times*, May 28, June 4, and December 30, 1978, January 17-19, January 21, February 18, and March 16, 1979, October 30, 1980, May 8, 1981, February 12, June 22, September 29, and November 27, 1983; "Pardon Me, Ray," *Newsweek* (January 29, 1979); "A Pardoner's Legal Legacy," *Newsweek* (July 16, 1979). MMM

Lamar Alexander (Credit: Office of the Governor, Tennessee)

ALEXANDER, Lamar, 1979-

Born on July 3, 1940 in Blount County, Tennessee, the son of Andrew and Flo Alexander, both of whom were teachers. (Andrew was also a principal.) A Presbyterian, Alexander married Leslee Kathryn "Honey" Buhler, a former aide to United States Senator John Tower, on January 4, 1969. He is the father of Leslee, Kathryn, Will, and Drew.

Alexander attended public schools and was graduated from Maryville, Tennessee High School in 1958. The previous year, he had been selected "Governor" of the Tennessee American Legion Boys State, and heard Tennessee Governor Frank Clement predict that one of the delegates could one day become the "real Governor." Alexander was graduated Phi Beta Kappa from Vanderbilt University and nominated twice for a Rhodes Scholarship. New York University eventually awarded him a Root-Tilden Scholarship, and he was graduated from its law school in 1965, after serving as an Editor of the school's *Law Review*.

Alexander returned to Knoxville, and for a short time practiced with a firm before becoming a Clerk for the eminent Judge John Minor Wisdom of the United States Fifth Circuit Court of Appeals. A pianist of some talent, he supplemented his clerk's pay by appearing in a local club. In 1966 he was a campaign aide to Republican Howard Baker, and he became his Legislative Assistant when Baker was elected to the United States Senate. In 1969 Alexander became Executive Assistant to Bruce Harlow, President Richard Nixon's Congressional relations advisor. He also managed the successful campaign of Winfield Dunn for Governor of Tennessee in 1970.

A period in private law practice and work with groups devoted to revenue sharing and crime and deliquency control ended when Alexander ran for Governor in 1974. An upset victor in the Republican primary, he lost to Ray Blanton in the general election, largely because of the Watergate scandals. Alexander then became political commentator for WSM, a Nashville television station, and joined Baker as Special Counsel when the Senator became Minority Leader in 1977. Between January and July of 1978, Alexander, whom some had characterized as "too aloof" in his 1974 gubernatorial campaign, walked over 1,000 miles throughout the state. He easily won the Republican primary that year and went on to defeat Knoxville banker Jake Butcher in the general election by a vote of 661,959 to 523,495. Alexander took every part of the state, not only the traditionally Republican Appalachian region, by making particular use of the scandals of the administration of Ray Blanton and Butcher's lavish campaign spending.

Developments after election night, however, constitute one of the stranger stories in American politics. Blanton was the first Tennessee chief executive eligible for re-election to a consecutive term, but he had declined to run again. Earlier in his administration he had created a controversy by announcing that he would pardon Roger Humphries, the son of a former staff aide, who was in state prison for the murder of his ex-wife and her lover. Blanton then changed his mind when a public outcry ensued. Soon after the 1978 election, he granted clemency to a number of prisoners. The Federal Bureau of Investigation grew more suspicious, and Blanton chose to leave the country briefly in December 1978. He returned shortly before his term was to end on January 20, 1979. On January 15, 1979, Blanton granted executive clemency to 52 inmates, 24 of them murderers and including Humphries. Although under the Tennessee constitution a governor's power to grant clemency is absolute and personal, the Federal Bureau of Investigation had by now concluded that clemency was being sold. With Tennessee's government in disarray, Alexander was persuaded to take the oath of office on January 17, 1979. Blanton attempted to run the state for the next three days, but he was barred from his Capitol office.

Alexander's first term as governor was preoccupied with the scandals associated with Blanton's administration. Certain of Blanton's aides were sentenced for their role in selling clemency, and others were later freed when another Blanton aide, a star federal witness, admitted lying to the Federal Bureau of Investigation. Blanton's brother and uncle were indicted for mail fraud and bid rigging. Finally, in June 1981, Blanton was sentenced to three years in prison for selling liquor licenses while in office.

Tennessee managed to divert itself from these problems to some extent by staging the rather successful World's Fair at Knoxville in 1982. That same year Alexander ran for re-election against Knoxville Mayor Randy Tyree. While the incumbent governor was vulnerable on the issue of the state budget deficit, which had increased from $80 million to $150 million, Tyree focused his attack on President Ronald Reagan's economic program and high unemployment. Polls showed that Tennesseans were concerned about these issues, but they indicated that voters saw them as national and not state problems. Tyree did poorly throughout the state, even losing the Knoxville area by a margin of two to one. He was also defeated in the Memphis area, where Alexander made television commercials with *Roots* author Alex Haley and pledged to redevelop the region. The final vote in the election was 737,963 for Alexander and 500,937 for Tyree.

By 1983 Jake Butcher, Alexander's former gubernatorial opponent, was under scrutiny for alleged financial irregularities. The Tennessee Valley Authority, venerable but somewhat inconsistent with free-market economic theory, celebrated its golden anniversary the same year. Alexander's term ends in 1987.

Bibliography: Nashville Tennessean, November and December 1978, January 1-20, 1979, and November 3, 1982; Richard M. Scammon and Alice V. McGillivray, eds., *America Votes,* 13 (Washington, D.C., 1979); *Tennessee Blue Book, 1979-1980* (Nashville, n.d.). JH

Dolph Briscoe

TEXAS

BRISCOE, Dolph, 1973-1979

Born in Uvalde, Texas on April 23, 1923, the son of Dolph and Georgie Briscoe. An Episcopalian, Briscoe married Betty Jane Slaughter on August 10, 1941. He was graduated with a B.A. degree from the University of Texas, and served with the United States Army from 1942 to 1946.

After his military service Briscoe, a Democrat, ran for the Texas House of Representatives, where he served for four terms, from 1949 to 1957. A millionaire rancher and banker who campaigned in a private plane, he was first elected Governor of Texas in 1972. The race was closely watched by feminists around the country, because Briscoe first had to fend off a strong challenge from outspoken liberal Frances Farenthold to win the Democratic nomination. Defeating Farenthold, a state legislator, with 54 percent of the vote in the primary runoff, Briscoe edged ultraconservative Republican Hank C. Grover in the general election by a margin of 48 percent to 45 percent. Independent Ramsey Muniz of the La Raza Unida Party drew about six percent of the vote.

A major accomplishment of Briscoe's first term was the restoration of confidence in government following the corrupt and scandal-ridden administration of his predecessor, Preston Smith. Other developments during his early years in office were an increase in funding for public and higher education, and the reorganization of state government.

In his bid for re-election in 1974 (for a four-year rather than a two-year term, due to a change in state law), Briscoe again defeated Farenthold in the Democratic primary, this time by a margin of 70 percent to 30 percent. He also captured the general election easily, defeating Republican Jim Granberry and Ramsey Muniz of La Raza Unida with 63 percent of the vote.

Ideologically, Briscoe is what Texans call a "Tory Democrat," one whose views on substantive issues are closer to a traditional Republican rather than a Democratic stance. Believing that the interests of the state are best served by meeting the needs of its richest and most successful citizens, Tory Democrats have long dominated Texas state government and its Congressional delegation in Washington. They have aimed to keep taxes and public services low, and to provide incentives and inexpensive labor to business.

Once in office, however, Briscoe demonstrated none of the activism of his predecessors, such as erstwhile Tory Democrat John Connally. Indeed, some political observers have characterized his years in office as being marked by "ennui." A quiet, conservative administrator who took a decidedly *laissez-faire* approach to government, he was fortunate to preside over a state whose biggest economic problem was how to dispose of large budget surpluses. Oil taxes gave the Texas Treasury a $3 billion surplus, enabling him to pledge more than $500 million for new highways and to spend more on education. After coming into office because other, better-known state Democrats had been tainted by scandals, and easily re-elected in 1974 because of high prosperity levels throughout the 1970s, Briscoe might not have fared so well had the state faced severe problems, economic or otherwise. Some Texans were beginning to wonder by 1978 whether the state could afford the Briscoe approach any longer. "He presides over an exploding Texas economy like a useful inert gas," the *Economist* of London wrote in 1977. And in 1978, a national Democratic committeeman from Houston put it more irreverently: "If Texans wanted a governor, they'd elect one."

The low profile Briscoe fared badly in 1978. Seeking to become the first chief executive of Texas to serve a full decade, he was defeated in a bitter primary battle by populist Attorney General John Hill. Although Hill was not an especially charismatic figure, it was thought that he would be more of an activist governor than Briscoe had been. As attorney general, he had established consumer complaint offices across Texas, and personally and successfully argued in court the state's claim to tax revenues from the estate of the late Howard Hughes. A liberal on matters of human welfare and a conservative in fiscal matters, Hill attacked Briscoe's ineffective, "do-nothing" administration. Lamenting that Briscoe's policies had allowed governors of other petroleum-producing states, David Boren of Oklahoma and Edwin Edwards of Louisiana, for example, to emerge as spokesmen for the region, Hill also claimed that the incumbent had let government drift at a time when the state's booming economy and increasingly complex social order required clearer guidance and stronger direction from Austin. Briscoe responded to these charges by warning that Hill's activist programs would set Texas on the road to a state income tax. "Briscoe for Texas, Hill for taxes," the incumbent's button read. While Hill admitted that he favored increased state spending for education, purely to raise teachers' salaries to the national average, he insisted that this could be financed out of existing state revenues. By making education his top issue, Hill was launching a direct appeal to the state's increasingly important Chicano voters, for whom the question was an important one and who had voted for Briscoe in previous elections.

Political observers continued to predict that Briscoe would remain in office, but his critics mounted as the primary neared. Besides the charge of general inactivity, others attacked his absenteeism, his slowness to act, and his inaccessibility. Members of the American Agriculture Movement were embittered by his failure to rush to the International Bridge near McAllen in March 1978, when 210 protesting farmers were arrested. Hill, by contrast, was on the scene almost immediately, and he benefited from the television coverage. Briscoe was also hurt by two scandals erupting in the weeks before the primary. The United States Justice Department dispatched a special team of federal agents to Texas to assist in an expanding inquiry into misallocation of federal manpower training funds by the Briscoe administration. At the center of the investigation was the governor's Office of Migrant Affairs, a state agency created by Briscoe in 1974 to dispense federal manpower funds provided to the state under the Comprehensive Employment and Training Act of 1973. The funds were used for job-training programs for migrant farm workers in and around South Texas, Briscoe's home base. His creation of the office by executive order was viewed by some observers as a frankly political attempt to reverse recent inroads by the minority La Raza Unida Party among traditionally Democratic Hispanic voters. Also hurting Briscoe was the public disclosure, prior to the primary, that the Occidental Petroleum Corporation had made illegal domestic political contributions to him, along with other southern politicians. Nor could Briscoe count on help from the Carter administration. He was no favorite of the President, partly because of his attacks on Carter energy policies, but also because of his early support for Texas Senator Lloyd Bentsen, who had made an abortive bid for the 1976 Democratic Presidential nomination.

Hill's primary victory, however, was a Pyrrhic one. His upset win over Briscoe paved the way for the election of Republican William P. Clements, Jr. in the general election.

In the intervening period between his defeat in the primary and the inauguration of Clements, Briscoe called the Texas Legislature into a 30-day special session on tax relief. Although critics charged that he was determined to deplete an estimated $2.9 billion revenue surplus before his successor took office, Briscoe insisted that the tax cut measure was essential because the new Legislature, in his opinion, would ignore the issue.

Once in retirement, Briscoe was elected to the executive boards of two corporations—General Portland, Inc., a Dallas-based cement manufacturer, and Southland Financial, a Texas holding company.

Bibliography: "Texas: Boss Lady," *Newsweek* (January 27, 1975); Michael Barone *et al.*, eds., *The Almanac of American Politics, 1978-82* (New York and Washington, D.C., 1977-81); *Who's Who in American Politics, 1977-78* (New York, 1977); *New York Times*, March 26, April 12, 22, May 4, 8, and August 12, 1978, May 21, 1979, April 29, 1980, April 29, 1982. MMM

William P. Clements, Jr. (Courtesy: William P. Clements, Jr.)

CLEMENTS, William P., Jr., 1979-1983

Born in Dallas, Texas on April 13, 1917. An Episcopalian, Clements and his wife Rita have two children.

After attending Southern Methodist University, Clements was a "roughneck" in the oil fields and a driller of oil rigs from 1937 to 1947. He founded Sedco, Inc., in 1947, a firm that manufactures oil drilling equipment. That venture made Clements a multi-millionaire. He worked as a Deputy Secretary at the United States Department of Defense from 1973 to 1977, receiving a Distinguished Public Service Award from the Defense Department in 1975. Clements was also awarded the Bronze Palm by President Gerald Ford in 1976.

The spread of prosperity in Texas throughout the 1970s, as well as a population boom and a large in-state migration from rural to urban areas, gradually altered the state's traditional voting patterns, and paved the way for Clements' election in 1978 as the state's first Republican governor since Reconstruction. Spending heavily in his first bid for elective office, the conservative Clements portrayed the election as a referendum on the policies of the Carter administration, which was highly unpopular in Texas. He easily defeated Dallas lawyer and former Texas Republican Chairman Ray Hutchinson in the primary, gaining 73 percent of the vote to Hutchinson's 24 percent (with a third candidate polling three percent). Clements then turned his attention to incumbent Democrat Dolph Briscoe, whom he attacked for not taking "an active role in Washington for the state." Clements' criticisms of Briscoe were premature, however, for in a startling upset the incumbent lost his own bid for the Democratic nomination to the liberal Attorney General John Hill in a bitter primary battle. Hill's victory gave Texans a choice that they had never really had before—a contest between a liberal Democrat and a *laissez-faire* Republican.

Presenting himself as a conservative businessman who believed in less government, Clements campaigned on a platform promising to reduce state spending and taxes, and to streamline the state's bureaucracy. Despite a staggering lead by the better known Hill in early polls, Clements came back to win a narrow victory, gaining 50 percent of the vote to Hill's 49 percent. Aided by his conservative views, the unpopularity of the Democratic administration in Washington, a high turnout in the affluent urban areas of the state, and a $7 million war chest, Clements gained national attention with his narrow victory. Unlike the retiring Governor Briscoe, he seemed a force to be reckoned with in national politics, as he boldly advocated policies to encourage free enterprise and to reduce the size of government on all levels. Clements was the first chief executive to endorse Ronald Reagan publicly in 1980, and during his term in office he attempted to make the Republican Party a major force in state politics.

During his term Clements tried to cut the state payroll by five percent a year, and vetoed a record $250 million from the $21 billion biennial budget. He streamlined the bureaucracy, encouraged a tough, anti-crime stance in state government, and attempted to work out a plan with Mexico to curb the flood of illegal aliens across Texas borders.

Clements alienated many voters, however, with his outspoken views. For example, when during the campaign he was asked to express his opinion on the problems of Mexican-Americans, he replied gruffly that he was not running for governor of Mexico. In his campaign for re-election in 1982, much was made of this so-called "meanness issue," and of Clements' personal style. Although he easily overcame the challenge of Duke Embs, a San Antonio insurance broker, to win the Republican nomination with more than 90 percent of the vote, he was not as fortunate in the general election. Clements' opponent was the moderate Attorney General Mark White, a Democrat with strong name recognition around the state. In 1978 White had defeated James A. Baker, President Reagan's Chief of Staff, to become Attorney General, and in that office he gained widespread publicity as a champion of law and order and as a protector of consumers.

The 1982 gubernatorial campaign was a rancorous one, with Clements attempting to portray White as a "bumbling incompetent" and White hoping to capitalize on the meanness issue, a charge revived when a Clements campaign tabloid ran a story about White's arrest for drunk driving almost 20 years earlier. Polls indicated that voters were increasingly annoyed not only with Clements' style, but also with his handling of the state's faltering economy. Although the Texas economy had been booming during most of his administration, and unemployment, at 6.7 percent, was lower than in any other large state, the recession was beginning to hit Texas hard. Rising unemployment rates, that set records by Texas standards, soon put Clements on the defensive. With world-wide petroleum prices depressed, drilling for new gas and oil wells slowed dramatically, and nearly every state business depending on the oil industry was affected. The Democratic platform attacked Clements' "callous," "short-sighted," and "morally bankrupt leadership." White also criticized high utility rates, low teacher salaries, looming water shortages, prison crowding, and rising interest rates. Adopting a neopopulist stance, he made the issue of soaring utility rates the symbol of his attempt to link Clements to the wealthy and privileged.

Although Clements raised and spent nearly $12 million in his re-election bid, possibly the largest campaign fund ever devoted to an American gubernatorial election, he lost to White by a rather large margin, 46 percent to 54 percent. The Democrats took more than 85 percent of the Hispanic vote, an increasingly important factor in Texas elections. This, said the neopopulist White, "was a victory of the people."

The election was closely watched by political observers because of the important role that Texas plays in national politics. Although Clements lost by 200,000 votes, most of the Republican strongholds in the state stayed that way, and in most areas he managed to poll as many votes as he had four years earlier. His defeat was attributed to a surprisingly high voter turnout, which has always favored the Democrats in Texas. As for the Democrats, their hopes for remaining in control of the state hinged on keeping the party united, and on maintaining the traditionally Democratic coalition of labor, minority, and urban voters. Already, however, there are signs that the coalition is becoming unglued, with Democratic State Controller Bob Bullock, an outspoken critic of White, announcing in 1983 that he would run for governor in 1986, even if White seeks a second term.

Clements eventually returned to his oil drilling equipment business. A member of the Board of Trustees of Southern Methodist University and of the National Executive Board of the Boy Scouts of America, Clements is also a member of the Independent Petroleum Association of America and of the American Association of Oil Well Drilling Contractors.

Bibliography: *New York Times*, March 26, May 4, August 18, and November 8, 1978, January 17 and September 23, 1979, June 29, 1980, September 9 and September 22, 1981, April 29, May 3, 28, June 16, September 13, October 12, 14, 31 and November 3, 1982, January 19, 1983; "Ups and Downs of the Newest Governors," *U.S. News and World Report* (September 24, 1979); Michael Barone *et al.*, eds., *The Almanac of American Politics, 1980-82* (New York and Washington, D.C., 1979-81); *Who's Who in American Politics, 1981-82* (New York, 1981); Alan Ehrenhalt, ed., *Politics in America, 1982* (Washington, D.C., 1981); "From Bragging to Begging," *Time* (September 20, 1982); "Texas: Jobs vs. Competence," *Newsweek* (October 4, 1982); "Did Money Talk? Sometimes," *Newsweek* (November 15, 1982); "Fresh Faces in the Mansions," *Time* (November 15, 1982). MMM

Scott Milne Matheson (Credit: Rusath Photography)

UTAH

Born on January 8, 1929 in Chicago, Illinois, the son of Scott Milne and Adele (Adams) Matheson. A Mormon, Matheson is married to the former Norma Louise Warenski. They have four children—Scott Milne III, Mary Lee, James, and Thomas.

Matheson spent his early years in southern Utah and was graduated from Salt Lake City's East High School in 1946. He was graduated with honors in political science from the University of Utah in 1950, and took his law degree from Stanford University in 1952. A City Attorney in Parowan, Utah and a Deputy Attorney with Iron County, Utah from 1953 to 1954, he was a law clerk with a United States District Court Judge in Salt Lake City between 1954 and 1956, before entering private practice with a Cedar City firm. Matheson joined the legal department of the Union Pacific Railroad in 1958, eventually becoming Solicitor General for the company. Except for a brief period (1969-71) during which he served as Assistant General Counsel for Anaconda Copper Company, he worked continuously for the Union Pacific Railroad until his election as Governor of Utah in 1976.

Matheson had been a long-time Democratic fund raiser in Utah and was well known in legal circles, having served as President of the Utah State Bar Association from 1968 to 1969, but except for a youthful post as President of the University of Utah Young Democrats in 1948, he had never before held a political or politically-related office. Yet his candidacy was personally endorsed by retiring Democratic Governor Calvin Rampton, who had held office since 1964 and who remained immensely popular in the state. Political observers agreed that Rampton would probably have been re-elected with more than 70 percent of the vote had he chosen to run again in 1976. With his support, Matheson defeated John Preston Creer, 59 percent to 41 percent, to win the Democratic gubernatorial nomination. Advocating a ''preparedness growth plan'' and exuding an attitude of competence and efficiency, Matheson was able to defeat a better known opponent in the general election, Republican Attorney General Vernon Romney, by a margin of 53 percent to 47 percent. Unopposed in the 1980 Democratic primary, Matheson easily won his bid for a second term. Despite Republican gains elsewhere in the state and nation in 1980, he handily defeated Republican Bob Wright, 55 percent to 44 percent.

During his years in office, Matheson has acquired a reputation as being possibly the best of all the governors in the West. Under his leadership, a record $1 billion appropriations bill was passed by the Utah Legislature, and state sales taxes on electricity, natural gas, coal, and fuel oil have been reduced. He has gained extensive publicity as the leading spokesman for a group of western governors who are demanding and building a new kind of partnership with the federal government on issues of water conservation, energy development, and the use of western land. The hard-working, "70-hour-a-week" governor has a "passion" for what he calls "returning the state of Utah to traditional federalism, Henry Clay federalism, full partnership" with the national government on these matters. Political observers have called him a "technician...with a real enthusiasm for the arcane tedium of working out inter-governmental relations."

Matheson became interested in this problem early in his first gubernatorial term, when fellow Democrat Jimmy Carter tried to cancel a key portion of a central Utah water project without consulting state officials in 1977. Matheson forced the Carter administration to restore the funding, and since then has worked to ensure that states and their elected officials have a voice in such national planning. Speaking for a group of western governors, he has also disagreed publicly with the Reagan administration, eventually getting Interior Secretary James Watt to agree to broad changes in federal coal leasing regulations. Outside of Utah, he is best known for his efforts in bringing the federal government to admit the probable connection between southern Utah's abnormally high cancer rates and the nationally sanctioned atomic testing programs in nearby Nevada during the 1950s. Matheson has also led his state in questioning the benefits of its selection as a site for the MX intercontinental ballistic missile system, going to Washington, D.C. to testify before Congressional committees as to the system's effect on health, grazing, mining, and the regional economy.

As Chairman of the National Governors' Association in 1982-83, Matheson called on the federal government to reduce the growth of military spending, to maintain the current level of social welfare appropriations, and to consider raising taxes to slash the federal budget deficit over the next five years. He also served as Chairman of the Agenda for the 80s Task Force of the National Governors' Association in 1982, and was President of the Council of State Governments in 1982-83. Matheson was the first Chairman of the Subcommittee on Water Management of the National Governors' Association from 1977 to 1982, and is a former Chairman of the Four Corners Regional Commission (1978-79) and of the Western Governors' Policy Office (1979-80). In 1977 he was one of four chief executives named by former Secretary of the Interior Cecil Andrus to serve on the Intergovernmental Task Force on Water Policy; in 1983 he was named by President Ronald Reagan to the Advisory Council on Intergovernmental Relations.

Matheson remains immensely popular in Utah. Public opinion polls conducted in 1982 showed him enjoying a popularity rating of 85 percent in a predominantly conservative and Republican state. In the opinion of political analysts, one of Matheson's strengths is that he had never been a politician before and, apparently, is not particularly concerned whether he will continue to be. His attitude is revealed by his favorite political dictum—"You get in, you give it your best shot, and then you get out again."

In keeping with his views on public service, Matheson chose not to run for a third term. He is scheduled to be succeeded as chief executive in 1985 by Norman H. Bangerter, the Republican Speaker of the Utah House, who defeated former Democratic Congressman Wayne Owens for the governorship in November 1984 by a margin of 56 percent to 44 percent.

Bibliography: Michael Barone *et al.*, eds., *The Almanac of American Politics, 1978, 1982* (New York and Washington, D.C., 1977, 1981); "Rising Voice of the West," *Newsweek* (September 17, 1979); *New York Times*, May 27, 1979, March 14 and November 5, 1980, February 24 and November 6, 1981, February 18, August 11, and November 22-23, 1982, January 1, February 28, March 1, April 2, 1983, and November 8, 1984; Alan Ehrenhalt, ed., *Politics in America, 1982* (Washington, D.C., 1981); *Who's Who in American Politics, 1981-82* (New York, 1981); National Governors' Association, *Governors of the American States, Commonwealths, and Territories* (Washington, D.C., 1983); biographical information, Governor's Office, State of Utah. MMM

Richard Arkwright Snelling (Credit: Office of the Governor, Vermont)

VERMONT

Born on February 18, 1927 in Allentown, Pennsylvania, the son of Walter Otheman, a doctor, and Marjorie (Gahring) Snelling. A Unitarian, Snelling married Barbara Weil in 1947; he is the father of Jacqueline Taylor, Mark Hornor, Diane Bryant, and Andrew Preston Snelling.

Snelling attended Lehigh University and the University of Havana in Cuba; he received an A.B. *cum laude* from Harvard University in 1948. After entering the United States Army as a Private in 1944, he served in the Infantry in the European theater of operations from 1945 until his discharge in 1946. Snelling served as a member of the Vermont Development Commission from 1959 to 1961, and as a Delegate to the Republican National Convention in 1960 and 1968. The President of Shelburne Industries, Inc. of Shelburne, Vermont since 1959, he was also President and Chairman of the Executive Committee of the Greater Burlington Industrial Corporation from 1961 to 1964. Snelling was a member of the Vermont State Republican Executive Committee from 1963 to 1966, and he has been on the Vermont State Republican Committee since 1970.

Although he was an unsuccessful candidate for Lieutenant Governor of Vermont in 1964 and for Governor in 1966, Snelling did serve as a member of the Vermont House of Representatives between 1973 and 1977. As the Republican gubernatorial candidate following his victory over William G. Craig in the primary, Snelling was elected governor of Vermont on November 6, 1976, when he defeated the Democratic candidate, Stella B. Hackell, by a vote of 99,268 to 75,262. He was inaugurated in January 1977. Snelling's first term was marred by a dispute over the selection of a lieutenant governor, after the Vermont Legislature was required to consider the matter because no candidate had received a majority in the general election.

In the 1978 gubernatorial contest Snelling overcame light opposition in the primary and defeated Edwin C. Granai, a member of the State Legislature, by a vote of 78,181 to 42,482 in the general election. By virtue of his victory, Snelling became the only Republican to win a governor's seat that year in New England. Snelling's second term was marked by a serious secession movement involving residents of the islands located in Lake Champlain, who had become bitter over the elimination of a State Attorney's Office in the county that held jurisdiction over the island.

In 1980 Snelling suggested to Canadian officials that they speed up construction of Canada's hydroelectric projects and sell any surplus electricity to New England. In that year's primary election he overwhelmed Clifford Thompson and then went on to defeat Jerome Diamond, an old political foe and State Attorney General, by 123,229 votes to 77,363 in the general election. Snelling became Chairman of the National Governors' Conference in 1981. Meanwhile, Vermont established a five-year transportation plan to cope with the loss of federal funds incurred during the Reagan administration. In 1982 the governor vetoed a bill which would have raised the drinking age to 19.

Although Snelling had announced that he would not seek a fourth term, he eventually changed his mind and defeated Lieutenant Governor Madeleine Kunin in the 1982 general election by a vote of 93,111 to 74,394. Kunin, who had promised to raise the drinking age to 19, contended that the governor had ignored the safety of Vermonters by permitting certain nuclear waste shipments to pass through the state. Snelling responded by pointing to the influx of jobs and businesses into Vermont. Snelling continues to be a prominent member of the National Governors' Conference, using that forum and others to make his case that the individual states cannot provide services lost through recent federal budget cuts.

Snelling, who elected not to seek a fifth term, is scheduled to be succeeded in 1985 by Mrs. Kunin. Kunin defeated her Republican opponent, Vermont Attorney General John J. Easton, Jr., in the state's 1984 gubernatorial contest by the narrow margin of 50.8 percent to 48 percent.

Bibliography: *New York Times*, November 3, 1976, January 4, 1977, January 14, 1979, and November 8, 1984; Bob Hollingsworth, ed., *Facts on File Yearbook, 1976* (New York, 1977); Richard M. Scammon and Alice V. McGillivray, *America Votes*, 13-14 (Washington, D.C., 1979, 1981); *Vermont Legislative Directory and State Manual* (Montpelier, 1981). JH

John Nicholas Dalton (Credit: Virgina State Library)

VIRGINIA

DALTON, John Nicholas, 1978-1982

Born on July 11, 1931 in Emporia, Virginia, the son of Ted R., a Virginia State Senator and Federal Judge, and Mary (Turner) Dalton. A Baptist, Dalton married Edwina Jeanette Panzer on February 18, 1956; he is the father of Katherine Scott, Ted Ernest, John Nichols, and Mary Helen.

After earning an A.B. degree from William and Mary College in 1953, Dalton served in the United States Army from 1954 to 1956, rising to the rank of First Lieutenant. He received a J.D. degree from the University of Virginia in 1957, and was admitted to the Virginia bar the same year. A partner in the Radford, Virginia law firm of Dalton and Jebo from 1957 to 1974, Dalton was also Vice President and Director of Meredith and Tate in Pulaski, Virginia in 1961, Director of the Sutton Development Corporation in Radford, and Director of the First and Merchant Bank in Radford. Dalton's political offices include service as President of the Young Republican Federation of Virginia in 1960, Treasurer of the Virginia Republican Committee in 1960, and General Counsel of the Virginia Republican Committee from 1961 to 1972. He was a member of the Virginia House of Delegates from 1966 to 1972, and a member of the Virginia Senate in 1973. Virginia's Lieutenant Governor between 1974 and 1978, Dalton ran as the Republican candidate and defeated Henry Howell, his Democratic opponent, to win that state's gubernatorial contest on November 8, 1977. His convincing victory was by a margin of 699,302 votes to 541,319. Dalton took office on January 14, 1978.

During his administration Dalton vetoed Medicaid abortions for rape and incest, cut back on Medicaid payments in general, and eliminated federally-funded programs for the mentally disabled. He signed a bill reducing the penalty for marijuana sales, but increased the legal age for certain liquor sales. When the Virginia Treasury showed a surplus in 1981, however, Dalton proposed to spend the funds on Medicaid and to give state employees a raise. He also established a plan to help indigent persons pay their heating bills. Dalton approved a bill requiring automobile emission inspections, and refused to abandon that policy in the face of the Legislature's threat to ban testing. He sought and obtained an increase in Virginia's gasoline sales tax to fund highway construction and the Washington, D.C. metropolitan area's subway system. During his tenure the Carter administration approved a Virginia college desegregation plan, and in 1981 the Legislature held twelve special sessions, but still could not produce a redistricting plan that Dalton believed would be accepted by the courts and the United States Department of Justice.

Unable to succeed himself as chief executive, Dalton rejected unspecified offers of an appointment in the Reagan administration and returned to private life in 1982. He has been a member of the American Legion, the Masons, the Moose, and the Odd Fellows.

Bibliography: Congressional Quarterly, Inc., *Guide to U.S. Elections* (Washington, D.C., 1975); Bob Hollingsworth, ed., *Facts on File Yearbook, 1976* (New York, 1977); *Times-Dispatch* [Richmond, Va.], November 9, 1977; *News-Leader* [Richmond, Va.], November 9, 1977; *Washington Post*, March 9, 1979 and December 31, 1981. Dalton's papers are at the State Library, Richmond, Virginia. JH

Charles Spittal Robb (Credit: Office of the Governor, Virginia)

ROBB, Charles Spittal, 1982-

Born in Phoenix, Arizona on June 26, 1939, the son of James Spittal and Francis Howard (Woolley) Robb. An Episcopalian, Robb attended Cornell University in 1957 and 1958; he then transferred to the University of Wisconsin, which granted him a B.A.A. in 1961. While a member of the United States Marine Corps, Robb married Lynda Bird Johnson, the daughter of President Lyndon B. Johnson, in a White House ceremony on December 9, 1967. The ceremony was the first White House wedding in 53 years. The Robbs are the parents of Lucinda Desha, Catherine Lewis, and Jennifer Wickliffe.

A few months after his marriage, Robb left for Vietnam. He was discharged from the Marines in 1970, and entered the University of Virginia Law School. While there, he became a Director of the LBJ Company. In 1973, the year in which President Johnson died, Robb was graduated from law school and was admitted to the Virginia bar. After serving as a law clerk for Judge John D. Butzner, Jr. of the United States Court of Appeals, he joined in 1974 the staff of the Washington law firm headed by Edward Bennett Williams (the noted criminal lawyer and President of the Washington Redskins professional football team), John Connally (the former Governor of Texas), and Joseph Califano (the former Secretary of Health and Human Services).

Robb quickly became active in civic organizations in the District of Columbia and in northern Virginia. By 1976, he had become Deputy General Counsel and Assistant Parliamentarian for the Democratic National Committee's Platform Committee. He was elected to the post of Lieutenant Governor of Virginia in 1977, despite the fact that a Republican, John Dalton, won the gubernatorial race that year. In 1981 Robb ran as a Democrat for Governor and defeated Virginia Attorney General J. Marshall Coleman by a vote of 760,357 to 659,398. President Ronald Reagan had campaigned actively for Coleman, but Robb defended himself from charges that he believed in lavish public spending and projected a conservative image similar to that of Coleman. Agreeing with the need for the Reagan administration's budget cuts in domestic spending, Robb portrayed his opponent as soft on drug pushers. Coleman unwisely returned the insult by running an ad that asked "What has Robb been smoking?" In the election Robb took most of Virginia handily. He captured his home territory, the usually Republican Fairfax County, and won the rest of the state except for Coleman's home base in the Shenandoah Valley. Robb's victory marked the first time that a Virginia governor had been elected while residing in the northern part of the state.

During Robb's administration Virginia raised the interest ceiling on credit card transactions, and provided for "no-fault" divorces after a six-month waiting period. At the national NAACP convention in 1983, he characterized the state as a leader in racial progress. (Robb's own children attended predominantly black public schools.) Since he cannot succeed himself, Robb has expressed a desire to return to private life in McLean, Virginia when his term ends in 1986. His wife has established a career for herself as a fashion writer.

Bibliography: *New York Times*, December 10, 1967; *Washington Post*, November 4, 1981, July 1, 1982, and July 12, 1983; *Who's Who in America* (Chicago, 1983). JH

Dixy Lee Ray (Credit: Atomic Energy Commission, Washington, D.C.)

WASHINGTON

RAY, Dixy Lee, 1977-1981

An unusual and unorthodox political figure who never ran for public office before her election as Governor in 1976, Ray is only the second woman in American history to win a governorship that her husband had not previously held, and the first woman to be elected chief executive of Washington. Born in Tacoma on September 3, 1914, she is the daughter of Alvis Marion, a commercial printer, and Frances (Adams) Ray. A marine biologist and among the most academically credentialed of United States politicians, Ray received a B. A. (1937) and an M. A. (1938) from Mills College and a Ph. D. from Stanford University (1945). She was a Professor of Zoology at the University of Washington from 1945 to 1976, and has garnered awards and recognition from learned societies all over the world, including a Guggenheim Fellowship in 1952-53. She has also received honorary degrees from more than 20 colleges and universities. In 1977 Ray was chosen as one of the ten most influential women in the nation by *Harper's Bazaar* magazine.

Director from 1963 to 1972 of the Pacific Science Center, a Seattle museum that successfully reached out to the community, Ray has held a variety of prestigious positions. The most important came in 1972 when President Richard Nixon appointed her to the Atomic Energy Commission, the first woman to be named either to a full term on the commission or to its chairmanship, which she held from 1973 to 1975. By federal appointment, she also served as Special Consultant in biological oceanography for the National Science Foundation (1960-62), Special Assistant to the Director of the National Science Foundation (1963), member of the Presidential Task Force on Oceanography (1969), Assistant Secretary of State for the Bureau of Oceans, International Environmental and Scientific Affairs (1975), and Chairman of the Education Commission of the States (1978).

Ray's scorn for bureaucracy grew during her Washington years, and when she returned to her home state in 1976 she decided to enter politics. Casting herself as a ''non-politician'' in a year when that label appealed to many voters, she conducted a low-budget, populist campaign for governor, running on a platform of fiscal austerity and government reorganization. Ray stressed the need for economic development and the controlled use of nuclear power, and backed the construction of a Trident submarine base on Puget Sound, an action opposed by environmentalists. Startling the experts, she narrowly defeated Wes Uhlman, the popular Mayor of Seattle, in the Democratic primary; she then went on to beat the Republican gubernatorial candidate, King County Executive John Spellman, by winning 53 percent of the vote to his 44 percent in the general election. A moderate Republican with a reputation as a skilled administrator, Spellman had the support of liberals from both parties, while Ray attracted a bipartisan coalition of conservatives, big businessmen, and independents.

The gruffly outspoken Ray soon drew national media attention. Colorful to say the least, the unmarried scientist shared a mobile home on Puget Sound with her pet dogs, wore tweeds and knee socks in the halls of power, and once gave herself a chainsaw for Christmas. She radiates a charm, one reporter observed, "that makes her seem like a benevolent pixie, a chubby Peter Pan."

Ray's years in the Statehouse, however, were stormy ones, and her popularity plummeted. She turned out to be something of an autocrat, who heartlessly replaced the staff at the governor's mansion at will, intimidated aides, and antagonized local political writers. She even feuded with the dean of Washington Democrats, Warren G. Magnuson, who had been in the United States Senate since 1944. Needing the support of Gordon Walgren, a Democratic leader in the State Senate, to block a bill on prison expansion, Ray offered to appoint him to the United States Senate should Magnuson "die in office." Magnuson, of course, was incensed when the comment was made public. Farmers, fishermen, and even businessmen were worried that Ray wanted the state to grow too quickly, and she angered many by insisting on keeping open a dump at Hanford for nuclear wastes, including atomic waste shipped in from other states. Clearly, her chief opponents were environmentalists, who condemned her support for nuclear power and her willingness to allow supertankers to carry oil from Alaska through Puget Sound. Critics charged that Ray handled bills from the Legislature on an *ad hoc* basis, and that she had no real legislative program of her own. Even her political appointments backfired. Her choice for Director of Washington's Transportation Agency turned out to have been convicted of drunken driving.

Nevertheless, when she stood for re-election in 1980, some political observers believed that Ray would succeed. Not only was her political style unique and genuine, but there had been a general improvement in the state's economic condition. She also received high marks for her decisive crisis management during the eruption of Mount St. Helens in 1980. During the campaign, however, Ray herself became the issue, with bumper stickers unceremoniously proclaiming "Ditch the Bitch." She was eventually defeated in her own party's primary, losing to State Senator Jim McDermott, a liberal Seattle psychiatrist. Ray received only 41 percent of the vote to McDermott's 59 percent. McDermott himself was soundly defeated by Republican John Spellman in the general election.

Ray's defeat was highlighted in the national news media, and many speculated on her political future. Living with a sister on her Fox Island farm, she is writing a book about her experiences as governor. In retirement, she has also done consulting work for TRW Engineering, and broadcasted a radio show, "Speaking Out," over Seattle station KVI. In 1981 Ray was named in a civil suit filed by the families of eight people who died in the eruption of Mount St. Helens. These litigants maintained that the state should have declared more of the area off limits when the mountain first began to rumble.

Bibliography: G. A. W. Boehm, "Extraordinary First Lady of the AEC," *Reader's Digest* (July 1974); R. Gillette, "Conversation with Dixy Lee Ray," *Science* (July 11, 1975); D. Chu and W. J. Cook, "Whistling Dixy," *Newsweek* (October 4, 1976); "Statehouse Turnabouts," *Newsweek* (November 15, 1976); T. Matthews *et al.*, "Governors: New Faces of 1977," *Newsweek* (April 11, 1977); Joan Libman, "Woman at the Helm: Dixy Lee Ray's Style," *Wall Street Journal* (December 6, 1977); "Dixy Rocks the Northwest," *Time* (December 12, 1977); Parris Emery, *America's Atomic Sweetheart: Dixy Lee Ray* (Seattle, 1978); Michael Barone *et al.*, eds., *The Almanac of American Politics, 1980* (New York, 1979); "Can Dixy Rise Again?," *Newsweek* (July 14, 1980); "Defeat for Dixy Lee Ray," *Time* (September 29, 1980); Esther Stineman, *American Political Women* (Littleton, Colo., 1980), pp. 129-32; "Dixy Lee Ray Is Still Speaking Out," *Newsweek* (June 8, 1981). MMM

John Dennis Spellman

SPELLMAN, John Dennis, 1981-

Born in Seattle, Washington on December 29, 1926, the son of Sterling B. and Lela (Cushman) Spellman. A Roman Catholic, Spellman is married to the former Lois Elizabeth Murphy, by whom he is the father of Margo, Bart, David, Jeffrey, Theresa, and Katherine.

Spellman is a graduate of Seattle University, where he was valedictorian of his class. After serving in the United States Navy during World War II, he completed his education at Georgetown University, where he received his law degree in 1953. Spellman, a Republican, was a practicing attorney in Seattle for 13 years before embarking on a career in public service. After an unsuccessful campaign for Mayor of Seattle in 1965, he was a King County Commissioner from 1967 to 1969, and was elected King County Executive in 1969. Re-elected in 1973 and 1977, he won wide acclaim for completing Seattle's domed stadium, the Kingdome, with no cost overruns. During his tenure as county executive, Spellman also served as First Vice President of the National Association of Counties, Chairman of the King-Snohomish Manpower Consortium, and Chairman of the State-wide Citizens Committee for Revenue Sharing. He made his first bid for state-wide office in 1976 when, as the Republican candidate for Governor, he was defeated by Dixy Lee Ray, who gained 53 percent of the vote to his 44 percent. The key to her victory, political observers believed, was the fact that she was able to attract votes from conservative Republicans who were dissatisfied with the more moderate Spellman.

Conservative opposition to Spellman continued, and when he again sought his party's gubernatorial nomination in 1980, he captured barely 41 percent of the vote to Duane Berentson's 39 percent and Bruce K. Chapman's 18 percent, but his margin was enough to make him the Republican candidate. Although he had acquired a reputation as a competent but rather colorless administrator, Spellman was helped during the campaign by tension within the Democratic ranks. When the tempestuous Governor Ray was rejected by her own party, with Washington Democrats choosing instead State Senator James McDermott, a liberal Seattle psychiatrist, as their gubernatorial candidate, more traditional and conservative Democrats defected to Spellman. This development allowed the Republicans to capture the Statehouse, with Spellman receiving 57 percent of the vote to McDermott's 43 percent.

Spellman is Chairman of the National Governors' Association Task Force on Export Finance, Vice Chairman of the National Governors' Association Committee on International Trade and Foreign Relations, founding Co-Chairman of the business and labor Coalition for Employment Through Exports, and national state government Chairman for the United States Savings Bonds Campaign. In 1981 he was awarded an honorary LL. D. by his alma mater, the University of Seattle. Governor Spellman is a lover of jazz music and an avid fisherman.

In the November 1984 gubernatorial race, Spellman unexpectedly lost his bid for re-election against the Democrat Booth Gardner. Despite Ronald Reagan's landslide Presidential victory that year, Gardner attracted 53 percent of the vote, compared with Spellman's 47 percent.

Bibliography: Michael Barone and Grant Ujifusa, eds., *The Almanac of American Politics, 1982* (Washington, D. C., 1981); National Governors' Association, *Governors of the American States, Commonwealths, and Territories* (Washington, D. C., 1983); *New York Times*, November 8, 1984; biographical information, Western Governors' Conference. MMM

John Davison Rockefeller, IV (Credit: Office of the Governor, West Virginia)

WEST VIRGINIA

ROCKEFELLER, John Davison, IV ("Jay"), 1977-

Born on June 16, 1937 in New York City, New York, the son of John Davison, III, a philanthropist, and Blanche Ferry (Hooker) Rockefeller. Jay Rockefeller is the great-grandson of John D. Rockefeller, founder of the Standard Oil Company, and nephew of Winthrop Rockefeller, who was a Governor of Arkansas, and Nelson A. Rockefeller, who was a Governor of New York and Vice President of the United States. A Baptist, he is the brother of Sandra, Hope, and Alidra. Rockefeller married Sharon Percy, the daughter of United States Senator Charles Percy of Illinois, on April 1, 1967; he is the father of Jamie, Charles, Valerie, and Justin Rockefeller.

After graduating from Phillips Exeter Academy in 1954, Rockefeller received an A. B. degree from Harvard in 1961. He was also a student at International Christian University in Tokyo in 1957, and did post-graduate work at the Yale University Institute of Far Eastern Languages. Appointed a member of the National Advisory Council of the Peace Corps in 1961, Rockefeller served as Special Assistant to the Director of the Peace Corps in 1962. He was an operations officer in charge of work in the Philippines until 1963, an assistant to the Assistant Secretary of State for Far Eastern Affairs, and desk officer for Indonesian affairs in the State Department's Bureau of Far Eastern Affairs in 1963. Rockefeller served as a consultant on the President's Commission on Juvenile Delinquency and Youth Crime in 1964, was employed as a field worker in the Action for Appalachian Youth Program beginning in 1964, and sat as a Democratic member of the West Virginia House of Delegates from 1966 to 1968. After serving as West Virginia Secretary of State from 1968 to 1972, he spent two years, from 1973 to 1975, as President of West Virginia Wesleyan College. Rockefeller has also served as a Trustee of the University of Chicago from 1967 until the present.

Rockefeller lost his initial bid for the West Virginia governorship in 1972, when he was defeated by the Republican Arch A. Moore by a vote of 423,817 to 350,462. Four years later he again became the Democratic Party's gubernatorial candidate, and this time defeated his Republican opponent, former West Virginia Governor Cecil H. Underwood, by a popular vote of 495,661 to 253,420 on November 2, 1976. Rockefeller was inaugurated on January 17, 1977.

During his first term Rockefeller devoted much of his attention to the nation's energy problems. The energy crisis had led to a renewed interest in West Virginia as a source of fossil fuels, and wildcatting for oil and natural gas in the state was frequent and at times successful. In 1978 West Virginia sought to condemn land in Mingo County owned by a development corporation, in order to relocate residents who were living in an area that experienced persistent flooding. West Virginia also took title that year to a 52-mile branch line of the Chessie System, at the time probably the largest purchase of a non-commuter rail line by a state. West Virginia sought to become the site of the first commercial plant to extract synthetic fuel from coal in 1979; the same year, Rockefeller appealed to the United States Civil Aeronautics Board to protest cuts in air service to the state.

Challenged in the 1980 Democratic primary by John Rogers, Rockefeller defeated his opponent by a margin of about four to one. An acrimonious battle followed with the Republican candidate, former Governor Arch Moore. Moore criticized Rockefeller's lavish campaign spending, which came to over $11.7 million, a considerable amount even for a man with a net worth estimated at $90 million. Rockefeller replied that the spending was needed in order to overcome Moore's lead in the polls. Attempting to depict himself as an expert on coal, which he saw as the energy source of the future, Rockefeller also took advantage of the fact that Moore had been tried for extortion during his administration from 1969 to 1977. Though Moore had been acquitted on that charge, an aide's admission early in 1980 that he had accepted kickbacks from the liquor industry and channeled the money into Moore's campaign also weakened his candidacy. Rockefeller eventually won the general election by a vote of 401,863 to 337,240, fueling speculation that he would run for President in 1984 and that Sharon, who became Chairwoman of the Corporation for Public Broadcasting in 1981, would seek the West Virginia governorship.

Rockefeller awarded state employees a salary increase in 1982, though he himself drew no salary. His current term expires in 1985.

Unable to succeed himself as governor, Rockefeller entered West Virginia's United States Senate race in 1984, where he defeated Republican John Raese by a margin of 370,762 votes to 339,871. Meanwhile his former rival, Arch Moore, regained the West Virginia governorship that year by defeating the Democrat Clyde M. See, Jr., 388,739 votes to 344,386.

Bibliography: Peter Collier and David Horowitz, *Rockefellers* (New York, 1976); *New York Times*, November 3, 1976, January 13, 1977, and November 8, 1984; Bob Hollingsworth, ed., *Facts on File Yearbook, 1976* (New York, 1977); *Washington Post*, July 29 and October 13, 1978, March 24, 1979, October 4, 1980, January 10, 1982; *Charleston Gazette*, November 5, 1980. JH

Martin J. Schreiber (Courtesy: Martin J. Schreiber)

WISCONSIN

SCHREIBER, Martin J., 1977-1979

Born on April 8, 1939 in Milwaukee, Wisconsin, the son of Emeline (Kurz) and Martin E. Schreiber, a long time alderman on the Milwaukee Common Council. Schreiber was graduated from Milwaukee Lutheran High School, studied at Valparaiso University and the University of Wisconsin—Milwaukee, and received an LL. B. from Marquette University in 1964. He married Elaine Thaney in 1961, and is the father of Kathryn, Martin III, Kristine, and Matthew.

Before finishing his education Schreiber was elected as a Democrat to serve an unexpired term in the Wisconsin Senate in 1962; he was re-elected in 1964 and 1968 to represent the Sixth Senatorial District. Schreiber ran unsuccessfully for Lieutenant Governor in 1966. He served as Democratic Caucus Chair in 1967 and 1969, before winning a five-way vote to become once again the Democratic Party's choice for Lieutenant Governor in 1970. Running on the same ticket as Patrick J. Lucey, the Democrats' gubernatorial candidate that year, Schreiber was the first Wisconsin lieutenant governor ever elected to a four-year term. He was re-elected in 1974.

During the Lucey administration Schreiber served as the state's Nursing Home Ombudsman, Chairman of the Governor's Council for Consumer Affairs, Chairman of the Wisconsin American Revolution Bicentennial Commission, Chairman of the Legislative Council's Insurance Law Revision Committee, Chairman of the Affirmative Action Executive Commission, and as a member of the Interstate Cooperation Commission. The press speculated that he would challenge Lucey for the governorship in 1978, but Lucey resigned to become United States Ambassador to Mexico. Schreiber became Acting Governor on July 7, 1977, just as a 15-day strike by state employees had begun. State employees, represented by the American Federation of State, County, and Municipal Employees, were unhappy with the settlement, especially in light of Wisconsin's budget surplus, and helped discourage labor support for Schreiber's subsequent re-election bid.

At his inauguration Schreiber enunciated as his major goals tax and welfare reform, economic development, and natural resource preservation. New legislation passed during his administration, however, reflected to some extent the agenda of his predecessor. Major legislation included a $10 million income tax relief for low income and elderly persons, a more stringent code of ethics for public employees, stricter lobbying regulations, and a ''clean campaign fund'' that limited campaign contributions and spending. Schreiber also signed into law a nursing home enforcement bill, a property tax limit bill, changes in the farmland tax program, a bill prohibiting sexual exploitation of children, and a code to improve the juvenile justice system. In addition, he approved a single-level trial court system, a tough drunk-driving law, funding for a new veterinary school as part of the University of Wisconsin system, and appropriations for cleaning up the state's waterways—the "Wisconsin Fund."

Schreiber was credited with appointing strong and effective administrators to key agency positions. He expressed particular pride in his "Prevention and Wellness Initiative," a $1 million program which would provide grants to local government for model projects to promote wellness. Schreiber's plan to return part of an approximately $750 million state budget surplus through a $20 per person rebate was rejected, as was his effort to retain the law requiring motorcyclists to wear helmets. Although he at first opposed it, he eventually signed a controversial bill prohibiting the use of state funds for non-therapeutic abortions. During his 18 months in office, Schreiber took action on 444 bills.

In the 1978 Democratic primary Schreiber defeated David Carley, a businessman and former President of the Medical College of Wisconsin. He was defeated in the fall 1978 elections by Lee Sherman Dreyfus, whose colorful style and articulate speech contrasted with Schreiber's mild-mannered and cautious approach, a difference that became particularly evident in televised debates. Although interested in a federal judgeship, Schreiber eventually became a Vice President of Sentry Insurance in Stevens Point. Shortly after Dreyfus declined to stand for re-election in 1982, Schreiber declared his own candidacy for the Democratic nomination, but he was defeated in the primary by Anthony Earl. Schreiber then returned to work at Sentry.

Bibliography: *Wisconsin Blue Books, 1966–77*; Frank Ryan, "Schreiber's Record Was a Good One," *Milwaukee Journal*, November 24, 1978; Eugene C. Harrington, "Did My Best, Schreiber Says," *Milwaukee Journal*, December 26, 1978; *Milwaukee Journal* Library. Some of Schreiber's papers are on deposit at the State Historical Society of Wisconsin in Madison. NCB

Lee Sherman Dreyfus (Courtesy: Lee Sherman Dreyfus)

DREYFUS, Lee Sherman, 1979-1983

Born in Milwaukee, Wisconsin on June 20, 1926, the son of Woods Orlow, a radio program director, and Clare (Bluett) Dreyfus, who was a member of the Milwaukee School Board in 1944; he received his B.A. in 1949, M.S. in 1952, and a Ph.D. in 1957 in communications from the University of Wisconsin—Madison. From 1944 to 1946 he served in the United States Navy as an electronic technician. Dreyfus married Joyce Mae Unke on April 5, 1947; he is the father of Susan Lynn Fosdick and Lee Sherman Jr.

While attending school, Dreyfus worked as a radio actor on station WISN in Milwaukee, and then as an instructor at the University of Wisconsin from 1949 to 1952. During the next ten years he served as General Manager for radio station WDET in Detroit, Assistant Professor and later Associate Professor of Speech and Associate Director of Mass Communications at Wayne State University. Dreyfus then returned to the University of Wisconsin—Madison as General Manager of WHA-TV (1962-65), Professor of Speech, and Chairman of the Radio-TV, and Films Division (1962-67) and Director of Instructional Resources (1965-67). He was selected by the Wisconsin State University Board of Regents as President (later called Chancellor) of Wisconsin State University—Stevens Point (following merger of the two university systems, called University of Wisconsin—Stevens Point), where he served from 1967 to 1979.

During his career in education Dreyfus was Chairman of the national Army Advisory Panel on ROTC Affairs, Chairman of the Wisconsin Governor's Commission on CATV, consultant to the National Educational Television and Radio Center, and Director of Sentry Broadcasting Corporation. He also was a member of the Board of Directors of the American Association of State Colleges and Universities and the Board of Directors of the Wisconsin Ballet Company. His dissertation dealt with "Persuasion Techniques in Modern Congressional Debate," and his scholarly publications included *Televised Instruction* (co-authored, 1962), "The University Station" in *The Farther Vision* (1967), and "The Evolution and Promise of Educational Technology," in the *Journal of Animal Science* (1968). Dreyfus was a member of numerous professional fraternities and service organizations, including Phi Beta Kappa, Phi Eta Sigma, Phi Kappa Phi, Phi Tau Phi, Kappa Sigma, and the American Legion. He was a 33rd degree Mason and recipient of the United States Distinguished Public Service Medal.

Although a latecomer to politics, Dreyfus cultivated contacts around Wisconsin and eventually entered the Republican gubernatorial primary in 1978 after months of newspaper speculation that he would run. Even though the party's state convention endorsed his opponent, Robert Kasten, Dreyfus organized a grass-roots campaign launched from an old red bus in which he toured the state, resulting in his victory over Kasten by a vote of 197,279 to 143,361. Working to Dreyfus' advantage was his education and experience as an effective communicator, and the fact that he was new to elective politics. He also gained popularity by promising to reduce state taxes, reform the vocational school system, increase energy production, and overhaul the Department of Natural Resources. In televised debates with his Democratic opponent, Acting Governor Martin J. Schreiber, Dreyfus made the projected state budget surplus an issue by characterizing it as a reflection of the state's burdensome level of taxation. In the fall election he defeated Schreiber by a vote of 816,056 to 673,813.

Dreyfus was a popular chief executive because of his charm, affability, openness to the press, and penchant for suggesting new ideas. For instance, he always wore a red vest, a custom he adopted while Chancellor during the Vietnam War protest to increase his visibility and access to students. At frequent press conferences and interviews he often made off-the-cuff suggestions, such as barring freshmen from the University of Wisconsin—Madison, selling Great Lakes water to the West, creating two "czars" to oversee education, eliminating the school tax for the elderly, closing gas stations once a week to reduce gasoline shortages, and offering students admission to the University in exchange for oil from Alberta, Canada. Dreyfus also appeared to enjoy campaigning and ceremonial duties more than the routine responsibilities of government, leaving much of the latter to his Secretary of Administration, Kenneth Lindner.

During his term Dreyfus faced a Democratically-controlled Legislature, and differences between the two made cooperation difficult. Even so, he was able to decrease taxes—first by reducing the state surplus by temporarily suspending the withholding of state taxes from employee wages and salaries, and then by having the state income tax indexed so that taxpayers were not forced into higher tax brackets simply through inflation and by eliminating the inheritance tax on spouses. Dreyfus was also responsible for deregulating the trucking industry, creating the Department of Development, reducing the term of Wisconsin's adjutant general to five years, and supporting a constitutional amendment to toughen preventive detention of criminals. He signed into law bills prohibiting discrimination because of sexual preference (the so-called gay rights bill), requiring children to be properly protected in automobiles, creating the Citizens Utility Board, providing programs for witness rights and crime victims, and establishing competence testing in the schools. As the state's economy deteriorated during the national recession, Dreyfus imposed reductions on state spending and proposed a five cent-a-gallon increase in gasoline taxes and an increase from four to five percent in the state sales tax. At the time he declined to seek re-election, choosing instead to become President of Sentry Insurance, the state deficit was projected at $350 million.

Bibliography: Wisconsin Blue Books, 1979-82; Charles E. Friedrich, "The Words vs. Deeds of Dreyfus' 2 Years," *Milwaukee Journal*, January 11, 1981; Eugene C. Harrington, "Dreyfus' Star Lost Some of Its Glitter," *Milwaukee Journal*, December 12, 1982; Matt Pommer, "Dreyfus Endows Us with Rhetoric, Red Ink," *Capital Times* [Madison], December 20, 1982; *Who's Who in America, 1982-83; Milwaukee Journal* Library. Papers relating to the Dreyfus administration are on deposit at the State Historical Society of Wisconsin in Madison. NCB

Edgar J. Herschler (Credit: Peterson's Portrait Studio)

WYOMING

Born on October 27, 1918 on his grandfather's pioneer homestead in the Fontenelle Creek region of Lincoln County, near Kemmerer, Wyoming. The son of Edgar F. and Charlotte (Jenkins) Herschler, Herschler married Kathleen ("Casey") Colter in 1944; he has two children, Kathleen and James. Herschler is an Episcopalian.

A product of Kemmerer public schools, Herschler was graduated in 1941 from the University of Colorado as a pre-law student; he received an LL.B. from the University of Wyoming Law School in 1949. During World War II he served with the United States Marine Corps in the South Pacific. Wounded in action, he received both the Purple Heart and the Silver Star.

Herschler's political career began soon after his graduation from law school. Serving as Kemmerer Town Attorney from 1949 until his election as Governor in 1974, he was also the Lincoln County Prosecuting Attorney from 1951 to 1959 and a member of the Wyoming House of Representatives from 1959 to 1969. He was a member of the State Parole Board from 1972 to 1974.

Despite an unsuccessful attempt to become the Democratic candidate for a United States Congressional seat in 1970, Herschler decided in 1974 to try and succeed Wyoming's popular Governor Stanley Hathaway, a Republican who had resigned to become United States Secretary of the Interior. After defeating Harry E. Leimback and John J. Rooney in the Democratic primary (where he captured 47 percent of the vote), Herschler faced conservative State Senator Dick Jones of Cody in the general election. One of the major issues in the race was the construction of a slurry pipeline—a device to mix coal with water and pipe it out of state to market. Outgoing Governor Hathaway favored the plan, as did Jones, but Herschler opposed it on the grounds that the pipeline would deplete Wyoming's scarce water resources. The voters obviously agreed. Herschler carried the traditionally Democratic southern counties of the state by large margins and ran almost even with Jones in the usually Republican north, where farmers and ranchers feared coal companies would bid up the price of water should the pipeline become a reality. Losing significantly only in Casper (because of his opposition to transforming a local junior college into a four-year school), Herschler won the election with 56 percent of the vote to Jones' 44 percent. He thereby became Wyoming's first Democratic governor since 1963, and the first actually elected to the position since 1958.

During his first term in office, Herschler identified the energy shortage, environmental protection, drought assistance, water development, aid to farmers and ranchers, and problems associated with industrial impact as the most important issues facing Wyoming. He favored an increase in the mineral severance tax and emphasized states' rights in regard to water, public land, and mining laws, and tried to make himself and his office more accessible to Wyoming citizens. Despite these accomplishments, Herschler barely retained his office in his 1978 bid for re-election. He was caught in the backlash of scandals coming out of Rock Springs, one of the major mineral boom towns of the state. The site of much prostitution and gambling, some of it apparently controlled by organized crime interests, the town and its problems were featured on the CBS television show "60 Minutes," where one of the state's leading investigators charged that Herschler himself was involved in improprieties. Several of his political associates were also implicated. A grand jury investigating Rock Springs indicted Attorney General Frank Mendecino, a Herschler appointee, and there were charges that Don Anselmi, a Rock Springs hotel owner and State Democratic Chairman, was involved in corruption. In 1978 the Rock Springs police chief shot and killed an undercover agent who was looking into crime in the area.

Although few voters thought that Herschler himself was guilty of wrongdoing, his Republican gubernatorial opponent, State Senator John Ostlund of Gillette, criticized Herschler's failure to do anything about the widening scandal. After his own re-nomination was secured with a victory over Margaret McKinstry in the Democratic primary by a margin of 65 percent to 35 percent, Herschler responded by firing Mendecino and obtaining Anselmi's resignation. He also shifted the focus of the campaign to his proposal to increase Wyoming's severance tax on minerals by five percent and to use the proceeds to reduce state property taxes, a move opposed by Ostlund. This allowed Herschler to charge that his opponent was a "mouthpiece" for the big mining companies, a charge that seemed to ring true when it was revealed that Ostlund had had profitable business dealings with at least one of the companies. The contest was a real cliffhanger, with Herschler re-elected by a margin of 51 percent to 49 percent, or less than 2,400 votes. With his re-election, Herschler became the first Democratic chief executive of Wyoming to serve more than one term since Governor Lester C. Hunt's tenure from 1943 to 1949.

During his second term Herschler obtained widespread publicity as a spokesman for the increasingly alienated West. He has angrily informed federal officials of his opposition to Wyoming's becoming the "energy breadbasket of the nation" or an "energy colony of the nation," speaking up against an amendment that would weaken federal environmental curbs on the strip mining of coal. Because the federal government owns vast tracts of land in Wyoming, Herschler has also bitterly denounced federal red tape and bureaucratic regulations that reflect ignorance of the realities of Wyoming life.

With his ability to balance the requirements of growth and environmental protection, Herschler was easily re-elected to a third term in 1982, defeating Republican Warren Morton, a former Speaker of the Wyoming House, with 63 percent of the vote. Currently, Governor Herschler is Chairman of the Interstate Oil Compact Commission and is immediate Past Chairman of the Western Governors' Policy Office and the Western Governors' Conference. He is Co-Chairman of the National Governors' Association Subcommittee on Range Resources Management and Chairman of the Subcommittee on Coal. He has served as Chairman of the Corrections Project of the Education Commission of the States, and is Past Co-Chairman of the Old West Regional Commission. Herschler is a supporter of the Reagan administration's plan to deploy the MX missile system in his state.

A staff member of the American Legion Boys' State for nine years, Herschler has been a member of the Board of Directors for the Wyoming Heart Association, a member of the Board of Directors of the American Lung Association of Wyoming, and a member of the Board of Directors of the Goettche Rehabilitation Center in Thermopolis. He is a life member of the VFW and a member of the Disabled American Veterans and AMVETS. A Past President of the Wyoming Bar Association, he is also a member of the American Bar Association, the International Society of Barristers, and the American Judicature Society. Herschler is Past Executive Secretary of the Wyoming State Democratic Central Committee, and was a Delegate to the Democratic National Convention in 1976 and 1980.

Bibliography: Michael Barone *et al.*, eds., *The Almanac of American Politics, 1978-82* (New York and Washington, D.C., 1977-81); *New York Times*, March 18, 1979, August 20, 1980, September 19 and November 23, 1982; "The Angry West vs. the Rest," *Newsweek* (September 17, 1979); Alan Ehrenhalt, ed., *Politics in America, 1982* (Washington, D.C., 1981); *Who's Who in American Politics, 1981-82* (New York, 1981); biographical information, Governor's Office, State of Wyoming. MMM

APPENDIX

First-time U.S. Governors elected in or after fall 1982:

California	George Deukmejian (seat up in 1986)
Delaware	Michael N. Castle (term expires Jan. 1989)
Georgia	Joe Frank Harris (term expires Jan. 1987)
Iowa	Terry E. Branstad (term expires Jan. 1987)
Kentucky	Martha Layne Collins (term expires Dec. 1987)
Michigan	James J. Blanchard (term expires Jan. 1987)
Mississippi	Bill Allain (term expires Jan. 1988)
Nebraska	Robert Kerrey (term expires Jan. 1987)
Nevada	Richard H. Bryan (term expires Jan. 1987)
New Hampshire	John H. Sununu (term expires Jan. 1987)
New Mexico	Toney Anaya (term expires Jan. 1987)
New York	Mario M. Cuomo (term expires Jan. 1987)
North Carolina	James G. Martin (term expires Jan. 1989)
Ohio	Richard F. Celeste (term expires Jan. 1987)
Rhode Island	Edward D. DiPriete (term expires Jan. 1987)
Texas	Mark W. White, Jr. (term expires Jan. 1987)
Utah	Norman Bangerter (term expires Jan. 1989)
Vermont	Madeleine Kunin (term expires Jan. 1987)
Washington	Booth Gardner (term expires Jan. 1989)
Wisconsin	Anthony S. Earl (term expires Jan. 1987)

INDEX

A

B

C

D

L

M

N

O

P

Q

R